CW01433063

Nationalism and Political Liberty

Redlich, Namier, and the Crisis of Empire

AMY NG

CLARENDON PRESS · OXFORD

This book has been printed digitally and produced in a standard specification
in order to ensure its continuing availability

OXFORD
UNIVERSITY PRESS

Great Clarendon Street, Oxford OX2 6DP

Oxford University Press is a department of the University of Oxford.
It furthers the University's objective of excellence in research, scholarship,
and education by publishing worldwide in

Oxford New York

Auckland Cape Town Dar es Salaam Hong Kong Karachi
Kuala Lumpur Madrid Melbourne Mexico City Nairobi
New Delhi Shanghai Taipei Toronto
With offices in
Argentina Austria Brazil Chile Czech Republic France Greece
Guatemala Hungary Italy Japan South Korea Poland Portugal
Singapore Switzerland Thailand Turkey Ukraine Vietnam

Oxford is a registered trade mark of Oxford University Press
in the UK and in certain other countries

Published in the United States
by Oxford University Press Inc., New York

ISBN 0-19-927309-X

ACKNOWLEDGEMENTS

First of all I would like to thank my supervisors Professor Robert Evans, Professor Richard Crampton, and Dr David Rechter for all their help and support throughout the writing of my doctoral dissertation which is the basis for this book. I would also like to thank my college advisor Dr Martin Conway for encouragement at difficult times, and my two examiners, Professor Peter Pulzer and Dr Robin Okey for their trenchant criticism which I have tried to incorporate into my book. I am indebted to Professor Fritz Fellner for permission to use and quote from the Redlich Papers in his possession, and for freely sharing his expert knowledge on Redlich. Thanks are also due to Professor Christopher Seton-Watson for permission to consult and to quote from the R. W. Seton-Watson archives, to Professor Solomon Wank and Dr Franz Adlgasser for their advice on American and Austrian depositories containing Redlich material, to Professor Linda Colley for help with Namier sources, and to the Houghton Library and the Harvard Law School Library for permission to cite Redlich manuscript material deposited at the respective libraries. Citations from the Lewis Namier Papers and the Manchester Guardian Archives are by courtesy of the the Director and Librarian, John Rylands University Library of Manchester. Last but not least, I would like to thank Rhodes Trust for three years of generous financial support as well as Balliol College for a research grant.

CONTENTS

NOTE ON TERMINOLOGY

Both Redlich and Namier used the terms 'Austria', 'England', and 'Great Britain' inconsistently and carelessly. Redlich, and to a lesser extent Namier, labelled British foreign policy 'English'. Both, however, clearly limited themselves to English parliamentary and political history in their scholarly works and regarded the British parliament as a product of English parliamentary and government practice. Hence, their use of the term 'English parliament' instead of 'British parliament', although not technically accurate, was consistent with their own understanding of British parliamentary history. By 'Austria', Redlich and Namier sometimes meant the entire Dual Monarchy and at other times referred only to the non-Hungarian part of the Monarchy. I have tried not to replicate this confusion of nomenclature in my own writing whilst respecting their original usages both in direct quotations and in paraphrasing their ideas.

LIST OF ABBREVIATIONS

AHY	*Austrian History Yearbook*
AVA	Österreichisches Staatsarchiv, Allgemeines Verwaltungsarchiv, Vienna
BOD	Bodleian Library, Oxford
HHStA	Österreichisches Staatsarchiv, Haus-, Hof-und Staatsarchiv, Vienna
HLS	Harvard Law School Library, Harvard University
JMH	*Journal of Modern History*
LOC	Library of Congress, Washington, DC
MGA	Manchester Guardian Archives, in John Rylands Library (Deansgate), Manchester University
NP	Namier Papers, in John Rylands Library, Manchester University
ÖNB	Österreichische Nationalbibliothek, Vienna
PRO	Public Record Office, London
FO	Foreign Office
CA	Cabinet
RP	Redlich Papers, in the private possession of Professor Fritz Fellner, Neustiftgasse 47, Vienna
SSEES	London University School of Slavonic and East European Studies Library
SPOR	*Stenographische Protokolle über die Sitzungen des Hauses der Abgeordneten der österreichischen Reichsrates, (1867–1918)*
WSLB	Wiener Stadt-und Landesbibliothek, Vienna

Introduction

'This is just a line to enclose a reprint from the 4th volume of the History of the Peace Conference . . . and at the same time to introduce its author, Mr L. B. Namier . . . You will find that he has a very remarkable knowledge of Habsburg history and politics',[1] wrote R. W. Seton-Watson to Josef Redlich in October 1921.[2] Redlich replied politely six days later that Namier's visit would 'give me great pleasure'.[3] This is the only clue I have found pointing to a possible meeting between my two protagonists, nor do I know if the meeting ever took place. Redlich never referred to Namier outside this letter, while Namier mentioned Redlich twice in passing—once in the very article that Seton-Watson sent to Redlich.[4] Although they did have mutual friends and acquaintances—Seton-Watson, *The Times* editor Wickham Steed, Thomas Masaryk, Eduard Beneš, and Sidney and Beatrice Webb, to name a few—a comparison of Redlich and Namier on the basis of personal relationship and mutual influence would be rather fruitless.

We are thus left with the path of systematic comparison, of elucidating the major similarities and differences in the content and method of their works, their dilemmas and their responses to these dilemmas in their lives. On the surface, however, Redlich and Namier seem to have little in common. Redlich is best known as a giant amongst Austrian historians, whose magisterial *Das österreichische Staats- und Reichsproblem*, biography of Franz Joseph, and study of Austrian war government are still definitive,[5] or else as the keen social observer in his political diary, one of the principal sources for Austrian political history and Viennese social history from 1908 to 1919.[6] Even those few who remember Redlich's reputation in his own lifetime as an expert on English administrative and parliamentary

---

[1] The article in question is Namier's 'The Downfall of the Habsburg Monarchy', in H. W. V. Temperley (ed.), *A History of the Peace Conference of Paris*, 6 vols. (London, 1920–4), vol. iv, part 3, pp. 58–119.
[2] SSEES, Seton-Watson Papers, SEW/17/22/7, Seton-Watson to Redlich, 22 Oct. 1921.
[3] Ibid., Redlich to Seton-Watson, 28 Oct. 1921.
[4] Namier, 'The Downfall of the Habsburg Monarchy', 110; L. B. Namier, *In the Margin of History* (London, 1939), 82.
[5] Josef Redlich, *Das österreichische Staats- und Reichsproblem*, 2 vols. (Leipzig, 1922, 1926); id., *Kaiser Franz Joseph von Österreich* (Berlin, 1928); id., *Austrian War Government* (New Haven, 1925).
[6] Josef Redlich, *Schicksalsjahre Österreichs 1908–1919: Das politische Tagebuch Josef Redlichs*, ed. Fritz Fellner, 2 vols. (Graz and Cologne, 1953).

history—Asquith quoted Redlich in parliament and the Carnegie Institute commissioned him to conduct a study on the teaching of the Common Law in American law schools[7]—would find the idea of comparing Namier with Redlich puzzling. Redlich moved in Fabian circles in Britain and was a proponent of the left-liberal democratic version of Whig history, celebrating the 1832 Reform Act as the just victory of democracy over a corrupt aristocratic parliament, whereas Namier is of course known as the ultra-conservative historian of the eighteenth century who glorified the English aristocracy, and whose name—unique amongst all historians—was immortalized by the *Oxford English Dictionary* in the term 'to namierize'.[8] Namier's Fabian and socialist past, his lifelong (albeit ambiguous) admiration for the Soviet experiment, and the affection which many English radicals bore him, have all been obscured by the larger-than-life legend of his incorrigible conservatism. His Habsburg past, too, and indeed, his works on European history, with the important exception of his Raleigh lecture on 1848,[9] have largely been ignored.

Before embarking upon my research, the little I knew about Redlich conformed to the conventional image of him as a German centralist empire reformer. I first came across Namier, however, not in his incarnation as conservative English monarchist, but as a young socialist radical with revolutionary tendencies and Pan-Slav sympathies, recently emigrated from Galicia but working for the British Foreign Office, pushing for the dismemberment of the empire. It appeared to me that Redlich and Namier constituted a pair of polar opposites—the one culturally German, pro-Habsburg, working to save the empire through reform from within; the other pro-Slav, anti-Habsburg, campaigning for the dismemberment of the empire from without. I had hoped that a comparison of the two would cast light on the origins of the debate about the viability and the desirability of the Habsburg empire that now looms so large in Habsburg historiography.

In the course of my research, however, I realized that the relationship between Redlich and Namier was far more complicated than one of opposition. World War I marked the period of greatest divergence between the

---

[7] Josef Redlich, *The Common Law and the Case Method in American University Law Schools*, The Carnegie Foundation for the Advancement of Teaching, Bulletin 8 (1914).

[8] *Oxford English Dictionary*, 2nd edn. (Oxford, 1989). The dictionary quotes several definitions of 'to namierize', including one from the *Observer*, 28 Aug. 1960: 'a vigorous substitution of accurate detail for the generalizations which had contented older historians'; and from the *Sunday Times*, 30 May 1971: 'a well known historical technique of constructing multiple biographies of inarticulate men whose common but unconscious aims may be a force, even a determining force in history.'

[9] L. B. Namier, *1848: Revolution of the Intellectuals* (London, 1992).

two men, but even then there was a joint allegiance to supranational ideas which transcended either a German centralist hegemonic conception of the Austrian empire or the pro-Slav, nationalist view of the oppressed nationalities. Neither Redlich's identification with the Germans nor Namier's with the Slavs was unproblematic—the former struggled with Austrian versus German allegiances, whilst the latter was divided between Polish, Ukrainian, and socialist internationalist loyalties, complicated in both cases by rising anti-Semitism which made Jewish identification with either the German or Polish nation increasingly problematic.

A pattern began to emerge as I surveyed their lives as a whole and not merely through the narrow window of the Great War—a pattern not of polar opposition, but of divergence and convergence. Redlich and Namier were both from upper-middle-class, politically liberal, assimilated Jewish families in Moravia and Galicia respectively. They grew up in an era of escalating anti-Semitism, integral nationalism, and nationality conflict which witnessed the eclipse of liberalism and made the position of assimilated Jews increasingly untenable. They responded differently not only to the nationality conflict in Austria but to anti-Semitism as well—Redlich disassociated himself from the Jewish community and Namier became a Zionist.

Their historical interests, however, are remarkably similar—the revolutions of 1848, nationalism and liberalism in nineteenth-century continental European history, English parliamentary and political history, and the history of the Habsburg monarchy. Both became great anti-nationalist historians—a minority position in an age when nationalism was at its apogee in Central and Eastern Europe. Moreover, Redlich and Namier were both anglophiles and passionate advocates of representative self-government. They increasingly saw Great Britain as an extraordinarily stable island of liberty in stark contrast to a dark, despotic Europe, where authoritarianism was intermittently broken by revolutions and peace ripped apart by nationalisms. Their scholarly interests encompassing both British and European history were reflected in their lives—cosmopolitan, straddling the continental European and Anglo-American worlds, a rare phenomenon at the beginning of the twentieth century, although increasingly common in the inter-war years. Ultimately, however, their differences in personal temperament and philosophical assumptions led them to opposing conclusions about the viability of multinational federations, international comity, and the prospects of parliamentary democracy in continental Europe.

Throughout my research, I have been struck by the force and cogency of their arguments against nationalism, their concern for political liberty and for parliamentary democracy—all unpopular positions in Central and Eastern Europe during their lifetimes. Given the prominence accorded to historians both in the construction of nationalist narratives and nationalism, as well as the role of German historians in the construction of an ideology of state supremacy,[10] I thought it important both to re-examine the case against nationalism and the absolutist state as well as to emphasize this alternative mode of political activism by two prominent historians.

I have found William Johnston's delineation of three distinct disciplines within intellectual history to be very useful in this study. The first discipline is the 'internal history of ideas'—to expound ideas for their own sake, and to locate them in relation to other ideas. The second, the 'sociology of thinkers', examines the influence of milieu, both on the micro-biographical level of childhood, youth, parents, and profession, as well as the macro-societal level of an entire city, nation, or state. The third, the 'sociology of *engagé* intellectuals', explores the way intellectuals try to instigate social change.[11] Intellectually, Redlich and Namier sought answers to very similar questions: why was political liberty so much better entrenched in Great Britain than in the rest of Europe? In what ways was nationalism inimical to the development of parliamentary government? Why did German history take such a fatal turn? What caused the downfall of the Habsburg Monarchy, and how does the Habsburg experience reflect upon the viability of multinational empires in general? On the sociological-biographical level, Redlich and Namier present a fascinating contrast in terms of how they dealt with the problems of identity, allegiance, and political upheavals in the face of integral nationalism and anti-Semitism. What do their different experiences and responses indicate about the options available to Jews in the early twentieth century? How did their experiences as Jews shape their understanding of nationalism? Their political activism raises two fascinating questions: first, the relation between political convictions and

[10] R. W. Seton-Watson, *The Historian as a Political Force in Central Europe: An Inaugural Lecture Delivered on 2 November 1922* (London, 1922); Stefan Berger, Mark Donovan, and Kevin Passmore (eds.), *Writing National Histories: Western Europe Since 1800* (London and New York, 1999); Georg G. Iggers, *The German Conception of History: The National Tradition of Historical Thought from Herder to the Present* (Middletown, Conn, 1968). See R. J. W. Evans, 'Historians and the State in the Habsburg Lands', in Wim Blockmans and Jean-Philippe Genet (eds.), *Visions sur le développement des états européens: théories et historiographies de l'état moderne* (Rome, 1993), 203–18, for a discussion of the role of historians in constructing state, imperial, and national histories in the Habsburg Monarchy.
[11] William Johnston, *The Austrian Mind: An Intellectual and Social History* (Berkeley and Los Angeles, 1972), 2–5.

actions; secondly, the efficacy of intervention by intellectuals in the political sphere.

The first four chapters are primarily chronological, although, as in all intellectual biographies, chronological sequence must sometimes be interrupted by more integrative discussions of their ideas. The first two chapters cover Redlich's and Namier's lives respectively from childhood until World War I, with special emphasis on their evolving attitudes towards the Habsburg Monarchy and Great Britain. In Chapter 1, I trace the increasingly critical attitude Redlich takes towards the Habsburg Monarchy, and his attempts to reform Austria in accordance to his understanding of British history, whereas in Chapter 2, I trace Namier's rejection of Austria, which results in his becoming naturalized as a British subject. The third chapter deals with Redlich's and Namier's activities during World War I. Since this is the period of greatest divergence between their views, I have discussed Redlich and Namier in two discrete blocs. The fourth chapter, however, is comparative throughout, since this is the time when their views converged. Chronologically it covers the inter-war years, with a postscript on Namier's World War II activities and post-war scholarly life until his death in 1960. Thematically, it covers their reactions to post-war chaos, their ideas on possible Danubian federations, their views on Nazism, and deep concern about the fate of political liberty in the face of the totalitarian threat. Although Zionism is a major preoccupation for Namier at this time, the political side of his Zionist activities is very well served by Norman Rose's monograph;[12] hence, I have only analyzed his Zionism in so far as it relates to his own Jewish identity, his ideas on nationalism, and his rejection of liberalism. The fifth and final chapter is the only non-biographical chapter. It is based squarely on their historical oeuvre, and is structured around common themes such as nationalism, liberalism, political liberty, British parliamentary government, the nature of the modern state, German political development, the rise of the nationality conflict in Europe, and the 'inevitability' of the fall of Austria. My primary purpose is not to examine their findings in detail or to test the validity of their conclusions, but to understand their political ideas and historiographical assumptions.

The only source we have for Redlich's early childhood is an unpublished, incomplete memoir written by Redlich in 1928[13]—a very nostalgic

---

[12] Norman Rose, *Lewis Namier and Zionism*, (Oxford, 1980).
[13] RP: J. Redlich, 'Aus dem alten Oesterreich. Erinnerungen und Einsichten'. A copy of Redlich's memoirs can also be found in HHStA: Redlich Nachlass.

document, but nevertheless one that appears to be factually accurate in the parts I could verify independently. The memoirs break off at age 18, but fortunately, in that very same year (1887) the correspondence between Redlich and his first love Flora Darkow-Singer, a cousin of the philosopher Edmund Husserl, commenced. Over 200 letters from Redlich to Flora Darkow-Singer have survived, covering a span of nearly fifty years (the last letter was dated September 1936, two months before Redlich's death).[14] These letters are remarkable for their frankness and comprehensiveness—their importance as sources can hardly be overestimated. They are also the only substantial source for Redlich's life from 1888 until 1907, after which we have Redlich's celebrated political diaries from 1908 to 1919. Redlich embarked upon his political career in 1907. The post-1907 era is accordingly rich in primary sources such as parliamentary speeches, letters to other politicians like Joseph Maria Baernreither and Ernst Plener, Redlich's published letters to Hermann Bahr,[15] as well as the very substantial archive of the imperial administrative reform project (1911–17),[16] a brainchild of Redlich's. Moreover, we have his two volumes on English local government[17] and three volumes on English parliamentary government,[18] invaluable for understanding his evolving ideas on parliamentary government and bureaucracy.

The paucity of sources for Namier's early years contrast bleakly with the richness of the Redlich sources. Overall, the researcher on Namier is severely hampered by the fact that Namier burnt many of his papers at the beginning of World War II, a move dictated by fear of a German invasion of Great Britain.[19] Almost the only source we have for Namier's childhood and early youth is his biography, written by his wife Julia Namier, based substantially on memoirs dictated by Namier in the last sixteen months of his life. Although beautifully written and profoundly moving, Julia Namier's biography must be regarded with a double caution on both the autobiographical as well as the biographical fronts. The adult Namier was fascinated by psychoanalysis and his memories of his childhood are accordingly rather

[14] WSLB, Handschriftensammlung: I.N. 198.547–I.N.198.743, letters from Josef Redlich to Flora Darkow-Singer.
[15] Fritz Fellner (ed.), *Dichter und Gelehrter: Hermann Bahr und Josef Redlich in ihren Briefen, 1896–1934* (Salzburg, 1980).
[16] AVA, Verwaltungsreform-Kommission 1911–17.
[17] Josef Redlich, *Local Government in England*, ed. with additions by F. W. Hirst, 2 vols. (London, 1903).
[18] Josef Redlich, *The Procedure of the House of Commons: A Study of its History and Present Form*, trans. A. E. Steinthal, 3 vols. (London, 1908).
[19] Linda Colley, *Lewis Namier* (London, 1989), 107.

Freudian. Linda Colley has rightly cautioned against accepting the Freudian structure of Namier's biography at face value, pointing out that the mature Namier, after years of Freudian analysis, undoubtedly remembered his childhood as a titanic struggle against his father, but that Namier's relatives remembered his father as a weakling and wastrel, and his mother as the strong one of the family.[20] Secondly, Julia Namier herself was a religious mystic, and this strongly religious attitude coloured her account of Namier's own religiosity.[21] Moreover, her personal dislike of Chaim Weizmann influenced her treatment of Namier's Zionism. Furthermore, the biography is obviously an apologia for Namier, a polemical attempt to set the record straight against what Namier and his wife regarded as unfair attacks or biased portrayals.

For the period after Namier's arrival at Balliol in 1908, we have Arnold Toynbee's reminiscences of Namier, a few essays published by Namier before the Great War, and a handful of letters deposited in the Yale University Library from his year in America in 1913. I have also drawn on material from the beginning of World War I on the assumption that such comprehensive views on the German–Slav conflict in Central and Eastern Europe must have had their roots in pre-war years.

For Chapter 3, sources include Redlich's political diaries, letters, and speeches, as well as relevant parts of *Das österreichische Staats- und Reichsproblem* which cast light on his ideas on empire reform during the war.[22] The trickle of Namier sources swells to a flood in World War I in the form of memoranda and reports he wrote for the Foreign Office, supplemented by articles for *New Europe* and other journals, as well as propaganda pamphlets for Wellington House.

With Redlich's call to the Harvard Law School, American archives become important, especially the papers of Felix Frankfurter, Charles C. Burlingham, and Roscoe Pound. Redlich wrote many articles for a variety of journals, which are important for understanding the evolution of his political thought in this final phase of his life. Article-chasing is also important for tracing Namier's development in the inter-war years. He was a special correspondent for the *Manchester Guardian Commercial* from 1921 to 1924, and supported himself partially through journalism throughout the period. The Namier Papers in the John Rylands Library in Manchester University include not only letters and drafts of lectures, but also a valuable

---

[20] Ibid. 8–9.
[21] Ibid. 7. See also Constance Babington-Smith, *Julia de Beausobre: A Russian Christian in the West* (London, 1983).
[22] The first volume was finished in 1920 and published in 1922.

8 *Introduction*

collection of newspaper articles written by Namier (many of which would otherwise be difficult to trace because of their anonymity). A most informative correspondence with W. P. Crozier, editor of the *Manchester Guardian*, is to be found in the *Manchester Guardian* Archives.

Historians, unless they have been pioneers in historiography or in the philosophy of history, have been relatively neglected in intellectual history, because their original insights tend to be embedded in commentary and analysis of past events rather than developed in sustained abstract exposition. For instance, Redlich's ideas on empire reform are largely to be found in his examination of competing models of empire reform in the Habsburg past, although he did make one important attempt to systematize and put into practice these ideas—namely in the imperial administrative reform project of 1911–17. Like the empire reform schemes of Karl Renner and Aurel Popovici, Redlich's project ran aground on insurmountable political opposition. Since Redlich only published his extremely technical proposals on financial reform, and since his would-be popularizer, Hermann Bahr, ran afoul of war censorship,[23] Redlich's achievements in this area were largely ignored at the time and have been ignored since.

Indeed, for such an important historian and *engagé* intellectual, Redlich has been sadly neglected. The latest book on Austro-German liberalism by Pieter Judson omits Redlich almost completely.[24] Ironically, John Boyer's history of the Christian Socialist party is the only recent account to have discussed Redlich's political career and administrative reform project at any length.[25] Namier's historiographical innovations, in particular his prosopographical methods, have received more attention. British historians have been debating the pros and cons of Namier's historiography and methodology and his contributions to eighteenth-century British history ever since the mid-twentieth century, albeit mostly in the form of articles or even extended obituaries. Linda Colley's book on Namier is the latest and best example of this genre, with the added distinction of including a short intellectual biography.[26] Namier's role as political secretary to Zionist leader Chaim Weizmann has also been covered by Norman Rose.[27]

---

[23] Redlich, *Schicksalsjahre Österreichs*, 1 June 1915, II, 42.
[24] Pieter Judson, *Exclusive Revolutionaries: Liberal Politics, Social Experience, and National Identity in the Austrian Empire, 1848–1914* (Ann Arbor, Mich., 1996).
[25] John W. Boyer, *Culture and Political Crisis in Vienna: Christian Socialism in Power, 1897–1918* (Chicago, 1995), 357–63, and John W. Boyer, 'The End of the Old Regime: Visions of Political Reform in Late Imperial Austria', *Journal of Modern History*, 58 (1986), 159–93.
[26] Colley, *Lewis Namier*.
[27] Norman Rose, *Lewis Namier and Zionism* (Oxford, 1980).

However, no other study of Namier has paid attention to his pre-war and World War I socialism,[28] looked at his intellectual debt to Pareto, or related his views on rationality and mass psychology to the *fin-de-siècle* 'revolt against positivism'. Moreover, the existing accounts have tended to locate Namier within the context of British intellectual life or Zionist debates rather than in relation to his own Central and East European roots. Just as Janik and Toulmin insisted that Wittgenstein's philosophy had to be seen in the light of Viennese political, cultural, and philosophical preoccupations instead of in the context of the Cambridge school of philosophers,[29] so also much that was puzzling about and seemed unique to Namier is illuminated when considered in the light of his Habsburg background. Significantly, Isaiah Berlin alone, another anglophile Jew from the East, grasped the importance of this background to Namier's work in a short reminiscence on the historian.[30]

This neglect is unfortunate. Redlich and Namier were profoundly interesting people whose lives illustrate, with great poignancy, the dilemma of assimilated Jews serving as cannon-fodder in the nationality conflict, and the personal impact of conflict and loss in Central and Eastern Europe. Their political activities raise the question of the relation between scholarship and political action. Most importantly, their insights into nationalism, political liberty, parliamentary government, and the nature of the modern state are still very pertinent to the Danubian region, and offer fresh insights into the political forces at work in our time. One of the purposes of this book is to rescue Redlich and Namier from the semi-oblivion of a faded veneration, so that we can truly wrestle with their ideas and engage with their passions.

---

[28] One of the few references to Namier's socialism occurs in a Polish work which implies that Namier, with his 'pseudo-social, class-based judgement of Poland's situation', was actually a Bolshevist agent. See Stanisław Zochowski, *Brytyjska polityka wobec Polski 1916–1948* (London, 1979), 20.

[29] Allan Janik and Stephen Toulmin, *Wittgenstein's Vienna* (London, 1973).

[30] Isaiah Berlin, 'Lewis Namier: A Personal Impression', in Martin Gilbert (ed.), *A Century of Conflict: 1850–1950. Essays for A. J. P. Taylor* (London, 1966), 229.

I

Josef Redlich and the Critique of Austria

Der Österreicher hat ein Vaterland und allen Grund, es—zu beklagen. [1]
(The Austrian has a fatherland and every reason—to complain.)

It was the best of times, it was the worst of times for Austro-German liberals at the time of Josef Redlich's birth in 1869. It was the best of times because the German Liberals had finally attained power in 1867, a success enhanced by the accompanying industrial boom, the so-called *Gründerzeit*. It was the worst of times because Prussia had defeated Austria in 1866, giving rise to Austria's subsequent exclusion from the unified Germany in 1871.[2] Liberal confidence proved misplaced, as the economic crash of 1873 ushered in several years of economic depression and the liberals fell permanently from power in 1879.[3] The trauma proved lasting, assuaged by an alliance with Germany but more and more manifesting itself in an alienation from the state and a deep feeling of inferiority to the Germans in Germany.[4] Thus, despite a happy childhood and a family ascending swiftly and smoothly up the social and economic ladder, Redlich grew up in an atmosphere in which liberalism and Austria both seemed increasingly in crisis. In many ways, this contrast between personal prosperity and a pervasive sense of crisis and anomie is a microcosm of the often remarked-upon paradox of the late imperial Habsburg Monarchy—the fact that economic growth and cultural achievement went hand in hand with increasingly intractable political problems and social alienation.[5]

Unlike so many of his generation who rejected liberalism, escaped into aestheticism, or increasingly replaced Austrian state patriotism with

[1] WSLB, Handschriftensammlung: I.N.198.605, Redlich to Darkow-Singer, 21 Dec. 1903.

[2] Pieter Judson, *Exclusive Revolutionaries*, 117–142.

[3] Ibid. 165–91; Adam Wandruszka, Peter Urbanitsch, and Alois Brusatti (eds.), *Die Habsburgermonarchie 1848–1918: Die Wirtschaftliche Entwicklung*, vol. I (Vienna, 1973), 337–51, 1,867–92.

[4] Redlich, *Emperor Francis Joseph of Austria* (London, 1929), 3768.

[5] See Robin Okey, *The Habsburg Monarchy c. 1765–1918: From Enlightenment to Eclipse* (London, 2001), 194, and Gerald Stourzh, 'The Multinational Empire Revisited: Reflections on Late Imperial Austria', *AHY* 23 (1992), 13.

nationalism,[6] Redlich's attitude was one of both affirmation and sharp critique. Although he never rejected liberalism, he vehemently criticized Austrian liberalism and its hypocrisies. Similarly, he never traded his Austrian patriotism for nationalism, but characterized himself as one who affirmed the Austrian state idea but combated Austrian reality.[7] This dual pattern of affirmation and critique would dominate Redlich's politics and thought.

Born the second son of Adolf and Rosa (née Fanto) Redlich in Göding,[8] Moravia, Redlich belonged through both sides of his family to the affluent strata of the assimilated German-speaking Jewish bourgeoisie. Commercial farming formed the foundation of wealth for both the Redlichs and the Fantos, but the industrial revolution in Austria propelled the Redlichs into sugar factories, construction, river regulation, and the national railroads, whilst the Fantos established themselves in the petroleum industry. Both managed to expand beyond their regional base (Göding, Moravia for the Redlichs; Holics, a large Slovakian village, in Hungary for the Fantos), and to establish an economic presence in Vienna.

Like the majority of the Jewish bourgeoisie, Redlich's family benefited enormously from the political victories of liberalism. Nathan Redlich, grandfather of Josef, bought land in 1848 in the heady but all too brief days of full Jewish emancipation. Although formal ownership of the land had to be transferred to a Slovakian friend until the final emancipation of the Jews in 1867, the land nevertheless served as the foundation of the Redlich family fortune. To Redlich's family, then, liberalism meant political emancipation, and its laissez-faire economic policies the road to wealth and modernization.[9]

The Jewish religious tradition was still strong on the Redlich side of the family, but had died out amongst the Fantos, giving place to a secularized rationalist ethos with a very strong emphasis on ethics and duty. Adolf Redlich was religiously observant, but his wife and children did not observe kosher dietary rules. A stern woman, Rosa Redlich instilled duty and ethics into her children, adhering to the motto that 'one should not

---

[6] See Carl E. Schorske, *Fin-de-siècle Vienna: Politics and Culture* (Cambridge, 1981), introduction, for the classic account of liberal bourgeois alienation from politics.

[7] Redlich, *Das österreichische Staats- und Reichsproblem*, i. p.v.

[8] Now Hodonín.

[9] Peter Pulzer, 'The Austrian Liberals and the Jewish Question, 1867–1914', *Journal of Central European Affair*, 23: 2 (July 1963), 131–42.

show the children too much how much one loves them'.[10] Nevertheless, Redlich remembered the family as a close-knit one, united by an 'inner tenderness'.[11] He attributed 'the best of what we have . . . mental and physical health, the highest good',[12] to his parents' influence, and indeed, his mother's rationalism, his father's business pragmatism, and both parents' strong ethical beliefs served as guiding stars for Redlich throughout his life.

Into this sober household of emotional restraint, hard work, thrift, and small-town propriety, Redlich's uncle Ignaz came every Saturday, trailing clouds of Vienna. Based in Vienna, where he took care of the family's business interests in railroads and river regulation, Ignaz Redlich was fond of wine, women, and song, cutting a flamboyant swathe through the Jewish middle classes in Vienna. Josef Redlich remembered him with awe as the first 'great gentleman' in his life. He fired his nephew with a burning desire for the sensual, hedonistic lifestyle of Vienna, and a burning ambition to attain it.[13]

Redlich's curiosity about Vienna was soon satisfied when his parents decided to send Josef, aged 8, and his brother Fritz, aged 9, to Vienna to continue their education whilst boarding with various relatives and landlords. What seems to have struck him most about the great change was the huge contrast between his austere upbringing, which was quite 'alien' in the Austrian context,[14] and the affectionate volubility of the various families, 'more Viennese than Jewish',[15] that he encountered.

Young Redlich was experiencing the clash between two different cultures—the culture of law, represented by his parents, and the culture of grace in Vienna. In his analysis of Austrian intellectual history, Robert Kann distinguished between two dominant and opposing cultures which have shaped Austrian intellectual life—the one, religious and aesthetic, embodied in the plastic and sensuous culture of grace derived from the baroque Counter-Reformation—in Carl Schorske's words, an aristocratic 'amoral *Gefühlskultur*';[16] the other, a rational culture of law and the word, derived from the Enlightenment and the province primarily of the bourgeoisie.[17] Steven Beller has argued that the primary representatives of

[10] RP: Redlich, 'Aus dem alten Oesterreich', 66.
[11] WSLB, Handschriftensammlung: I.N.198.578, Redlich to Darkow-Singer, 14 Mar. 1896.
[12] RP: Redlich, 'Aus dem alten Oesterreich', 6–7.   [13] Ibid. 28–30.
[14] Ibid. 66.   [15] Ibid. 82.
[16] Carl E. Schorske, 'Grace and the Word: Austria's Two Cultures and Their Modern Fate', *AHY* 22 (1991), 21–34.
[17] R. A. Kann, *A Study in Austrian Intellectual History, from Late Baroque to Romanticism* (New York, 1960).

Enlightenment values and the culture of law in late imperial Austria were the Jews.[18] As such, Jews always felt somewhat outside the mainstream of Austrian life, which was dominated by the culture of grace.[19] Whilst we may dispute the general validity of Beller's argument that Judaism had a special affinity with the Enlightenment,[20] Redlich himself attributed the strong emphasis on duty and ethics in his family to a secularized Judaic ethical code,[21] and regarded these parental characteristics as somewhat un-Austrian.[22] Beller further argues that the clash was especially sharp for immigrants to Vienna from the Bohemian crownlands (where the culture of law rather than grace predominated), that this cultural clash spurred great creativity, and that the great cultural renaissance in Vienna around 1900 was the work disproportionately of those Viennese who had ties to Bohemia or Moravia.[23]

Redlich's reaction to the new culture of grace was ambivalent. On the one hand, he responded rapturously to the affection, sensuality, and artistic pleasures of his new environment. He frequented theatres, the opera, and concerts; went ice-skating, dancing, and to *Fasching* balls. All his life he had a great need and capacity for affection. Redlich was a fond father to his son Hans Ferdinand, retained sole custody over his son after his divorce in 1908, and gave his son the artistic exposure and musical training which his own childhood had lacked.[24] Hans Ferdinand Redlich later became a distinguished conductor and musicologist.

Josef's yearning after the aesthetic, enchanting side of Vienna was matched by his repulsion towards its poverty-stricken aspects. Redlich's first residence and Gymnasium were in the Second District of Vienna, home to the Jewish lower and lower-middle classes. He spent three rather unhappy years there, and recalled that he did not make a single friend at school. 'The Jewish lower middle classes are socially impossible!' he would

---

[18] Steven Beller, *Vienna and the Jews 1867–1938: A Cultural History* (Cambridge, 1989), ch. 9.

[19] Ibid. 165–87.

[20] See M. L. Rozenblit, 'The Jews of the Dual Monarchy', *AHY* 23 (1992), 178, for the argument that Beller based his theory on Jewish apologists of the nineteenth century rather than on traditional Judaic beliefs.

[21] RP: Redlich, 'Aus dem alten Oesterreich', 20.

[22] Ibid. 66.

[23] Beller, *Vienna and the Jews*, 168–9. Beller lists Victor Adler, Otto Bauer, Richard Beer-Hofmann, Hermann Broch, Egon Friedel, Karl Kraus, Stefan Zweig, Sigmund Freud, Gustav Mahler, and Ludwig Wittgenstein as having Bohemian or Moravian ties.

[24] Redlich managed to engage Carl Orff as a composition teacher for Hans Ferdinand Redlich. See *Catalogue of the Hans Ferdinand Redlich Collection of Musical Books and Scores* (Lancaster, 1976), introduction.

later exclaim.[25] To his great delight, he was transferred to the Akademisches Gymnasium in 1881, whilst his brother Fritz, designated to run the family business, was sent to a Realschule, where sciences and modern languages were emphasized instead of classical studies.[26]

The Akademisches Gymnasium was one of the leading educational institutions in the empire, alma mater of Hugo von Hofmannsthal, Arthur Schnitzler, Hans Kelsen, Peter Altenberg, Richard Beer-Hofmann, Ludwig von Mises, the nuclear physicist Erwin Schrödinger, and Thomas Masaryk, amongst others.[27] Socially, its students came from privileged backgrounds—a fact Redlich noted with satisfaction. Through his school-mates, Redlich came into contact with the circles of the '*Ringstrasse* Jewish bourgeoisie'—wealthy Jewish financiers and industrialists, some of whose ancestors were already 'tolerated' during the time of the Emperor Franz—in other words, the Jewish bourgeois liberal elite.[28] The much noted cohesiveness of the Viennese elite, in which writers, artists, philosophers, and musicians mixed with 'a business and professional elite proud of its general education and artistic culture',[29] meant that by gaining access to the bourgeois liberal elite Redlich came to know men like Hermann Bahr and the literati of the Café Griensteidl,[30] Hugo von Hofmannsthal, Theodor Herzl, Gustav Mahler,[31] Arthur Schnitzler, and Arnold Schoenberg.

His own social ascent paralleled that of his parents, who had started spending their summer vacations in Reichenau alongside the wealthiest Jewish families from Vienna, Bohemia, Moravia, and Budapest.[32] In Reichenau Redlich became familiar with the circles for whom he coined the term the 'Third Society'[33]—the established Jewish families of the banking

---

[25] WSLB, Handschriftensammlung: I.N.198.599, Redlich to Darkow-Singer, 8 Apr. 1902. See Rozenblit, *The Jews of Vienna, 1867–1914* for the social structure of Viennese Jewish society.

[26] Gustav Strakosch-Grassmann, *Geschichte des Unterrichtswesens in Österreich*, (Vienna 1905), 249, 276, 321.

[27] Beller, *Vienna and the Jews*, 50; Rozenblit, *The Jews of Vienna*, ch. 5.

[28] Beller has calculated that over 40% of students at the Akademisches Gymnasium came from Jewish backgrounds. See also Rozenblit, *The Jews of Vienna*, 104–5, Table 5:1.

[29] Schorske, *Fin-de-siècle Vienna*, p. xxvii.

[30] Redlich to Bahr, 12 Mar. 1923, in Fellner (ed.), *Dichter und Gelehrter*, 484.

[31] Gustav Mahler wrote most of *Das Lied von der Erde* while staying with Redlich's parents in Göding. See Kurt Blaukopf, 'Mahler in Göding', in *Neue Zürcher Zeitung*, 14 Sept. 1969, quoted in H. Fußgänger (ed.), *Hugo von Hofmannsthal, Josef Redlich, Briefwechsel* (Frankfurt am Main, 1971), 162, n. vii.

[32] RP: Redlich, 'Aus dem alten Oesterreich', 92.

[33] The 'First Society' consisted of the hereditary nobility, the 'Second' of recently ennobled families.

and stock-exchange world, who were already 'rich and cultivated' before the crash of 1873.[34]

Yet despite the seduction of Vienna, the 'city of dreams', the influence of his parents was impossible to shake off. The 'deep-rooted Puritanism' of his parents' household, their earnestness, and their sense of duty led him to judge the Viennese Jewish circles as too 'windy' and 'superficial.'[35] He remembered himself from his schoolboy days as 'too earnest' for his age, never satisfied with himself, always engaged in serious academic and philosophical pursuits. He was 'not an affable youngster, unlike the typical Viennese youth of good family, amusing and easily amused, always good humoured and witty'.[36] Although Redlich loved music ('Wagner is a necessity to me', he noted),[37] art (he was a fan of Klimt's *Secession*),[38] and read widely in belles lettres (Shakespeare, Heine, Grillparzer), his intellectual tastes inclined most of all towards history and politics, which was indeed atypical in the prevalent Viennese milieu of aesthetic absorption. He studied Mommsen, Ranke, and Gregorovius,[39] read parliamentary debates and Heinrich Friedjung's *Deutsche Wochenschrift*, and followed the activities of Gladstone and Bismarck with great interest.[40]

Redlich's criticisms of the Viennese bourgeois way of life swelled to a flood in the 1890s. He pronounced himself hostile to Viennese conversation and society, and complained about the indolence, superficiality, and over-refinement 'to the point of deformity' of the Viennese bourgeoisie. Underneath the glittering surface of balls, dinners, dances, and the never-ending round of engagements and marriages which used to enchant him, Redlich now discerned weakness, debauchery, and nervous discontent. The heroes of the Burgtheater were getting older and more mannered, Abbazia was still no world spa,[41] and Austrian political life was so schematic that one knew in advance the speech of the next 'liberal' candidate.[42] The coalition of the United German Left with the Poles and the Hohenwart conservatives in 1893–5 was 'the union of all the evil, meanness, thoughtlessness and hypocrisy, which together constitutes the philharmonic

---

34 RP: Redlich, 'Aus dem alten Oesterreich', 92.　　35 Ibid. 82–3.
36 Ibid. 79.
37 WSLB, Handschriftensammlung: I.N.198.599, Redlich to Darkow-Singer, 8 Apr. 1902.
38 Redlich to Bahr, 19 Nov. 1903, in Fellner (ed.), *Dichter und Gelehrter* 18–19.
39 RP: Redlich, 'Aus dem alten Oesterreich', 91.
40 Ibid. 115.
41 WSLB, Handschriftensammlung: I.N.198.572, Redlich to Darkow-Singer, 5 Feb. 1893. Abbazia, present-day Opatia.
42 WSLB, Handschriftensammlung: I.N.198.574, Redlich to Darkow-Singer, 27 Feb. 1894.

concert of our public life . . . too unethical, incompetent and weak to accomplish anything good but strong enough to hinder that which is better'.[43] Everywhere Redlich discerned signs of over-ripeness and decay, of habit hardened into compulsion, of a chasm between appearances and reality, in himself as much as in the society around him. 'Underneath the cover of amiability and cheerfulness I am full of anxiety, torment, uneasiness',[44] he wrote.

Scholars have pointed to the existence of a group of *fin-de-siècle* Viennese intellectuals and artists who attacked the solipsism and hypocrisy of Austrian culture, society, language, and politics from the standpoint of the culture of law. Much about Austria at the time defied both rationality and ethics. The Habsburg Empire was a multinational state which masqueraded as a dynastic centralist state; it was formally a constitutional monarchy but was in actuality still governed by the emperor and his bureaucracy. The rift between the façade of Austrian life and its inner reality expressed itself in every sphere of public activity, sensitizing a whole generation of intellectuals to the discrepancy between official ideology and reality.[45] Redlich's friend Wickham Steed, the perceptive Vienna correspondent for *The Times*, noted that in the Monarchy 'most things have another than their surface meaning, fulfil another than their ostensible function',[46] and argued that the most pressing problem of Austria was 'how to adjust appearances to reality and to bring more sincerity into life'.[47]

The urge to bridge the gap between appearance and reality inspired Loos to strip the ornamental façades from Viennese architecture, Schönberg to rid music of all superfluous elements, Freud to explode bourgeois hypocrisy over sexual matters, Kraus to inveigh against public corruption and the corruption of language—and Josef Redlich to later denounce 'bureaucratism' as 'form without substance . . . appearance without truth',[48] vowing to tear off the 'fabric of deception'[49] that covered the administrative forms of the public life of the empire. Together with a

[43] Ibid., I.N.198.577, Redlich to Darkow-Singer, 6 Mar. 1895.
[44] Ibid., I.N.198.573, Redlich to Darkow-Singer, 12 Sept. 1893.
[45] E. Timms, *Karl Kraus: Apocalyptic Satirist: Culture and Catastrophe in Habsburg Vienna* (New Haven and London, 1986), 10–29; Janik and Toulmin, *Wittgenstein's Vienna*, 33–66; I. Barea, *Vienna: Legend and Reality* (London, 1966), 323–4; A. Janik, 'Vienna 1900 Revisited: Paradigms and Problems', *AHY* 28 (1997), 1–27.
[46] H. Wickham Steed, *The Hapsburg Monarchy*, 2nd edn. (London, 1914), p. xx.
[47] Ibid. 205.
[48] *SPOR*, XXI, 1227: Redlich parliamentary speech, 26 Oct. 1911.
[49] AVA, Verwaltungsreform-Kommission 1911–1917, Box 11, Vol. 29: 12 June 1913, Auschüsse I and IV, 19.

group of young bourgeois democratic radicals who were united by disgust with the current state of Austrian politics, a desire to 'make everything clean from the ground up',[50] and an interest in universal suffrage and social politics, Redlich founded the Viennese Fabian Society,[51] which later became the core of the Social Political party.[52]

The Fabian mouthpiece was the weekly newspaper *Die Zeit*.[53] Founded in 1894 by Isidore Singer, Heinrich Kanner, and Hermann Bahr, the aims of *Die Zeit* were very similar to those of Kraus's *Die Fackel*—to break the virtual monopoly over educated public opinion enjoyed by the *Neue Freie Presse* and to create a more truthful climate of opinion.[54] Redlich was involved from the very beginning in *Die Zeit*, both as an investor and as the author of much of the social political criticism and reviews.[55]

Redlich's father had subscribed to the *Neue Freie Presse* from its very first issue. To him, as to most of the liberal bourgeoisie of his generation, it represented 'the light of the Enlightenment and of opposition against absolutism'.[56] By Redlich's time, however, the *Neue Freie Presse* had grown to be the most powerful newspaper in Austria. It was popularly said that, next to Moritz Benedikt (the editor of the *Neue Freie Presse*), the emperor was the most important man in the empire.[57] The *Neue Freie Presse* promoted the economic, social, and national interests of the Austro-German bourgeoisie, legitimized financially corrupt practices, such as the device of printing advertisements disguised as news items, but bowed to government pressure in its coverage of foreign affairs. It was dangerous precisely because its high standards and great prestige lent an aura of objectivity to news that was in fact filtered through the prism of class and German hegemonic interests.

The founders of *Die Zeit*, like Karl Kraus later with *Die Fackel*, hoped to start a tradition of critical, independent journalism in Austria, and aimed to make their newspaper independent of financial control, free from government manipulation, and radical in its coverage of the social and political

---

[50] WSLB, Handschriftensammlung: I.N.198.577, Redlich to Darkow-Singer, 6, 9 Mar. 1895.

[51] Eva Holleis, *Die Sozialpolitische Partei: Sozialliberale Bestrebungen in Wien um 1900* (Munich, 1978), 9–14.

[52] Ibid. 35.

[53] Edith Walter, *Österreichische Tageszeitungen der Jahrhundertwende: Ideologischer Anspruch und ökonomische Erfordernisse* (Vienna, 1994), 52.

[54] See Timms, *Karl Kraus*, 39–40, for similarities between *Die Zeit* and *Die Fackel*.

[55] WSLB, Handschriftensammlung: I.N.198.577, Redlich to Darkow-Singer, 6 Mar. 1895, and I.N.198.600, 7 July.1902. See too Walter, *Österreichische Tageszeitungen*, 51–8.

[56] RP: Redlich, 'Aus dem Alten Oesterreich', 50.

[57] Wickham Steed, *The Hapsburg Monarchy*, 187.

problems of Austria. *Die Zeit* was so radical in its attacks on the regime that the government intrigued against Kanner.[58] '[Kanner] has done more to damage the coalition and Austrian liberalism in six months than if they had lost thirty seats',[59] noted Redlich with satisfaction. The bitterness of Redlich's circle against Austrian liberalism arose out of the fact that this was a family quarrel. They were the sons of liberals who were disillusioned by the gap between what their fathers professed—the 1848 ideals of freedom and equality—and the reality of Austrian liberalism, which had become the protector of capitalist interests and German hegemony.

The Social Political party emerged out of the nucleus of the Fabians. It sought to build an alliance of the radical bourgeoisie with the working class against traditional liberalism and clerical reaction, and campaigned for universal suffrage and a comprehensive *Sozialpolitik*. Redlich was one of the founding members of the party.[60] But he had no instinctive sympathy for the working classes, and indeed had been repelled by the face of urban poverty he had seen in the Second District of Vienna. His support for social politics stemmed rather from a sense of fairness and indignation at liberal selfishness rather than any crusading zeal for the working classes.

His fellow Fabians and Social Political party members looked back towards the 1848 liberal ideals of democracy and equality. Redlich, however, was most interested in the 1848 struggle for freedom against absolutism, which he felt had been seriously compromised by the Austro-German Liberal party. Thrust into power by the Austrian defeat against Prussia and not by their own efforts, the Austro-German Liberals were forced to share power with the court and the bureaucracy. Like their counterparts in Germany, the National Liberals, the German Liberal party in Austria had reached a craven accommodation with the absolutist state rather than decisively resisting it. The result: Austria was still governed by the *ancien régime* 'that began with the accession of Franz II in 1792 and has only been intermittently interrupted by the Revolution (1848) and an episode of bourgeois-liberal ascendancy (1867–1877), but which in essence has not been disturbed'.[61] Redlich thought this obsequious attitude of German liberals towards the state had deep roots in German culture and philosophy. In the 'German school of legal history, led by Savigny, political metaphysic has been employed to justify and bolster up absolute monarchy,

---

[58] Walter, *Österreichische Tageszeitungen*, 53.
[59] WSLB, Handschriftensammlung: I.N.198.577, Redlich to Darkow-Singer, 6 Mar. 1895.
[60] Holleis, *Die Sozialpolitische Partei*, 35.
[61] Redlich to Bahr, 13 Oct. 1913, in Fellner (ed.), *Dichter und Gelehrter*, 92.

until the "Kaiser-idee" appears as the embodiment of a supreme and eternal State, divine and sacrosanct, enthroned above and beyond the reach of the subject people'.[62] Redlich's ancestors had identified themselves as Germans for several generations. Although a *kaisertreu* man,[63] Redlich's father expressed great admiration for the Prussians during the war of 1866 and may even have sympathized with them rather than the Austrians, as did other Bohemian and Moravian German Jews.[64] To the liberals of the 1848 generation, Germany was the great liberal hope, not reactionary Austria.[65] But Redlich's stay in Germany as a law student in Tübingen and Leipzig convinced him that contemporary Germany was not the Germany of liberal dreams, but an authoritarian militarized state with a hatred of individualism. He felt he could discern a 'visible or invisible uniform' on everyone around him, noted the prevailing military style of walking and behaviour amongst the men, and observed the propensity for group life which enforced a certain uniformity of outlook and opinion, and which pushed individuality as far back as possible into the background.[66]

From the beginning he repudiated the whole trend of 'German State scholasticism'. Despite a succession of outstanding professors such as Carl Menger, Eugen von Böhm-Bawerk, and Gustav Schmoller, he insisted that this 'original half-instinctive repudiation' was his 'best and only actual teacher'. His first visit to Britain, in 1891, the beginning of a lifelong association with that country, enabled him to convert this instinctive aversion to the German veneration of the state into a coherent political philosophy. His British friends included a circle of young Oxford liberals such as Francis W. Hirst, John Simon, L. W. Hammond, and Hilaire Belloc, the Fabian circle around the Webbs, and notable academics like F. W. Maitland,[67] Sir William Anson, Lord Bryce, and A. V. Dicey. In the company of these friends, and especially under the influence of Dicey 'whose work immunized me decisively against the Prussian-German state-rights school', he began to formulate a pair of oppositions: the free 'popular state' (*Volksstaat*) as embodied in Britain, versus the authoritarian state (*Obrigkeitsstaat*) of Austria and Germany.[68]

---

[62] Redlich, *Local Government in England*, ii. 394.
[63] RP: Redlich, 'Aus dem Alten Oesterreich', 62.
[64] Ibid., 85; Beller, *Vienna and the Jews*, 153.   [65] Beller, *Vienna and the Jews*, 154.
[66] WSLB, Handschriftensammlung: I.N.198.553, Redlich to Darkow-Singer, 14 Nov. 1887.
[67] See Maitland's letters to Redlich in *The Letters of Frederic William Maitland*, Vol. II, ed. P. N. R. Zutshi (London, 1995).
[68] Redlich to Bahr, 16 Nov. 1920, in Fellner (ed.), *Dichter und Gelehrter*, 434.

Redlich's fascination with Britain, or more precisely England, stemmed from his Gymnasium days.[69] Inspired by an anglophile tutor, Redlich taught himself English from brother Fritz's Realschule textbooks.[70] England represented for Redlich, as for so many other continental liberals, the land of freedom; her parliament, the mother of parliaments.

British positivism and political practice gave Redlich weapons with which to combat German idealistic philosophy and its authoritarian political structure. Despite the German idealistic influence, Austrian intellectual life still produced such outstanding nominalists as Mach, Brentano, Mauthner, and Freud.[71] Redlich's quest to refute political absolutism using nominalism and positivism had precedents as well—Bertrand Russell's theory of the 'logical construction' of abstract terms out of simpler, more concrete ones stemmed from his early interest in socialism and his suspicion of large political abstractions like 'the State'.[72] In Austria, Fritz Mauthner had been driven to his nominalist 'critique of language' as a reaction against the political mystification resulting from such grandiose abstract terms as *Volk*, *Geist*, and *Staat*. The tendency to reify abstractions led to 'conceptual monsters'—an obsession with notions like Race, Culture, and Language, and with their purity or profanity. Conversely, the conviction that there were no eternal truths led to tolerance and an ability to make compromises, which Redlich regarded as one of the key political virtues, and indeed the only basis on which parliamentary government could work.

His admiration for England extended not only to her culture of law and her political progressiveness, but also to her deeply aristocratic culture. Social conservatism was entrenched in Redlich, the source of which was probably the 'aristocratic-conservative' feeling of his family, proud of their pedigree vis-à-vis Jewish families which had emerged more recently from the ghetto.[73] Redlich was enchanted by the elegance of English society, the aristocratic ethos of Oxford and Cambridge and the English public schools. In England Redlich saw a happy marriage between the culture of law and the culture of grace.

---

[69] I have used 'England' and not Britain here because Redlich himself consciously limited himself to England and English political institutions in his works.

[70] Whilst Latin and Greek were taught in the Gymnasium, English was only taught in *Realschule*.

[71] David S. Luft, 'Austria as a Region of German Culture: 1900–1938', *AHY* 23 (1992), 142; Johnston, *Austrian Mind*, 77.

[72] Janik and Toulmin, *Wittgenstein's Vienna*, 121–2.

[73] RP: Redlich, 'Aus dem Alten Oesterreich', 11. Cf. Stefan Zweig, *Die Welt von Gestern: Ermmerungen eines Europäers* (Frankfurt am Main, 1970), 25.

Any German law student interested in English politics in the latter half of the nineteenth century was led inevitably to the works of Rudolf von Gneist.[74] Gneist's studies of English local government were regarded as definitive within the German-speaking world.[75] Yet Redlich soon began to question both the philosophical foundation of Gneist's theory as well as the historical accuracy of his analysis of English government.[76]

Puzzled by the disappointing results of parliamentary government in continental Europe as opposed to the English original, Gneist was drawn towards the study of English administration. He soon became convinced that English administration was essential to the smooth functioning of the English polity, and that unless continental countries reformed their own administrations according to certain English principles, they would never attain the same level of political maturity.

Gneist's philosophical foundation for his interpretation of English government rested on the distinction between State and Society constructed by Lorenz von Stein, himself a distinguished administrative reformer and scholar.[77] Stein had in turn drawn upon Hegelian philosophy. The State was the highest manifestation of the community as will and act, and aimed to secure the best possible development for all its individual members. However, the community also manifested itself economically as Society. Society was in permanent conflict with the State, since self-interest and class struggles predominate in Society. The State's function was to educate its members to transcend the selfishness of Society and attain the 'consciousness of the State'.[78]

Since the monarch was above class struggles and Society, his will embodied that of the State. Successive English monarchs in their wisdom had created the institution of Justices of the Peace, in which unpaid members of the local propertied classes were made responsible for local administration. By imbuing the local gentry with political powers, by obliging them to carry out their responsibilities out of a sense of duty and not for money, the State was educating them to forego their own self-interests and to think of the good of the whole.

---

[74] E. J. Hahn, 'Rudolf von Gneist (1816–1895): The Political Ideas and Political Activity of a Prussian Liberal in the Bismarck Period', Ph.D dissertation, Yale University (1971).

[75] See Heinrich Heffter, *Die Deutsche Selbstverwaltung im 19. Jahrhundert: Geschichte der Ideen und Institutionen* (Stuttgart, 1950), 372–403.

[76] See Redlich, *Local Government in England*, i. pp. v–vi, xxii; ii. 380–418.

[77] Heffter, *Die Deutsche Selbstverwaltung*, 276–80, 445–52.

[78] Giles Pope, 'The Political Ideas of Lorenz Stein and Their Influence on Rudolf Gneist and Gustav Schmoller', D.Phil. thesis, Oxford University (1985), ch. 2 and 3; E. Munroe Smith, *A General View of European Legal History and Other Papers* (New York, 1927), 231.

To Gneist, the State rested on the foundation not of rights, but of duties; the citizen was not born, but had to be trained. He regarded John Stuart Mill's theory of representative self-government as completely wrong-headed—instead of basing power on service and regarding all political power as duties and as a public trust, Mill held suffrage and eligibility to be rights based upon interests.[79] Gneist thought that voting in elections had no intrinsic educational value, since it could not engender political sense or the capacity for public activity. For that, nothing could replace habitual personal service. Thus he considered the nineteenth-century reforms in English administration extremely dangerous, for in place of unpaid public service, administration would now be run by paid officers subject to democratic, that is societal, control. Gneist also exhibited marked reservations about the value of parliamentary government, insisting that in Prussia at least a thorough system of self-government in the localities had to be established before the introduction of parliamentary government.[80]

Gneist rightly described his works on the English administration as 'epoch-making'.[81] His interpretation of English government was the definitive one in German jurisprudence. Moreover, with the support of Bismarck he managed to introduce reforms in the Prussian administration which pressed the propertied classes in the countryside into the service of the state. His influence was felt too amongst the bureaucracy in Austria in the 1850s, and amongst politicians such as Heinrich Clam, Leo Thun, and Hans von Perthaler, the man responsible for the February Patent of 1861. Perthaler was very much influenced by Gneist's theory of consultative liberalism—an autocratic version of liberalism in which the citizens had more 'duties' in implementing legislation on the local and regional levels than in policy determination and control on the national level, and which emphasized the duties and responsibilities of the bourgeoisie to the crown rather than its rights in civil society.[82]

To Redlich, Gneist had corrupted liberal theory from its original liberal democratic basis in the revolutions of 1848 to a much more conservative 'pseudo-liberalism'. He was the fitting political theorist for the generation of 'mild post-liberals' of the 1850s and 1860s in both Germany and Austria.[83] Gneist's 'liberalism' scarcely merited the name. His political

[79] Munroe Smith, *A General View of European Legal History*, 239, 255.
[80] Ibid. 240.   [81] Ibid. 221.
[82] Redlich, *Das österreichische Staats-und Reichsproblem*, i, 727–32, 786–7; id., *Austrian War Government*, 9.
[83] Redlich, *Austrian War Government*, 9.

philosophy was merely the old Roman concept of government being a good in itself, something superior to the governed in its nature and attributes, dressed up in Hegelian metaphysics.[84] Redlich thought that the separation between State and Society was metaphysical legerdemain, since the State could not exist apart from Society.[85] The true ideal should be the conversion of the old authoritarian state into 'the commonwealth of a society governing itself'.[86]

Redlich's condemnation of Gneist is fundamentally a philosophical disagreement about the nature of liberty and the nature of the state. Gneist maintained that the state's true purpose was to advance the cause of freedom and to bring about the highest stage of development. It followed, then, that obedience to the State was the path to freedom. Redlich, on the other hand, made no such teleological and metaphysical claims for the State. To him, the State should simply be society governing itself. According to Redlich, freedom was protected in the English state through the rule of law, a rule from which no one, not even the monarch, was exempt. Contrary to Gneist, who maintained that the evolution of local self-government in England was the result of positive legislation by a wise monarchy, Redlich thought that the success of English administration had been obtained at the expense of the monarchy. The supreme achievement of the English nation was in establishing a true *Rechtsstaat*, for in England there was no *droit administratif* in the continental sense. Throughout the centuries parliament repeatedly repulsed the monarch's attempts to bring administration under royal control, subject to special laws made apart from parliament. Instead, all administrators were both subjects as well as administrators of the one unified law of the whole country. 'Hence England never knew what it is to have government free and distinct from law.'[87]

Redlich's idea of freedom was notably more democratic than that of Gneist. Gneist argued that political liberty could only be safeguarded by the rule of the propertied oligarchy. Redlich the democrat, however, could not accept a theory which portrayed the great democratic progress of the nineteenth century as a process of decay and disintegration. He demonstrated energetically that the reforms had produced a much more effective, non-corrupt, and efficient administration, which had successfully risen to the challenge both of administering an industrial, capitalist state and of improving the conditions of the working class.

[84] Redlich, *Local Government in England*, ii. 393–4.
[85] Ibid., ii. 403.
[86] Ibid., i. p. xiii..
[87] Ibid., ii, 399.

Not surprisingly, such a ringing affirmation of the Whig interpretation of history won Redlich great acclaim within the English-speaking world, so much so that there was enough demand to warrant an English translation of his book. This success was followed four years later by another book on English government, this time on parliamentary procedure, which met with equal acclaim. Prime Minister Asquith even quoted Redlich as an authority in a parliamentary debate pertaining to the elimination of the House of Lords from financial legislation.[88] The historian G. P. Gooch praised Redlich as the only German who understood nineteenth-century England.[89] Redlich was invited to be a visiting professor at Harvard in 1910 and 1913, a guest lecturer at Johns Hopkins and Illinois Universities, and was commissioned by the Carnegie Foundation for the Advancement of Teaching to write a report on American legal studies.[90]

Within the German-speaking world, however, Redlich's ferocious attack on German political philosophy and on the hallowed Gneist made him rather unpopular, and involved him in some very public polemics with his former professor Georg Jellinek.[91] All this made it difficult for him to find an academic job. A call to a great German university was almost out of the question, since he was 'too well known as an adversary of the present Prussian-German system to be given official sympathy'. His reputation as a 'raging anglophile' did not help matters either. In Austria he was 'little loved because of [his] independence and critical sharpness', and besides that, no one cared about his subject.[92]

Faced with such unsatisfactory personal prospects in Austria, and under his great weight of pessimism concerning Austria's future, Redlich contemplated emigrating in 1903. 'When I am an old man, I will happily return to this country, where one can dream well and die calmly, but not create anything',[93] he wrote. Yet at other times he thought he could discern signs that there was hope for Austria after all. Klimt and Mahler, Hermann Bahr and Hugo von Hofmannsthal, were 'rejuvenating' Vienna's artistic life.[94] Most importantly, the Russian Revolution of 1905 inspired Austrian

[88] Redlich, *Schicksalsjahre Österreichs*, 14 Apr. 1910, I, 55.
[89] WSLB, Handschriftensammlung: I.N.198.612, Redlich to Darkow-Singer, 12 Mar. 1906.
[90] Redlich, *The Common Law and the Case Method in American University Law Schools*, Carnegie Foundation for the Advancement of Teaching, Bulletin 8 (1914).
[91] Redlich, *Schicksalsjahre Österreichs*, I, xv.
[92] WSLB, Handschriftensammlung: I.N.198.612, Redlich to Darkow-Singer, 12 Mar. 1906.
[93] Ibid., I.N.198.605, Redlich to Darkow-Singer, 21 Dec. 1903.
[94] Ibid., I.N.198.589, Redlich to Darkow-Singer, 11 July 1899.

workers to demonstrate in front of parliament, leading to the emperor's declaration of support for universal suffrage. 'God preserve the emperor!'[95] exclaimed this otherwise rather lukewarm supporter of monarchy. 'Great things are happening in Europe which still represents the world—or at least its best part.'[96]

Redlich had earlier rejected an opportunity to run for parliament in 1900. 'I don't see how this run-down country could be saved by an assembly of 425 people, elected on the principle that only the most stupid, incompetent individuals completely lacking in conscience are to be selected.'[97] But now, at this pregnant moment of Austrian history, Redlich chose successfully to run for the first Austrian parliament elected by universal suffrage.

Redlich entered parliament not as a Social Political or as one of the neo-liberal independents, but as a member of the *Deutschfortschrittlichen Partei*.[98] This marked the formal parting of ways with his original political associates, foreshadowed already by his break with *Die Zeit* in 1902, when he ceased to involve himself in the daily running of the paper, although he continued to contribute occasional articles. Redlich differed from main-stream Social Politicals not only in political interests, but also in political temperament. Many of the Social Politicals were radicals with strong ideo-logical positions, whereas Redlich's was always the voice of tolerance and pragmatism. He grew impatient with their ethical absolutist positions, especially their attacks on clericalism, which he thought a red herring distracting from more important issues. They differed especially in their responses to the new Christian Social movement created and led by Karl Lueger.[99]

Unlike many Jews, Redlich greeted Lueger's assumption of power with equanimity. He wrote reassuringly to a friend living in the United States that political life in Austria was not as dire as reported in the newspapers, for the 'rabble' whom 'clerical anti-Semitism' had defeated was even worse.[100] He regarded Lueger's anti-Semitism as an opportunistic political

[95] Ibid., I.N.198.611, Redlich to Darkow-Singer, 25 Feb. 1906.

[96] Ibid., I.N.198.610, Redlich to Darkow-Singer, 30 Nov. 1905.

[97] Ibid., I.N.198.592, Redlich to Darkow-Singer, 11 Oct. 1900.

[98] D. Harrington-Mueller, *Der Fortschrittsklub im Abg. Haus des oesterr. Reichsrat 1873–1910* (Vienna, 1972).

[99] See Holleis, *Die Sozialpolitische Partei*, 72, for Social-Political opposition towards Christian Socials.

[100] WSLB, Handschriftensammlung: I.N.198.581, Redlich to Darkow-Singer, 14 July 1896.

tool,[101] whereas German nationalist anti-Semitism he condemned as competitive envy against Jewish success in public life.[102] As a democrat, Redlich probably saw Lueger, denied the mayoralty time after time by the emperor, as a latter-day Wilkes,[103] a champion and near-martyr for democracy.

As we have seen, the young Redlich had been proud and happy to be associated with the Jewish liberal bourgeois elite whom he regarded as the bearers of political, artistic, and literary 'progress'.[104] During his year of study at Leipzig in 1887–8 he attributed the cultural and intellectual dullness of Leipzig after Vienna to the fact that there were 'no Jewish families in the style of Vienna'.[105] However, like many other assimilated Jews, such as Viktor Adler, Karl Kraus, and Heinrich Friedjung, Redlich had internalized much cultural anti-Semitism, especially the identification of Jews with capitalism, with liberalism, and with the press.[106] As he became critical of Austrian liberalism and the corrupt press, he began increasingly to distance himself from the Jewish community. 'I feel that I am the "last" of my tribe . . . any children I might have will no longer belong to Jewry', he wrote in 1896,[107] and in 1903 he formally exited the Jewish community through baptism.[108] Politically, he dissociated himself ever more from the 'Jewish liberalism à la Hock' and the Social Democrats.[109] This caused trouble for Redlich with Jewish voters in his subsequent political career. Redlich's rival at the polls, the Viennese Jewish nationalist Lucian Brunner,

---

[101] Whilst Redlich may have underestimated the virulence of Christian Social anti-Semitism, his mild evaluation of Lueger and his followers as moderate, almost harmless anti-Semites was widely shared. See M. Z. Rosensaft, 'Jews and Antisemites in Austria at the End of the Nineteenth Century', *Leo Baeck Institute Yearbook* (1976), 71–83; Stefan Zweig, *Die Welt von Gestern*, 82–3.

[102] Redlich, *Schicksalsjahre Österreichs*, 10 June 1911, I, 86.

[103] King George III compelled a servile House of Commons to declare John Wilkes, who had been elected to parliament, unfit to sit; whereupon the City of London made Wilkes an alderman and, with the country at its back, fought both king and parliamentary majority. See Redlich, *Local Government in England*, i. 66–7.

[104] RP: Redlich, 'Aus dem alten Oesterreich', 94.

[105] WSLB, Handschriftensammlung: I.N.198.553, Redlich to Darkow-Singer, 14 Nov. 1887.

[106] Robert S. Wistrich, *The Jews of Vienna in the Age of Franz Joseph* (New York, 1989), 498–536; Timms, *Karl Kraus*, 237–40; Allan Janik, 'Viennese Culture and the Jewish Self-Hatred Hypothesis: A Critique', in Ivar Oxaal, Michael Pollack, and Gerhard Botz (ed.) *Jews, Anti-Semitism and Culture in Vienna* (London, 1987), 75–88.

[107] WSLB, Handschriftensammlung: I.N.198.582, Redlich to Darkow-Singer, 22 Dec. 1896.

[108] See Rozenblit, *The Jews of Vienna*, ch. 6, for intermarriage and conversion amongst Viennese Jews.

[109] Redlich, *Schicksalsjahre Österreichs*, I, xvii.

designated Redlich 'the political house Jew (Hausjude) of the Christian Socials'.[110] Redlich never wrote about his reasons for baptism. It was certainly not a religious move, as he remained a freethinker all his life. Although his decision can partially be explained by its immense advantages for academic and political advancement,[111] it was probably also his way of symbolically extricating himself from Jewishness. We know that Redlich, like other assimilated Jews such as Karl Kraus, read Houston Stewart Chamberlain with approval.[112] Redlich's pronouncement that the Viennese Jews had 'corrupted, caricatured, and sterilized the old Austrian culture without replacing it with anything new and vital . . . in the tired and unproductive manner of Arthur Schnitzler',[113] echoes Chamberlain's idea of Jewry as a world-historical force undermining traditional European civilization. On the other hand, Chamberlain's interpretation of Jewry as a set of negative ideological characteristics rather than genetic traits suggested that enlightened Jews could rise above these characteristics.[114] Redlich's ultimate goal was a complete transcendence of his own Jewishness—he aimed not just at assimilation but at dissolution.[115] Not surprisingly, he found it hard to take Herzl's Zionism seriously, both on philosophic grounds and because he had long known Herzl socially in his role as a dandy—well enough that Herzl would telephone Redlich to discuss his famous audience with the pope.[116] '[Herzl] has made "Zionism" respectable in the salons, he wants to lead the Jews into Palestine whilst remaining in Vienna as the correspondent of the "Jerusalem *Neue Freie Presse*" ', quipped Redlich at the outset of Herzl's movement.[117] Later he would describe Zionism as an 'appalling swindle'.[118]

Redlich was impressed by Lueger's powerful personality and his struggle against 'Viennese idleness, Austrian faint-heartedness, the ridiculous "pseudo-liberal" fuss and drivel of Viennese Jewry'.[119] He also concurred

---

[110] 90: *Österreichische Wochenschrift*, 5 May 1911, quoted in Adolf Gaisbauer, *David Stern und Doppeladler* (Vienna, Cologne, and Graz, 1988), 294.

[111] Rozenblit, *The Jews of Vienna*, 132–7.

[112] Redlich, *Schicksalsjahre Österreichs*, 3 Dec. 1916, II, 163; 1 Jan. 1917, II, 176; Redlich to Bahr, 18 Apr. 1915, in Fellner (ed.), *Dichter und Gelehrter*, 112; Timms, *Karl Kraus*, 238.

[113] Redlich to Bahr, 10 Feb. 1918, in Fellner (ed.), *Dichter und Gelehrter*, 306.

[114] Wistrich, *The Jews of Vienna in the Age of Franz Joseph*, 516–7.

[115] Beller, *Vienna and the Jews*, 190–1.

[116] Redlich to Bahr, 2 Feb. 1904, in Fellner (ed.), *Dichter und Gelehrter*, 25.

[117] WSLB, Handschriftensammlung: I.N.198.582, Redlich to Darkow-Singer, 22 Dec. 1896.

[118] Ibid., I.N.198.601, Redlich to Darkow-Singer, 3 Dec. 1902.

[119] Redlich, *Schicksalsjahre Österreichs*, 10 Mar. 1910, I, 52.

with Lueger's attacks on 'Judapest'—Redlich himself characterized the Hungarian kingdom as 'an aristocratic republic with affiliated Jews'.[120] Politically, Redlich and Lueger shared many goals—indeed, Lueger and the Social Politicals had far more in common than either side would have cared to admit. Lueger had started his career as a left-liberal—championing the victims of capitalist interests, rejecting German nationalism in favour of a multinational Austria, forging ties with Slav politicians, and drawing inspiration from Fischhof's programme of national reconciliation and federation in Austria.[121] As mayor, Lueger successfully transformed Vienna by expanding the water supply, building hospitals, schools, and a publicly owned abattoir, and founding an employment exchange and savings bank—'all in a spirit of municipal Socialism that would have warmed the hearts of the Webbs'.[122]

But what especially drew Redlich towards Lueger's Christian Socials was their Austrian patriotism. 'Lueger made it possible for a new healthy Austrian state feeling to emerge once more: in this sense I have for many years felt myself to be his thankful student.'[123] As a true Austrian party, the Christian Socials tried to forge links with the Slavs on common socioeconomic interests, asserted Austrian interests against Hungary, and, most important of all, were not averse to supporting imperialistic adventures.

Redlich's patriotism had its roots in early childhood, and took on fiercely defensive overtones since it was born out of a feeling of humiliation for Austria. Stories of Austrian battles against Hungarians and Italians in 1848 and against Prussia in 1866 awoke strong patriotic feelings in the young Redlich, who often dreamt that he would one day assemble a great host to defend Austria against Hungary and Kossuth or against Prussia.[124] Later on his Austrian feeling was wounded by growing consciousness of the disdain or ignorance in which Austria was held abroad. Wounded pride and defensiveness made Redlich lash out at Hungary and dream of decisive Austrian military action abroad to restore her Great Power status in the eyes of herself and the world.[125] Hence, he supported foreign minister Count Aehrenthal's annexation of Bosnia and Hercegovina, both as the beginning

[120] Diary of Bahr, 24 Sept. 1905. Quoted in Fellner (ed.), *Dichter und Gelehrter*, 45.

[121] John W. Boyer, *Political Radicalism in Late Imperial Vienna: Origins of the Christian Social Movement 1848–1897* (Chicago, 1981), ch. 4.

[122] Peter Pulzer, *The Rise of Political Anti-Semitism in Germany and Austria*, rev. edn. (London, 1988), 198.

[123] Redlich, *Schicksalsjahre Österreichs*, 10 Mar. 1910, I, 52.

[124] RP: Redlich, 'Aus dem alten Oesterreich', 85.

[125] WSLB, Handschriftensammlung: I.N.198.622, Redlich to Darkow-Singer, 20 May 1909.

of a new active policy in the Balkans and as a means of reasserting Austria's Great Power status in the councils of the world, although he upheld the innocence of the Croatian Coalition during the Friedjung trial.[126] Moreover, Redlich believed that, ultimately, Austria would be safe only by including all of the South Slavs within her realm.[127]

Hungary was, to Redlich, the greatest stumbling-block to renewed Austrian greatness. He repudiated Dualism and viewed all attempts by Hungarian politicians to win more autonomy for Hungary as overt or covert attempts to establish Hungary's independence, warning that: 'Hungary now follows as short-sighted and frivolous a policy as in the sixteenth century, where the Hungarian nobles, despite the clear advantage Hungary would obtain through connection with the mighty Habsburg empire and its blooming lands with Ferdinand I as king, still elected a counter-king and plunged Hungary into a hundred and fifty years of catastrophe.'[128] The Austrian chauvinism manifest in such a sentiment prevented Redlich from understanding legitimate Hungarian national feeling. Redlich devoted much time and effort in parliament and in the 1908 Delegations to maintaining Austrian interests against Hungary's, arguing against an *Ausgleich* which sacrificed Austrian political interests in exchange for economic concessions from Hungary.[129]

Redlich's Austrian patriotism did not preclude a strong ethnic German identity, which emerged most clearly in political debates at the regional crownland level. He felt that the Germans were on the defensive against the Czechs in Bohemia and Moravia, and argued that an extension of suffrage in those two crownlands must be balanced by clauses to protect the Germans against Czech numerical supremacy.[130] (Despite his insistence on protective legislation, his qualified support for universal suffrage in Moravia angered the German nationals.[131]) He was also alarmed at the number of (in his view) formerly German towns, like Prossnitz, that were 'falling into the hands of the Czechs',[132] and worked with Joseph Maria Baernreither, the influential Bohemian German member of the Upper

---

[126] SSEES, Seton-Watson Papers, SEW/17/22/7, Redlich to Seton-Watson, 21 Dec. 1909; *SPOR*, XXI, 1144–9: Redlich parliamentary speech, 18 May 1909.
[127] *SPOR*, XVIII, 8119–28: Redlich parliamentary speech, 17 Dec. 1908.
[128] Ibid. 2363: Redlich parliamentary speech, 30 Oct. 1907.
[129] Ibid. 2359–68: Redlich parliamentary speech, 30 Oct. 1907; *SPOR*, XXI, 5066–70: Redlich parliamentary speech, 3 July 1912.
[130] *SPOR*, XVIII, 779–81: Redlich parliamentary speech, 5 July 1907.
[131] Redlich to Bahr, 28 June 1907, in Fellner (ed.), *Dichter und Gelehrter*, 56.
[132] Redlich to Darkow-Singer, 5 Feb. 1893.

House, on legislation to protect German schools both in Bohemia and in Lower Austria.[133]

Redlich believed that a strong ethnic identity (or what in the terminology of his time he would have called national or even racial identity) could coexist with a strong Austrian civic identity, an idea he might have derived as a schoolboy from reading Rabbi Josef Samuel Bloch's 'splendid' writings.[134] Redlich's concept of Austria was inclusive, like Bloch's, embracing all its nationalities within her borders, and his first allegiance was to this inclusive Austria rather than to his own 'race'.[135] Whilst at the Gymnasium Redlich had already read and rejected Heinrich Friedjung's German nationalist ideas in the *Deutsche Wochenschrift*. 'For that the Göding impression was too strong in me. I felt myself to be Austrian and therefore was in the last analysis loyal to the dynasty; I felt myself to be Moravian and therefore could not reject our Moravians and Slovakians.'[136] This ran contrary to the trend of German liberal and national politics, in which Germans increasingly perceived themselves no longer as the *Staatsvolk* but as an embattled nation grimly determined to protect their *Nationalbesitz*.[137]

Redlich's childhood had been blessed by national harmony, albeit within a national hierarchy. Redlich's first language was the Moravian dialect of Slovak prevalent in Göding, which he spoke with his brother, his mother, and his nurse.[138] However, the warmly remembered Slovaks in his childhood were all servants and field-hands, which inevitably led to a somewhat condescending yet idealized view of Slovak life. His father perceived the 'happy Slovak peasant' through the same rose-tinted glasses with which kindly landowners the world over viewed their peasant neighbours—they were a happy people for they had few needs, which were easily met: they grew their own food, made their own clothes, and built their own farm-

---

[133] HHFST, Baernreither Nachlass, Box 47: Redlich to Baernreither, 9 Sept. 1909; Redlich to Baernreither, 17 Sept. 1909.

[134] WSLB, Handschriftensammlung: I.N.198.572, Redlich to Darkow-Singer, 5 Feb. 1893. Bloch was a Galician-Jewish political activist, parliamentarian, and publisher of one of Austrian Jewry's most important weeklies, the *Oesterreichische Wochenschrift*. See Wistrich, *The Jews of Vienna in the Age of Franz Josef*, ch. 9.

[135] Ian Reifowitz, 'Inventing a Nation: Joseph Samuel Bloch and the Cultivation of a Supraethnic Austrian Identity, 1882–1918', paper given at the Fifth Annual Convention of the Association for the Study of Nationalities (ASN), Columbia University, New York, 14 Apr. 2000.

[136] RP: Redlich, 'Aus dem alten Oesterreich', 115.

[137] Pieter M. Judson. ' "Not Another Square Foot!" German Liberalism and the Rhetoric of National Ownership in Nineteenth-Century Austria', *AHY* 26 (1995), 83–97.

[138] RP: Redlich, 'Aus dem alten Oesterreich', 35.

houses and fences.[139] Yet his parents impressed upon their children the unquestioned superiority of German culture by forbidding them to speak Slovak after the arrival of their first German governess.[140]

From his childhood experiences, Redlich retained a great affection and respect for the Slavs. He defended Slav rights to cultural and economic development—indeed, amidst the general morass of Austrian politics in the 1890s Redlich thought the Slav peoples showed the only signs of youthful drive.[141] Redlich sought to allay German fears of the Slavs by arguing that Slav economic development would provide new markets for German goods, thus benefiting German industry and commerce.[142] He believed that Austria would have to be reorganized on a basis other than that of German bureaucratic and military hegemony, although he assumed that the Germans would retain their cultural leadership.[143] Redlich's outspoken condemnation of Magyar oppression of the Slavs in Hungary in parliament, and his efforts to promote Seton-Watson's book, *Racial Problems in Hungary*,[144] led to his being hailed as 'the sole German parliamentarian who protests often against the injustice suffered by the Slavs'.[145] He was regularly approached by Croatian and Slovak politicians for support—for instance, the Slovak politician Milan Hodža asked Redlich to use his influence with Aehrenthal to work against an Andrássy ministry,[146] and Redlich attended a meeting to protest an 'outrageous' sentence passed on the Croatian parliamentarian Lorković.[147] Thomas Masaryk recommended Redlich to foreign minister Count Berchtold for a semi-confidential mission to Belgrade, bearing the conciliatory offer of a possible free harbour in Neum, Klek, or Metkovic for Serbia.[148] Masaryk even went so far as to sound Redlich out about the possibility of joining the Foreign Ministry, adding that the Slavs were discontented with Berchtold and his men, and wanted a man like Redlich in the Ballhausplatz with 'connections to industry, the banking world and parliament, and who possessed an understanding of the new economic policies in the Balkan states'.[149]

[139] Ibid. 45–6.   [140] Ibid. 49.

[141] WSLB, Handschriftensammlung: I.N.198.581, Redlich to Darkow-Singer, 14 July. 1896.

[142] *SPOR*, XIX, 1264–84: Redlich parliamentary speech, 4 June 1909.

[143] Redlich to Bahr, 2 June 1909, in Fellner (ed.) *Dichter und Gelehrter*, 63–4.

[144] SSEES, Seton-Watson Papers, SEW/17/22/7, Redlich to Dr Erich Pistor, 12 Oct. 1908.

[145] Redlich, *Schicksalsjahre Österreichs*, 10 Dec. 1911, I, 116.

[146] Ibid., 5 June 1909, I, 14.   [147] Ibid., 10 Dec. 1911, I, 116.

[148] Ibid., 2 Nov. 1912, I, 166–9; 6 Nov. 1912, I, 175–6; 7 Nov. 1912, I, 176.

[149] Ibid., 10 Nov. 1912, I, 177.

Nevertheless, Redlich's distrust of Slav nationalism and pan-Slavism inevitably distanced him from the Slav politicians. Whilst Redlich thought it perfectly natural for groups of people of the same 'race' to establish cultural and other ties across political boundaries, he thought it reprehensible for an Austrian citizen to give one's political loyalty to another state.[150] Thus, he detested pan-Germanism as well as political pan-Slavism oriented towards Russia. He also distrusted nationalism, seeing it as one of those metaphysical constructions which led to dogmatism and intolerance. He condemned both German and Slav nationalism equally as reactionary. Nationalism which manifested itself as parliamentary obstruction and which degenerated into violence, he labelled 'terrorism'.[151]

The emperor had hoped that nationalist parliamentary obstruction would cease in a democratically elected parliament. He was to be sorely disappointed, however, as nationalist parliamentary obstruction proved even more intractable than before. Although Redlich had started his political career as a fervent democrat, he began to suspect that democracy alone would not solve the nationality problem—indeed, that democracy in an age of mass nationalist passions might even add fuel to the fire.

Parliamentary obstruction and nationalism formed one of the main themes in his second book.[152] Redlich had earlier celebrated the fusion of democracy and parliamentary government in the British political system. Now, however, he realized that parliamentary government had to fear not only the forces of the absolutist state but also democratic popular movements such as nationalism and socialism. Moreover, whilst the absolutist enemy was external, the adversaries of parliament were now internal, in the shape of 'organized, intentional obstruction—the systematic, often violent, negation of the parliamentary idea by the very representatives of the people'.[153] Throughout Europe, parliamentary obstruction was most likely to arise out of 'a conflict of nationalities, a struggle against the existing unions of states',[154] and nowhere was this problem more urgent than in Austria.

Representative self-government presupposes 'common loyalty' to the state, a common commitment to make 'mutual concessions and to strive for

---

[150] *SPOR*, XIX, 1277–81: Redlich parliamentary speech, 4 June 1909.
[151] Redlich, *Schicksalsjahre Österreichs*, 3 Nov. 1909, I, 27.
[152] Josef Redlich, *Recht und Technik des englischen Parlamentarismus. Die Geschäftsordnung des House of Commons in ihrer geschichtlichen Entwicklung und gegenwärtigen Gestalt* (Leipzig, 1905); id., *The Procedure of the House of Commons: A Study of its History and Present Form*, trans. A. E. Steinthal, 3 vols. (London, 1908).
[153] Redlich, *The Procedure of the House of Commons*, i. p. xxiv.
[154] Ibid., iii. 197.

peaceful compromises',[155] and a deep sense of political responsibility. Compromise was possible in the British parliament because the disagreements that divided parties and individuals were not irreconcilable principles, but concrete political, social, and economic issues.

The Catholic Emancipation Act of 1829 and the Franchise Reform Act of 1832 opened parliament to the Irish nationalists. For the first time, parliament included a party held against its will in the British Union. The effects were disastrous. Under Parnell's leadership, the Irish transformed parliamentary opposition from 'a method of parliamentary warfare' against specific legislation into a 'weapon . . . aimed at bringing to a standstill not only a single measure introduced by the majority or the Government, but the whole function of Parliament'.[156] Parliamentary obstruction was nothing less than 'a *repudiation of the existing constitution of the country*, intensified to the point of denying the right of its parliament to exist.'[157]

The success of the Irish nationalists in paralyzing parliament proved that parliamentary government is only possible 'when there is an *acceptance of the constitutional basis* upon which state and parliament are founded'.[158] When there existed 'political feelings of such depth as to threaten the allegiance of an individual to the state in which he lives'; when an individual's political views have 'deeper and firmer roots than his patriotism', whether these originate in 'religious emotion, or from a feeling of nationality; in the future, perhaps, a craving for social or economic equality'—'in all such cases *the majority principle*, a fundamental convention upon which all parliamentary government is built, must needs begin to lose its moral force. At the same time and to the same degree the principle of protection for the minority begins to suffer from decay.'[159]

The Irish nationalists, however, underestimated the determination of the 'national will of the British people, embodied in the corporate will of the House',[160] to break the obstruction, when they realized that Irish obstruction was 'parliamentary anarchy, a revolutionary struggle, with barricades of speeches on every highway and byway to the parliamentary market . . . It was no longer argument against argument, but force against force'.[161] Hence, both Liberal and Conservative parties agreed to a far-reaching reform of parliamentary procedure, which resulted in greater dictatorial powers for the Speaker that broke Irish obstruction.

[155] Ibid., i. 58.   [156] Ibid., 139–140.   [157] Ibid., iii. 197.
[158] Ibid., 197.   [159] Ibid., 197–8.   [160] Ibid., i. 162.
[161] Ibid., 154.

But Redlich also pointed out that the coercion was directed towards Irish obstruction, and not towards the Irish cause as such. Redlich was not blind to the historic injustice committed against Ireland or to the sufferings of the Irish people. Nor did he grudge the Irish their political organization and unity, for only through united political action could the Irish succeed in raising consciousness for the problems plaguing Ireland. Yet he felt that '[h]owever reasonable and practicable the objects of the Irish Nationalist party may have been—the next twenty years saw many of them attained—they were not to be won by open force, nor was it right they should be'.[162] In an act of poetic justice, it was Gladstone, leader of the battle against obstruction, who also led the movement for reform in Ireland and for Home Rule.

The lessons, then, that Redlich drew from what he regarded as the British parliamentary triumph over Irish nationalism may be summarized as follows: first, a working parliament rests on the principles of the rule of the majority and the protection of the minority—without the former, parliament cannot function; without the latter, a despairing minority would be driven to revolt. Secondly, all sides must practise pragmatism and mutual compromise to ensure a working parliament. Thirdly, if a minority intent on destroying the state tries to bring parliament to a halt altogether, the parliamentary majority is justified in using legal force against it as a measure of state defence. And fourthly, legal force is not a permanent solution, and must be accompanied by tackling the root of the problem—in the case of the Irish, the agricultural and the economic problem. That the solution to the problem of nationalism might be actual secession or de facto independence was shunted aside by Redlich on the grounds that it fell outside the scope of his enquiry. 'It is a question which may well be raised, but can hardly receive a theoretical answer, whether it is at all conceivable that struggles involving the existence or destruction of a state or of a union of states can be carried through under the forms of parliamentary government.'[163] Little did Redlich know, when penning those words, that one day he would have to find legal forms for the disintegration of his beloved Austrian state as a member of the last imperial ministry in Austria.

To Redlich, political liberty meant freedom from the authoritarian state, but not secession from the historically determined territorial state itself. The need to strengthen the Austrian state idea became the driving force behind all of his political activities.[164] Just *why* the Austrian state idea or the

---

[162] Redlich, *The Procedure of the House of Commons*, 162.
[163] Ibid., iii. 200.
[164] For the Austrian state idea, see Günther Ramhardter, *Geschichtswissenschaft und Patriotismus* (Munich, 1973), 57–62.

continual existence of Austria was so important was a question that scarcely troubled the pre-war Redlich. Redlich thought of Austria as a 'civilizing' force in Central and Eastern Europe. He also thought it impossible for the constituent peoples of Austria to live without Austria—an independent Hungary could not coexist with a strong South Slav state, nor could the Czechs and Poles do without the empire's protection.[165] Yet such considerations did not loom large in Redlich's thoughts. Austria was in danger; Redlich was Austrian; hence it was self-evident to him that he should do all in his power to rescue the Austrian state idea. '[Redlich] has a passionate feeling for Austria, and therefore feels the decline of our State far more acutely than do most other Austrian politicians',[166] wrote Baernreither.

Given the amount of ink and passion he had hurled at the German worship of the state, it might seem ironic that he was enthroning the Austrian state idea as his political ideal. But in all fairness it is important to note the distinctions between Redlich's Austrian state *idea* versus the German veneration of the actual *state*. Redlich wanted to strengthen the sense of belonging amongst the different peoples of Austria, and he believed that certain changes in the administrative structure of Austria could help foster such loyalty, but he was always very cautious about extending the actual administrative reach of the state. Moreover, the Austrian state of his visions was not an authoritarian state with rule imposed from above, but a popular state, based on popular sovereignty, with a strong parliament as true representative of the people at its centre.

Austria could not be ruled apart from parliament—that was axiomatic for Redlich. Parliament represented an attempt to solve the common problems of existence by common consensus, not force; its conventions exercised a restraint upon mass irrationalism; moreover, it lent itself to peaceable reform rather than violent revolution. History had proved that authoritarian rule in Austria could only weaken Austria by alienating her constituent peoples from the state idea itself. Nor should mass-based politics spill over into the extra-parliamentary arena—without the restraint exercised by parliament, the political passions in Austria would and did explode into violence. Commenting on the bloody street fight accompanying the Social Democratic demonstration on 17 September 1911, as well as the various outbreaks of nationalist violence throughout Austria, Redlich wrote that despite being a 'passionately good European', and 'very progres-

---

[165] Redlich, *Schicksalsjahre Österreichs*, 30 Oct. 1912, I, 166.
[166] J. M. Baernreither, *Fragments of a Political Diary*, ed. Josef Redlich (London, 1930), 18 Aug. 1913, p. 228.

sive and modern', he was very remote from radical methods and radical political goals. 'What radicalism has achieved in Austria can be seen [in the street fight], and I fear that this will spread to the whole of our political way of life, and not be confined to one party.'[167] Redlich was opposed to radicalism in thought as well as in deed. He rebuked Masaryk for his 'atomistic' advocacy of small parties in which members were united by common moral goals, rather than big parties held together by party discipline.[168] For Masaryk, liberal values could survive only by intensifying cultural combat between liberalism and reactionary forces in politics like clericalism. Any attempt to reconcile national conflicts on the basis of economic and class interests without addressing more fundamental questions such as religious, cultural, and national identity was morally suspect.[169] Despite his personal admiration and friendship for Masaryk, Redlich thought such an ethically absolute philosophy death to a working parliament. In place of the existing multi-party system, which was in essence a collection of lobby groups representing distinct interests, Redlich wanted large, disciplined parties similar to those of the British party system, which could act as state-wide parties representing trans-national and trans-regional interests. Only then could a parliamentarization of the regime take place.[170]

Hence Redlich rebuked those who opposed Christian Social leader Albert Gessmann's attempts to create a powerful new ministerial position for himself on the grounds of Gessmann's personal lack of ethics. Austria was on the threshold of parliamentary ministerialism in the West European sense, and Gessman deserved the ministry simply because he was the floor leader of the largest party in the parliament.[171] Redlich's perspective, as John Boyer has pointed out, was frankly *realpolitisch*—he would have sanctioned almost anything to achieve parliamentary stability.[172]

Redlich's *realpolitisch* perspective, although arising from pragmatism and a willingness to compromise, could easily lead to a dangerous moral relativism, a danger he himself recognized. 'In politics, will is everything,

---

[167] Redlich to Bahr, 18 Sept. 1911, in Fellner (ed.) *Dichter und Gelehrter*, 75–6.
[168] *SPQR*, XVIII, 5551–2: Redlich parliamentary speech, 10 June 1908.
[169] Boyer, *Culture and Political Crisis in Vienna*, 196–8.
[170] Redlich, *The Procedure of the House of Commons*, i. 129: 'To speak paradoxically, England possessed and still possesses its system of party government through a parliamentary cabinet, by reason of its *lack of parties in the Continental sense*' [italics in original]. See Peter Pulzer, *Political Representation and Elections in Britain*, 36–42, for a confirmation of Redlich's differentiation between the continental European multi-party and the British two-party systems.
[171] *SPQR*, XVIII, 4168–79: Redlich parliamentary speech, 9 Apr. 1908.
[172] Boyer, *Culture and Political Crisis in Vienna*, 125.

intellect worth little, ethics—nothing!'[173] For instance, his political alliance with the Christian Socials, which incidentally was not devoid of material advantage for Redlich, since Gessman obtained the coveted professorial appointment for him, did not blind Redlich to some of the Christian Socials' more unsavoury practices. Redlich judged the defeat of the Christian Social party at the polls in 1911 to be an 'unavoidable retaliation' for the 'shameless demagogy' of the people around Lueger, adding that Gessmann, Weiskirchner, and Lueger had 'smeared the great idea of a respectable Austrian, conservative-democratic party completely with filth'.[174]

Redlich's desire for political advantage and advancement also led to ethical dilemmas. Notwithstanding his campaign against the common parliamentary practice of relying on bureaucratic patronage to satisfy constituencies, Redlich's ' "corrupt" parliamentarian's heart' was delighted when Finance Minister Biliński informed him that Redlich's proposal to compensate those cities which had tobacco factories had been accepted, thus increasing Göding's annual income by 6,000 crowns.[175] Redlich also refrained from publishing a review of Kübeck's memoirs,[176] which exposed Austrian misrule from 1815 to 1848, for fear of 'barring the way to future political influence'.[177]

Nevertheless, Redlich managed to negotiate the fine line between pragmatism, moral relativism, and ethics. He supported Masaryk against Lueger's call for the expulsion of Jewish influence from academic life.[178] Although he labelled his own politics 'Great Austrian',[179] he refused to get drawn into the Archduke Franz Ferdinand's 'Great Austrian' group, on account of Franz Ferdinand's autocratic personality and feudal clerical convictions. 'I can only adhere to my own and no other man's politics. My politics: Austrian, anti-*Kulturkampf*, anticlerical, the imperial idea, nationality rights.'[180]

[173] Redlich, *Schicksalsjahre Österreichs*, 12 Nov. 1905, I, xvi.
[174] Ibid., 21 June 1911, I, 87.
[175] Ibid., 6. Nov. 1909, I, 30.
[176] Max Kübeck (ed.), *Tagebücher des Carl Friedrich Fr v. Kübeck* (Vienna, 1909).
[177] Redlich, *Schicksalsjahre Österreichs*, 28 July 1909, I, 21.
[178] SPQR, XVIII, 2938–48: Redlich *Dringlichkeitsantrag*, 'Die Freiheit der Wissenschaft und der Hochschulen', 4 Dec. 1907.
[179] For the 'Great Austrian' movement, see R. A. Kann, *The Multinational Empire: Nationalism and National Reform in the Habsburg Monarchy, 1848–1918*, 2 vols. (New York, 1950), vol. ii, ch. 11.
[180] Redlich, *Schicksalsjahre Österreichs*, 3 June 1909, I, 13.

Redlich's determination to remain true to his own convictions isolated him politically. His inner alienation from members of his own party was complete when the party was subsumed in 1910 in the Deutschen Nationalverband. After some debate about Redlich's eligibility for the Deutschen Nationalverband as a baptized Jew, he was accepted as a member and thus found himself belonging to the same coalition as the German nationalist radicals he despised.[181] He generally supported the Social Democrats on social political legislation, but maintained his distance from them otherwise. Even his political alliance with the Christian Socials was constrained by his uneasiness about their excesses and Christian Social hostility towards Redlich's administration reform project.[182] In other words, despite being nominally a member of the Deutschen Nationalverband, Redlich acted, like so many Viennese liberals, as a political independent, a *Wilde* in parliament, attaining prominence and influence without the power that comes from the backing of a major party.[183]

Realizing the need for an extra-party power-base to push through his pet project of administrative reform, Redlich successfully campaigned for an Imperial Commission for Administrative Reform in Austria.[184] Impressed by the role that Royal Commissions had played in the reform of English administration,[185] Redlich pinned high hopes on his new commission, which was the first of its kind in Austria. That he succeeded in forming one in 1911 is a measure of the respect and influence he had amassed in his short political career. From the start, Redlich was the guiding spirit of the commission.[186] He was motivated by three political passions—the Weberian fear of the threat to political liberty posed by bureaucratic absolutism and the expansion of state activity, the drive for integrity and public accountability in state finances, and the strengthening of the Austrian state idea through empire reform.

Bureaucratic management of the state had existed long before parliamentary government in Austria, and had retained its strength even in Austria's nominally constitutional period. Despite a guarded respect for the old Josephinist bureaucracy—incorruptible, economical, and imbued

---

[181] Ibid., 7 May 1911, I, 84; 6 July. 1911, I, 90. See Pulzer, *The Rise of Political Anti-Semitism in Germany and Austria*, 207–10.
[182] Redlich, *Schicksalsjahre Österreichs*, 25 Apr. 1910, I, 56.
[183] B. Morgenbrod, *Wiener Grossbürgertum im Ersten Weltkrieg* (Vienna, 1994), 27.
[184] AVA, Verwaltungsreform-Kommission 1911–1917.
[185] Redlich, *Local Government in England*, I, 98.
[186] SSEES, Seton-Watson Papers, SEW/17/22/7: Redlich to Seton-Watson, 21 Oct. 1911. See also Boyer, *Culture and Political Crisis in Vienna*, 351–64.

with a state loyalty that transcended national and regional boundaries[187]—
Redlich insisted, like Max Weber, on the tension between political and
bureaucratic modes of rule. Whilst he agreed with Weber that bureaucracy
was indispensable in a modern state, he believed that the function of the
bureaucracy should be to implement policies determined by parliament.
Bureaucracy was a good servant but a bad master.[188]

The transformation of the nature of Austrian bureaucracy in the second
half of the nineteenth century had exacerbated the bureaucratic problem
by introducing nationality conflict into the bureaucracy. The nationaliza-
tion of Austria's railroads necessitated an exponential increase in the
number of civil servants. The rising nationalities, especially the Czechs,
took advantage of this opportunity to flood the lower and middle ranks of
the civil service with their own members, with the result that the new mass
bureaucracy became thoroughly riddled with nationality conflict.[189] In
time, every party and nationality group took to measuring political success
by the ability to obtain bureaucratic appointments for members of their
own party or nationality. Instead of using parliament as a forum to push
through positive legislation, political parties preferred to rely on official
patronage to satisfy the demands of their constituencies. Since such practices obscured the need for acts of creative legislation in parliament, each
group could and did engage in parliamentary obstruction.[190] The
corrupted and corrupting bureaucracy was a 'living cancer' destroying the
nerve centres of Austrian society.[191]

With its power to award lucrative state contracts, the Finance Ministry
was a particularly attractive target for intervention and patronage by parliamentarians and parties, leading to widespread corruption.[192] From his
family, Redlich had learnt to regard financial matters with grave concern

---

[187] Redlich, *Austrian War Government*, 36.

[188] See Wolfgang Mommsen, 'Max Weber on Bureaucracy and Bureaucratization: Threat
to Liberty and Instrument of Creative Action', in *The Political and Social Theory of Max
Weber, Collected Essays* (Cambridge, 1989), 109–20.

[189] It is interesting that Redlich's analysis of the new bureaucracy was similar to that of
Heinrich von Tschirsky, the German ambassador in Vienna. Tschirsky reported that since the
disappearance of the old, centrally oriented German officials, bribery was rampant in the
bureaucracy. He blamed the corruption on the entrance into the civil service of Slavs who
constituted an educated proletariat from the Austrian *Mittelschulen*. See Boyer, *Culture and
Political Crisis in Vienna*, 355.

[190] See Joseph Redlich, *Emperor Francis Joseph of Austria* (London, 1929), 453–7, for
Redlich's description of parliamentary and bureaucratic collusion and corruption.

[191] *SPOR*, XVIII, 5549–60: Redlich parliamentary speech, 10 June 1908.

[192] Redlich, *Bericht . . . über die Entwicklung und den gegenwärtigen Stand der Österreichischen
Finanzverwaltung sowie Vorschläge der Kommission zur Reform dieser Verwaltung* (Vienna,
1913), 116–91.

and to treasure financial probity as one of the cardinal virtues. He spent almost one year single-handedly producing a fantastically detailed report on the Austrian financial administration.[193] Austria's weak finances dangerously compromised her military security. Moreover, the 'fabric of untruth' that veiled the financial administration of the empire made it impossible for Austria to pursue the sound fiscal and monetary policies necessary for her economic growth.[194] Redlich recommended that the accuracy, efficiency, and public scrutiny of the budget process be improved, thereby allowing parliament to fulfil its proper role of scrutiny over the budget, thus empowering it vis-à-vis the administration. Although Redlich did not participate directly in the family business, he was contributing just as surely as the Jewish commercial bourgeoisie to the modernization of Austria.[195] At times, Redlich singled out the financial question in Austria as the most threatening of all her ills.[196]

But the main preoccupation of the committee as a whole was with the organization of imperial administration.[197] Under Redlich's leadership, the committee tackled one of the most passionately debated political issues in the empire—the question of autonomy.[198] The centralizing bureaucratic absolutism of the pre-March and later the Bach administration's days in the 1850s brought about, in an almost Hegelian dialectical process, a yearning for autonomy on both ends of the political spectrum—demand for municipal autonomy from the liberals, and demand for *Länder* autonomy from the feudal conservatives.[199] Both kinds of autonomy made enormous strides in the second half of the nineteenth century, but at a huge price—the destruction of the Austrian state idea and the solidity of the state, so much so that Redlich described the history of autonomy in Austria

---

[193] Redlich, *Bericht . . . über die Entwicklung und den gegenwärtigen Stand der Österreichischen Finanzverwaltung sowie Vorschläge der Kommission zur Reform dieser Verwaltung* (Vienna, 1913), 116–91.

[194] AVA, Verwaltungsreform-Kommission 1911–1917, Box 11, Vol. 29: 12 June 1913, Ausschüsse I and III, 19.

[195] See Oskar Jászi, *The Dissolution of the Habsburg Empire* (Chicago, 1929), 170–6, for the role of the Jewish bourgeoisie in modernizing the Habsburg Monarchy.

[196] Redlich, *Schicksalsjahre Österreichs*, 27 Nov 1910, I, 72.

[197] For the administrative and constitutional background, see Adam Wandruszka and Peter Urbanitsch (eds.), *Die Habsburgermonarchie 1848–1918, Verwaltung und Rechtswesen*, Vol. II (Vienna, 1975).

[198] AVA, Verwaltungsreform-Kommission 1911–1917, Box 6, Vol. 11: 14 May 1912, Sitzung des verstärkten Enquete-Ausschuß.

[199] Redlich devoted much space to the history of administrative reform in his *Das österreichische Staats- und Reichsproblem*. See i. 250–70, 301–4, 360–80, 662–71.

as 'the conscious giving up of the Austrian state'.[200] Municipal autonomy
had been the battle-cry of Austrian liberals ever since 1848.[201] However,
with the franchise restricted to narrowly defined curias, local administration became in practice a one-class oligarchy, in which local elites could
profitably engage in corruption in important areas such as tax collection
and the administration of justice—a situation analogous to that prevailing
in the rotten boroughs of eighteenth-century England.[202] Even more disastrous, from Redlich's viewpoint, was the discovery by Austria's warring
nationalities that the state-free municipality could be a real asset in the
nationality struggle. The free municipality became the bulwark of parties
and the 'secure fortress' of nations. The municipality was the cell of political life—all party organizations in Austria, with the exception of the Social
Democrats, were based on the municipalities and the possession of the
municipality by a nation. No adequate protection existed for the rights of
individuals as state-citizens, especially the rights of those in the national or
political minority. The empire had 'dissolved into municipalities, each with
its own mayor, with the emperor as the mayor of mayors'.[203]

The success of the movement for increased autonomy in the *Länder*,
constructed on the basis of historical state rights, meant that Austria was
cursed not only with state-free administrative zones—the municipalities—
but also with state-free legislatures. Each provincial legislature acted in
isolation—women's suffrage in Carniola and proportional representation
in Moravia had both been discussed without regard to legislative trends
elsewhere in the empire or at the central level, and the question of municipal suffrage had been dealt with differently in different provinces. The
central regime seldom had any overview of the different legislative tendencies of the different crownlands. 'The whole thing gives an impression of a
complete lack of system and planning.'[204]

The central ministries still functioned as they had in the eighteenth
century—as an executive, interventionist power for the judgement of

[200] AVA, Verwaltungsreform-Kommission 1911–1917, Box 13, Vol. 37: 31 Mar. 1913,
Ausschüsse I und IV, 109.
[201] See Heffter, *Die Deutsche Selbstverwaltung im 19. Jahrhundert*, 180–4, for the influence of
Rottek and the *Pouvoir Municipal* on German liberals. See also AVA, Verwaltungsreform-
Kommission 1911–1917, Box 13, Vol. 37: 31 Mar. 1913, Sitzung des Referentenkomitees der
vereinigten Ausschüsse I und IV, 12–17, 109.
[202] Redlich, *Bericht . . . über die Entwicklung und den gegenwärtigen Stand der Österreichischen
Finanzverwaltung*, 116–91.
[203] AVA, Verwaltungsreform-Kommission 1911–1917, Box 13, Vol. 37: 31 Mar. 1913,
Ausschüsse I und IV, 177.
[204] Ibid., Box 11, Vol. 25: 19 May 1914, Auschuß III, 18.

individual cases. Yet although the central authorities could and did inter-
vene in local affairs, no matter how small (which made them such attractive
targets for politicians seeking to please their constituencies), they ignored
large issues such as the protection of the state rights of citizens and the
protection of state financial interests.

Drawing on his analysis of English administration, Redlich called for a
complete overhaul of the relation between centre and periphery. In
England, neither parliament nor the central administrative authority had
executive powers. Parliament legislated, local administration implemented
policy made by parliament, and the central administrative authority made
sure that local administration did not exceed the bounds of its authority as
defined by parliament. In addition to its supervisory tasks, the central
administration had two other functions—first, to collect the most precise
data from all parts of the country; secondly, to make available knowledge
acquired in one place to others, thus acting from its overall vantage-point as
a technical consultant.[205]

Redlich utilized the same principle of central authority as a supervisory
and consultative depository of information to unite the crownlands with
their diverse legislatures. He proposed to resurrect the institution of the
Staatsrat (Privy Council), not in its old incarnation as an administrative
organ, but as an organ for the overview of legislative trends in the different
crownlands. He pointed out that the Privy Council in Britain, rightfully
deprived of its administrative functions in the home country, nevertheless
played an important unifying role in the British empire by acting as a
central depository of legislative information from the different
Dominions. He also pointed to an equivalent body in the United States,
which was responsible for overseeing the activities of the judiciaries and
legislatures of the different states.[206]

Redlich maintained that his proposals did nothing to hurt local and
regional autonomy—indeed, he argued that provincial legislatures could
enjoy a vastly extended sphere of activity without injury to overall state
feeling if his proposals were implemented. He regarded himself as a true
friend of autonomy and freedom, pointing out that the relations between
central authority and local government as set out by British reformers in
the 1860s had drawn heavily on John Stuart Mill's philosophy of political

---

[205] Redlich, *Local Government in England*, i, 178–85; Redlich, *Bericht . . . über die
Entwicklung und den gegenwärtigen Stand der Österreichischen Finanzverwaltung*, 183.
[206] AVA, Verwaltungsreform-Kommission 1911–1917, Box 11, Vol. III: 19 May 1914,
Sitzung des Ausschuß für die innere Einrichtung und den Geschaftsgang der Behörden.
16–21.

liberty.[207] Mill had argued for centralized information and disseminated power, since a state in which everyone knows as much as possible but does not possess too much power is the best guarantee against absolute rule by the executive over a congregation of isolated individuals.[208]

Autonomous self-government was essential since the 'countless, fragmented but important tasks of living together in the community could never be decreed from above'.[209] The state was not something which should be imposed from above, a straitjacket binding together disparate elements, but an organic growth from below. In the last analysis, it was the concrete embodiment of a subjective feeling of belonging together, akin to Durkheim's conception of society as the manifestation of the *conscience collective*.[210] Since the state was the embodiment of a collective idea, a common pool of knowledge and a process of information-sharing between the different parts of the state could only strengthen the state idea.

The difference between the executive, interventionist mode of central government in Austria and Redlich's proposed supervisory mode in which knowledge played such an important integrative part bears more than a passing resemblance to Durkheim's categories of mechanical and organic solidarity, although there is no evidence that Redlich knew of Durkheim's work. Whereas mechanical solidarity discourages individual autonomy (and indeed Redlich was to complain that the hostility towards individualism in Austria was very great), organic solidarity encouraged differentiation and co-operation. Redlich's ideal state was not a 'mechanical' unity which consisted of a mere multiplication of homogeneous units, but an 'organic' unity in Durkheim's sense, in which individuals are highly differentiated yet unite through co-operation.[211] It was thus that Redlich could encourage local self-government in municipalities, accept the existence of legislatively autonomous crownlands, and insist that different nations could develop freely within the unity of the Habsburg empire.

Robert Kann has described Redlich as the heir of the German centralist liberal tradition.[212] There is some truth in this description, for Redlich

[207] Redlich, *Local Government in England*, i. 177–185.
[208] Isaiah Berlin, 'John Stuart Mill and the Ends of Life', in *Four Essays on Liberty* (Oxford, 1969), 200.
[209] AVA, Verwaltungsreform-Kommission 1911–1917, Box 11, Vol. 37: 31 Mar. 1913, Ausschüsse I und IV, 201.
[210] Steven Lukes, *Émile Durkheim: Life and Work: A Historical and Critical Study* (London, 1973), 4.
[211] Ken Morrison, *Marx Durkheim Weber: Formations of Modern Thought* (London, 1995), 129–130.
[212] Kann, *The Multinational Empire*, ii. 284.

rejected empire federalization as envisaged by the Slavs and aristocrats, looking instead to the introduction of *Kreise*—nationally homogeneous administrative units—as a solution to the nationality conflict in mixed-nationality crownlands.[213] He supported a unitary state with a strong central parliament and a nationally neutral administration. Municipal, *Kreise*, and *Länder* administration would be conducted in the local language, but Redlich assumed that German would be the language of the highest administrative circles, through sheer practicality and also as an acknowledgement of the historic role played by the Germans in the Habsburg state.[214]

However, Redlich's use of the British empire and the United States as structural models for the relations between autonomous crownlands with the centre and each other belongs to an alternative liberal model—the tradition of Fischhof, who read Hamilton, Madison, and Franklin in his quest for a federal yet united state.[215] Redlich's creative proposal on how to build a higher collectivity out of differentiated crownlands was a kernel from which federalization could, and did, grow. After all, Redlich's proposals were opposed by the bureaucracy precisely because they would have weakened the central ministries considerably at the expense of local authorities and parliament.

The imperial administrative reform commission sat for three years, produced an impressive weight of reports, and yet ultimately toiled in vain. Redlich's proposals were based on the democratic foundation of a true equality between the different parts of the empire and the centre, modelled in part on the example of the country with the longest tradition of representative self-government—Great Britain. Yet privately he expressed grave doubts as to whether or not Austria was ready for representative self-government or for democracy. He compared democracy in a country as 'socially and politically unripe' as Austria to an electric light-bulb, where 5 per cent of the expended energy is used and the other 95 per cent lost in heat.[216] At times he thought the state and empire so weak that only a strong assertion of monarchical power would help sustain it.[217] Given the private doubts of the author of the reform proposals, it is not surprising that many thought the reform commission's recommendations impossibly utopian.

[213] Redlich, *Schicksalsjahre Österreichs*, 30 Aug. 1913, I, 207–8.
[214] *SPOR*, XXI, 1239: Redlich parliamentary speech, 26 Oct. 1911.
[215] Kann, *The Multinational Empire*, ii. 148; Wistrich, *The Jews of Vienna in the Age of Franz Josef*, 149–160.
[216] Redlich, *Schicksalsjahre Österreichs*, 10 Apr. 1911, I, 82.
[217] Ibid., 20 Oct. 1909, I, 24.

Redlich was utopian too, in thinking that the proposal could ever have been adopted in the political circumstances of the time. He was attacking too many sacred cows—the power of the central ministries, the power of local notables, of bureaucracy, and finally of the politicians. His hopes that a revived parliament with large disciplined blocs could push through the reforms against bureaucratic opposition came to nothing. However much politicians of all parties might decry corruption in bureaucracy, no political party had any interest in curbing the practice of bureaucratic patronage.[218] Redlich lacked the support of any party, including his own. 'Redlich is a genius, but no politician', noted the German liberal leader Sylvester; 'no politician can let his party know that he feels himself above it. No party will tolerate that!'[219] How threatening his proposals were to the existing political system in Austria can be gauged by the fact that Hermann Bahr's articles describing Redlich's reform proposals in detail were completely suppressed by the censor during the war.[220]

Those threatened by the administrative reform project decided to bury it in silence rather than dignify it by open debate.[221] Redlich several times noted plaintively the 'dead silence' in the newspapers which surrounded the project; most notably the silence from the *Neue Freie Presse*.[222] By 1914 it was clear that the project was all but dead.[223]

For a while Redlich had maintained a sceptical optimism that his commission could actually change things. Now, however, his domestic reform programme in shambles, Redlich lapsed into apocalyptic mode. He was a liberal who had lost faith in the underlying philosophical tenet of liberalism—progress. 'The self-confidence of the "liberal-rational" worldview has become for us lifeless dust', he wrote.[224]

But in true Viennese style, Redlich's apocalyptic diary entries exist side by side with a minute chronicling of his social triumphs. If Redlich had not succeeded politically, he could at least look with satisfaction on his prowess at social climbing. He socialized regularly, not only with inhabitants of the

---

[218] John W. Boyer, *Culture and Political Crisis in Vienna*, 360–1, 363–4; Redlich, *Austrian War Government*, 68.

[219] Bahr to Redlich, 17 Jan. 1924, in Fellner (ed.), *Dichter und Gelehrter*, 517.

[220] Redlich, *Schicksalsjahre Österreichs*, 1 June 1915, II, 42.

[221] Redlich, *Austrian War Government*, 67–8, for Redlich's own analysis of the reasons for failure.

[222] Redlich, *Schicksalsjahre Österreichs*, 5 Dec. 1912, I, 184. Cf. the *Totschweigentaktik* (conspiracy of silence) around Freud and Kraus in newspapers. See Janik and Toulmin, *Wittgenstein's Vienna*, 35.

[223] Boyer, *Culture and Political Crisis in Vienna*, 364.

[224] Redlich to Bahr, 15 Sept. 1912, in Fellner (ed.), *Dichter und Gelehrter*, 81.

Second Society of Vienna, but occasionally with the First Society. 'Professor Redlich finds particular pleasure in the society of certain aristocratic circles, where he is especially welcomed by the ladies, since he is a most fascinating talker', wrote Baernreither.[225] Redlich's diaries are replete with accounts of dinners at the Hotel Sacher, banquets, glittering society, and elegant palaces. Truly, Redlich was experiencing Vienna's 'Gay Apocalypse' to its fullest.

He greeted the declaration of war on Serbia with delirious enthusiasm, seeing this as the only solution to the paralysis and despondency that afflicted the empire. Looking back after the war, he would write that, for Austria, the issue was: 'To be or not to be?'[226]—that this was an existential war, the last desperate hope to save a dying empire.

---

[225] J. M. Baernreither, *Fragments of a Political Diary*, 29 Jan. 1913, p. 158.
[226] Redlich, *Austrian War Government*, 74.

2

Lewis Namier and the Rejection of Austria

Austria has been, not a home for her nationalities, but a hotel or boarding-house.[1]

The relation between Redlich's and Namier's family backgrounds is a relation of theme and variations. The common themes arise from their common membership of the affluent assimilated Jewish strata in Central and Eastern Europe; the variations from differences in personalities and geography. Like Redlich, Namier's forebears had been assimilated for several generations, although they had assimilated to Polish rather than German culture. What Namier's and Redlich's ancestors shared was the desire to assimilate to Western high culture. In Moravia this meant German culture; in Russian Poland and Galicia it meant Polish culture. Whilst Redlich's family had an indulgent, patronizing attitude towards the Slovak peasants amongst whom they lived, and tolerated the use of Slovak when their children were still very young, Namier's parents seemed to have despised the Ukrainians who formed the majority population in Eastern Galicia. Redlich's father forbade his children to speak Slovak, to facilitate them learning German from their governess; Namier's father Joseph prohibited Ukrainian in his household on the grounds that Ukrainian was 'no language at all'[2]—merely a debased dialect spoken by peasants.

Redlich could boast of an ancestry of 'tolerated' Jews from Maria Theresa's times on his paternal grandmother's side. Similarly, Namier's forefathers, the Niemirowskis, had been granted, through a special decree, full rights of landownership in Congress Poland after the Napoleonic wars.[3] Redlich's ancestors had identified themselves as German for several generations, to the extent that his father sympathized with the Prussians in the 1866 conflict with Austria. The Niemirowskis were fervent Polish patriots, and greatly resented being compelled to substitute 'Bernsztajn' instead of 'Niemirowski' as their last name, an event which Namier's future

---

[1] L. B. Namier, *Germany and Eastern Europe* (London, 1915), 124.
[2] J. Namier, *Lewis Namier: A Biography* (London, 1971), 31. Unless otherwise indicated, all biographical facts in this chapter are taken from this work.
[3] Ibid. 3.

tutor and eminent historian Stanisław Kot surmised had probably taken place in the second half of the eighteenth century, when much of Poland was being fiercely Germanized.[4] However, they managed to retain the memory of their original family name by having 'vel Niemirowski' inserted after 'Bernsztajn'. Namier's paternal grandfather Jacob Bernsztajn vel Niemirowski took part in the 1863 Polish uprising against the Russians. He was imprisoned and later released, but neither his health nor the family's financial situation recovered from this blow.[5]

Not surprisingly, the 'aristocratic-conservative feeling' which imbued the Redlich family also featured amongst the Niemirowskis. The latter looked not only to the success of their Polish assimilation but also to their Jewish heritage as a source of family pride. The Niemirowskis delighted in the number of scholars through whom they could trace their ancestry to the Talmudic Era. Namier's paternal grandmother could boast of even more exalted forebears, for she was the direct descendent of the famous Elijah ben-Solomon (1720–97), the Gaon[6] of Vilna.[7]

Yet despite this glorious Jewish heritage, Namier's parents were determined to secularize. The Polish society in which they mixed regarded religious enthusiasm, either Catholic or Jewish, to be in bad taste. However, they encountered fierce opposition in the form of Namier's paternal grandmother, Balbina. Joseph quailed before his strong-willed mother, but Namier's mother, Ann, proved to be a match for her mother-in-law. Ann, like Redlich's mother, was a rationalist with no use for religion but a strong sense of duty. She and Rosa Redlich both held the torch of secularism firm against the forces of traditionalism in their families, but the opposition Ann faced was far more formidable. Balbina won the battle over the wedding of her son, which she insisted be conducted according to traditional Jewish rites, but Ann refused to give in to her mother-in-law's pressure to give her only son the obviously Jewish name of Jacob. Instead, Ann named him Ludwik. In the end, Balbina compelled Joseph to register Ludwik Bernsztajn vel Niemirowski (as Namier was known until 1910) as Jewish— something that would have enormous consequences in Namier's childhood. Balbina's coercion led to a temporary break between Namier's parents, as a greatly indignant Ann left for her father's house with her two children.[8]

[4] J. Namier, *Lewis Namier: A Biography*, 3–4.
[5] Ibid. 4.
[6] Literally, Gaon means genius, and was used as a reverential title among East European Jews.
[7] J. Namier, *Lewis Namier*, 3–5. See also p. 66.   [8] Ibid. 6–7, 11–12.

From the Niemirowskis Namier inherited a glamorous family heritage, but it was his maternal grandfather Maurice Theodor Sommersztajn who provided the foundation of material wealth for Namier's immediate family. With the deterioration of the Niemirowskis' financial fortunes after Jacob's imprisonment for his part in the uprising against Russia, Joseph Niemirowski relied greatly on his wife's substantial dowry and subsequent assistance from his father-in-law in the form of land and estates. Like Redlich's grandfather Nathan Redlich, Maurice Theodor Sommersztajn was a self-made man, who had become prosperous through large-scale cultivation of hitherto virgin steppe-lands in the Pantalicha region in East Galicia.[9] Although Namier's wife and biographer nowhere mentions the effect of the Jewish emancipations of 1848 and 1867 on the family, Sommersztajn's transformation into a large Galician landowner would have been impossible without Jewish emancipation.

The importance of landownership to both the Niemirowskis and Sommersztajn can hardly be overestimated—the right to landownership was a symbol of how successfully the Niemirowskis had integrated into Polish society. Although they derived their wealth from banking, the Niemirowskis attached great importance to their family estate at Wola Okrzejska, east of Warsaw, bought by Namier's great grandfather from Bishop Ciechanowski, Henryk Sienkiewicz's[10] uncle. It was a loss-making estate, but it elevated the family above other families of the Jewish commercial bourgeoisie.[11] In Galicia landownership by Jews was rare, and Jewish landowners distanced themselves from the rest of the Galician Jewish community, aspiring to join the Polish *Szlachta* (landowning nobility).[12]

As we have seen, landownership was also very important for the Redlich family's fortunes. The original joy in landownership of the newly emancipated Nathan Redlich found an echo in Redlich's delight in his old Viennese house set in two acres of garden overlooking the vineyards of Grinzing.[13] Yet landownership was never the overriding concern for Redlich that it became for Namier. Redlich's family had long diversified from landownership and agricultural-based wealth into industry and railroads, whereas the economic path of Namier's immediate family went in

---

[9] Ibid. 6.
[10] Great Polish novelist (1846–1916), author of *Quo Vadis*.
[11] J. Namier, *Lewis Namier*, 4.
[12] Tomasz Gąsowski, 'From Austeria to the Manor: Jewish Landowners in Autonomous Galicia', *Polin*, 12 (1999), 120–36; Piotr Wrobel, 'The Jews of Galicia under Austrian-Polish Rule, 1869–1918', *AHY* 25 (1994), 97–138.
[13] WSLB, Handschriftensammlung: I.N.198.615, Redlich to Darkow-Singer, 2 Dec. 1906.

the opposite direction—from commercial and professional pursuits to agriculture.

Namier's grandfather Jacob owned his own banking house in Warsaw. At the time of his wedding, Namier's father Joseph seemed to be on the threshold of a brilliant career as a lawyer. However, his mother Balbina soon decided that a law career in the city would overstrain the delicate Joseph, and sent him to administer the country estate in Wola Okrzejska, where Namier was born in 1888.[14] The reason for this move was ostensibly Joseph's bad health, but Balbina probably knew of Joseph's penchant for gambling and hoped that removal from urban temptations would benefit him. Joseph's gambling addiction never disappeared. Deprived of conventional channels of gambling, he invested in high-risk crops like clover, saddling his family with debts.

To get away from his overbearing mother, Joseph moved permanently with his family to Galicia in 1890, and settled on the first of two estates owned or leased by his father-in-law. This move from Russian to Austrian Poland was an important step to Namier's family. Warsaw gradually dimmed for Joseph Niemirowski, and Vienna became his *ville lumière*.[15] Namier had numerous relatives, both paternal and maternal, in Vienna, and spent extended periods of time there. Of the various languages Namier would speak in his lifetime, only two were perfect—Polish and 'Viennese German'.[16] In later years Namier would try to obscure his connection to the Habsburg empire—he described himself as a Russian subject by birth, a naturalized British subject, and a Jew by race in his first entry in *Who's Who*. Yet, however much he might have wished to dissociate himself from Austria, Namier and his family were decisively moulded by Austria and by Galicia.

Galicia was one of the most remote and undeveloped crownlands in Austria. The Polish *Szlachta* had been given de facto autonomy in Galicia since 1868. As one of the few Jewish landowners in Galicia, Namier's father shared the Polish gentry's perception of the importance of landownership and of the proper hierarchy between Poles and Ukrainians.[17] Yet he also adhered to an essentially bourgeois set of values, such as veneration for John Stuart Mill as the 'shining light of Liberalism',[18] and a great emphasis on education and culture.

---

[14] J. Namier, *Lewis Namier*, 5, 8.   [15] Ibid. 160–1.   [16] Ibid. 70.

[17] Stella Hryniuk, 'Polish Lords and Ukrainian Peasants: Conflict, Deference, and Accommodation in Eastern Galicia in the Late Nineteenth Century', *AHY* 24 (1993), 119–32; Piotr Wrobel, 'The Jews of Galicia under Austrian-Polish Rule, 1869–1918', 119.

[18] J. Namier, *Lewis Namier*, 53.

Namier's grandfather gave his children the best education that Warsaw could offer. All the children could play a musical instrument, speak French and German fluently, as well as some English, and the boys graduated from university. (Namier's paternal aunt, Anka Bernsztajn Landau, became an internationally well-known piano pedagogue. She taught at the Vienna Conservatory and later in New York.)[19] This milieu Namier's father attempted to reproduce for his children. In many ways, Namier's cultural environment was very similar to Redlich's, shaped by the same classical Gymnasium curriculum and the same bourgeois liberal values. Yet Namier was always alive to the incongruity of such an upbringing in the wilds of Galicia. 'Before the war the manor-houses on the big landed estates were centres of high culture and mainstays of modern economic life in Eastern Europe. They resembled Roman villas in semi-barbaric lands. Their inhabitants read the works and thought the thoughts of the most advanced civilisation in the midst of an illiterate peasantry.'[20] The claims of and problems presented by this illiterate peasantry were never far from Namier's mind.

The country estates on which Namier spent his childhood were all located in the steppes, away from urban centres. Namier's isolation was reinforced by his father's refusal to send him to local village schools.[21] Instead, Namier and his sister were educated at home by tutors. This profound isolation, punctuated only by visits to his grandfather or to relatives in Lwow and Vienna, magnified the influence of family on Namier's childhood. From the evidence of Namier's biography, this influence seems to have been predominantly negative, contributing to the extremeness of Namier's character—his misanthropy, irritability, and, in the words of his wife, 'his tendency to exaggerate daily vexations which piled up into violent resentments akin to hate'.[22]

It was not only the general atmosphere of conflict and anxiety that existed during his childhood which caused this malaise—conflict between his father and mother, between his parents and the formidable Balbina, his father's hypochondria, constant financial anxiety due mostly to his father's penchant for gambling, and his parents' peripatetic existence, which necessitated four moves between five different country estates before Namier was 18, from Wola Okrzejska near Warsaw in Russian Poland to Koszylowce in Galicia—unsettling though such circumstances were. Rather, it was Namier's sense of being a misfit and his father's unfeeling

---

[19] G. S. Rousseau, 'Namier on Namier', *Studies in Burke and his Time*, 13: 42 (1971), 2,016.
[20] L. B. Namier, *Skyscrapers and Other Essays* (London, 1931), 151.
[21] J. Namier, *Lewis Namier*, 30.
[22] Ibid. 31.

domination which darkened his childhood, and indeed decisively shaped his life. Whereas Redlich gratefully attributed everything good and healthy in his physical and mental life to his parents, Namier thought of Joseph as the plague of his existence. Throughout his life he observed himself obsessively for signs of Joseph's physical and moral weaknesses,[23] or of the insanity that had plagued some of his ancestors.[24]

Growing up in a supportive family and community, the young Redlich had never felt himself part of a lost world or a lost generation. Even after the dissolution of Austria-Hungary, Redlich perceived his altered situation vis-à-vis the world not as an identity crisis, but as a crisis of the world. He was never very interested in analysing himself, training all his powers of observation on the world outside—taking, however, much of the sorrow of the world personally. His was always the voice of hope and (a much-tried) faith in rational reform, despite all evidence to the contrary, until the last years of his life, when events during the 1930s became too much 'even for the Aristophanes in Redlich'.[25]

Namier, however, seems to have been born with an identity crisis, an existential void that he projected out onto the world. Feeling himself to be a misfit, he passionately identified with a series of underdogs—Ukrainian peasants, Czechs, Jews, and even the traditional landed ruling elites throughout Europe, driven almost to extinction in the inter-war years. Arnold Toynbee would later write that Namier became a Zionist for the 'chivalrous' reason of demonstrating solidarity with Jewry now that Jewry was suffering adversity.[26] Joseph Niemirowski's domination of his son engendered in Namier a loathing of bullies, coercion, and the abuse of power which he later extended to include militarism, imperialism, and class exploitation, and which impelled him to take up the cudgels on behalf of whatever underdog he identified with at the moment. He was so extreme, however, in the defence of his various causes that he ended up harming more than helping them. 'Politically he was as great a liability to his party as he was an asset to it intellectually',[27] wrote Isaiah Berlin of Namier's involvement with Zionism.

Regardless of the truth behind Namier's construction of his own life in terms of a lifelong Oedipal struggle with the phantom of his dead father,

---

[23] J. Namier, *Lewis Namier*, 98.

[24] Ibid. 99.

[25] Felix Frankfurter, 'Josef Redlich—Obituary', *Harvard Law Review*, 50: 3 (Jan. 1937), 389–91.

[26] A. J. Toynbee, *Acquaintances* (Oxford, 1967), 70.

[27] Isaiah Berlin, 'Lewis Namier: A Personal Impression', 223.

Namier's *perception* of his childhood as a titanic clash of wills between father and son profoundly influenced his life and the way he viewed history. In analysing key historical figures such as George III, Charles Townshend, and Talleyrand, Namier asserted that the pattern of their deeds and thoughts was forged through youthful conflict with and rebellion against their fathers. Whatever one thinks about the general validity of psycho-history or of Namier's uses of it, it is hard not to be struck by the curious parallels between Namier's psycho-historical portrait of Talleyrand and his own psycho-biographical understanding of himself.[28]

Namier's Talleyrand was both a misfit and a rebel against his parents and the aristocratic class they embodied. Born the lame son of an aristocrat, Talleyrand was rejected by his parents because of his disability, and farmed out to be raised by servants who impressed upon him the greatness of his family. Not surprisingly, Talleyrand acted very much the *grand seigneur* to the lower classes, and yet, 'devoid of any feeling for his own class—its primary representatives were to him his parents—contributed with cold indifference to its downfall'.[29] Talleyrand served first the French Revolution and then Napoleon, but developed an intense distaste for Napoleon's uncouthness. Eventually he brought about the restoration of the Bourbons at the Congress of Vienna in 1815, in the greater interests of France.

So puny that he was presumed dead at birth, Namier too was neglected in early childhood by his parents, who probably did not expect such a frail child to survive for long. Brought up by servants who 'coddled the boy to distraction', Namier did act the *grand seigneur* to peasants and others of the lower classes, sneering even during his early socialist days at their vulgarity and the meanness of their mental attainments. Nevertheless, his resentment against his parents who identified with the Polish landed gentry, and his familiarity with the Ukrainian peasants and servants engendered a sympathy for the oppressed Ukrainians which bore fruit during World War I, when he used his position in the British Foreign Office to fight against Polish imperialism and exploitation of the Ukrainians, as well as for the right of the East Galician Ukrainians to autonomy.[30] Yet Namier soon grew

---

[28] L.B. Namier, *Vanished Supremacies: Essays on European History, 1812–1918* (London, 1958), ch. 2.

[29] L.B. Namier, *Personalities and Powers* (London, 1955), 2.

[30] John Brooke, 'Namier and Namierism', *History and Theory: Studies in the Philosophy of History*, 3 (1964), 333: 'When I asked him [Namier] why he was interested in the lives of small men, he told me that as a child he had been neglected by his parents, had found companionship only with servants, and had thus developed an interest in the lives of people who never held the centre of the stage.'

alarmed at the brutality of nationalism after the war, and became a conservative. Unable to work for a literal restoration of pre-war society, he became the defender of the landowning class, especially in England, and argued that the destruction of the old social order in Europe would bring about disaster.

A querulous hypochondriac, Joseph was not so much overtly despotic as mocking towards his son, with no understanding of Namier's deepest desires, and was prone to sudden decisions that would drastically affect Namier's life. In search of a permanent cure for his son's chronic inflammation of the eyelids and blockages in the nose, Joseph insisted on subjecting Namier to operations on his nose and eyelids in Vienna, against the reservations of both Ann and Namier himself. The operations did permanent damage to Namier's health.[31] 'Joseph was a lightweight. Lightweights in positions of power generated corruption. They were a menace.'[32] With these damning words, Namier summed up the nature of his father's oppression.

To Namier, Joseph appeared 'overbred',[33] a poor financial manager plagued by physical and mental lassitude, and fundamentally an urban intellectual dilettante despite his gentry lifestyle, who preferred to devote his time to his library of rare books than to farming. Namier's later well-known distrust of rootless urban intellectuals perhaps stems from his dislike of his father. The real manager of their lands was Ann, who had inherited her father's practicality and love of the land. Namier revered his maternal grandfather, seeing in him the archetype of the self-sufficient country gentleman. Namier would come to believe that men rooted in the soil possessed a dignity unknown to restless urban intellectuals, and would later insist that Jewish settlement in Palestine should take on an agricultural character, and that all immigrants to Palestine should possess practical, not just theoretical, knowledge.

Plans for Namier to live with his maternal grandfather whilst attending the Gymnasium at Tarnopol came to nought with his grandfather's death. At home, Namier gradually formed a friendship with his mother which was nevertheless clouded by Ann's support of Joseph in arguments between father and son, and limited in time by the rigours of her schedule. From his earliest childhood, Namier felt himself a misfit in his parents' household, always in the shadow of his brilliant, charming, and healthy older sister. Joseph strengthened Namier's sense of being an outcast by emphasizing that it was his ill-health that prevented him from going to school with other boys. Years later Namier was to write of George III:

[31] J. Namier, *Lewis Namier*, 42–3.   [32] Ibid. 48.   [33] Ibid. 5.

He [George III] spent his young years cut off from intercourse with boys of his own age, till he himself ceased to desire it . . .

   So the boy spent joyless years in a well-regulated nursery, the nearest approach to a concentration camp: lonely but never alone, constantly watched and discussed, never safe from the wisdom and goodness of the grown-ups; never with anyone on terms of equality . . . The silent, sullen anger noted by Waldegrave, was natural to one who could not hit back or speak freely his mind, as a child would among children: he could merely retire, and nurture his griefs and grievances—and this again he continued through life.[34]

The autobiographical overtones in this passage are unmistakable.

Under such circumstances, Namier naturally turned towards the servants. The Niemirowskis did not have a resident staff, but instead employed many peasant girls who came in daily to cook, clean, and wash.[35] Despite his father's prohibition, Namier spoke with them in Ukrainian and developed a great love for the Ukrainian peasant. Above all, Namier's nanny Ella from Moravia exerted a formative influence on his life. As he accompanied her to various churches in the region, Namier discovered religion.[36]

Namier's wife, herself a deeply religious mystic, portrayed Namier's early religious experiences in his childhood as a personal quest for God. Yet we know that Namier's interest in religion, though abiding, was not so much in its mystical aspect as its sociological-communal one. '[N]ine-tenths of religion bear on relations between men and not on creed. Individual souls seek God, but communities and classes express in religion their own nature and aims, and adorn or burden it with their own peculiar signs and symbols; and it is not God who makes creeds differ.'[37] Like Weber, Namier was always interested in how secularized religious values shaped society; like Durkheim, Namier saw religion as an expression of the collective mind of society. The Protestant Ella, in the absence of any Protestant churches in the neighbourhood, went to both Roman Catholic and Greek Uniate churches, and Namier soon came to prefer the latter over the former.[38] Namier would come to associate Catholicism with despotism, over-elaborate ritual, and the baroque—everything that was hostile to progress and modernity. Later, during World War I, to differentiate the Greek-Catholic Church from mainstream Catholicism in the minds of his

34 Namier, *Personalities and Powers*, 50.
35 E. Buxton, 'A Dig Long Ago in Eastern Galicia', *The Times*, 21 Oct. 1963.
36 J. Namier, *Lewis Namier*, 17, 21–2.
37 Namier, *Skyscrapers*, 56–7.
38 J.Namier, *Lewis Namier*, 22.

superiors, he would provide the astonishing explanation that 'the Greek-Catholic Church is a kind of Ukranian [*sic*] National Protestantism'.[39] It is possible that Namier's preference for Protestantism over Catholicism was also influenced by his third tutor and lifelong friend, the historian Stanisław Kot,[40] whose speciality was the study of the Polish Reformation.[41]

In a region where national identity was so entwined with religion that Catholicism was known simply as the Polish religion, Namier's preference can be seen as an expression of solidarity with the Ukrainians. Namier's budding religious exploration was interrupted at the age of 10 by the devastating revelation that he was Jewish. Until then his parents had kept both their children in the dark.[42] Geographical isolation from traditionally minded relatives like Balbina (who died when Namier was very young) and from neighbours and school undoubtedly contributed to this state of ignorance—we may surmise that Namier's maternal relatives whom he frequently visited were also thoroughly secularized. Both Joseph and his daughter, slim, graceful, and fair of hair and complexion, looked down on the dark-haired, swarthy, stocky mother and son, probably because their features were so 'unmistakably Semitic'.[43] Linda Colley has speculated that one of the reasons for Joseph's insistence on operations on Namier's eyelids and nose was the cosmetic one of making him look less Jewish.[44]

The revelation was precipitated by the Austrian legal requirement of religious instruction. Namier, registered officially in Warsaw as a Jew, would have to be instructed in the Jewish religion, but his father made it clear that this was merely a formality, made easier by lenient rabbis. Joseph insisted that Namier was religiously neither Jewish nor Christian, in short, that he was 'nothing'. The choice of wording was unfortunate—the word 'nothing' precipitated an existential crisis in Namier. In place of the 'naïve, hodgepodge religion' that Namier had constructed out of church excursions with Ella, there now loomed a 'numinous void'.[45]

Julia Namier interpreted this existential crisis in religious terms. His father's revelation wantonly wrenched him 'away from Christ, his anchor of security, and away from Christ's mother, his one source of comfort',

[39] PRO: FO 371/2450/59791, Namier's criticisms of Pupin's letter, May 1915, p. 3.

[40] Kot was a member of the Polish government in exile in London and served for a time as Ambassador to Russia. See J. Namier, *Lewis Namier*, 52.

[41] MGA: B/N8A/301, Namier to Crozier, 13 Jan. 1944. 'The Polish Minister of Information, Professor Kot, is one of my closest friends—we have called each other by our Christian names for the last 40 years.'

[42] J. Namier, *Lewis Namier*, 35.   [43] Ibid. 95.

[44] Colley, *Lewis Namier*, 8.   [45] J. Namier, *Lewis Namier*, 35.

leaving him 'without respect for his parents and bereft of their celestial counterparts' protection'.[46] Yet it was almost certainly also a crisis of belonging. Namier's Jewishness excluded him from the Christian communities, both Polish and Ukrainian, among which he lived. He never went to church again with Ella. He did try to find out more about the Jews—he sought out an old Jewish servant on his father's estate who regaled him with tales of his glorious Jewish ancestors, particularly the Gaon of Vilna.[47] In the summer of 1911 he visited the Jewish community in Tredegar in South Wales, which had been a victim of the anti-Semitic resurgence following the republication of the *Protocols of the Elders of Zion*.[48] There he was greeted warmly by an orthodox small-town rabbi, who praised Namier for his 'good Jewish heart'[49]—a lasting memory of sweetness which assuaged some of the bitterness Namier felt in his conflicts with other Jews. For Namier would later discover that he had little in common with most Jews— at Oxford he tried attending Jewish meetings, but soon fled in incomprehension.[50] It was noted approvingly that Namier had 'no Jewish barnacles attached' on the occasion of his admittance to a prestigious undergraduate club in Yale University in 1913.[51]

He was tormented by certain anti-Semitic remarks about his father he inadvertently overheard in a train, when he became aware for the first time of 'the peculiarities with which the Jew is taunted (and sometimes tainted)'.[52] The worst of it was that Namier recognized in the description of the Jews' alleged sycophancy, dishonesty, and greed a living portrait of the Jewish factor on his father's estate. Redlich, in a strikingly similar phrase, described the characteristics of egocentric vanity, obsequiousness towards the wealthy and powerful, and pedantry as characteristics which were 'often, and not always unjustly, ascribed to the Jews', praising his father for being 'mentally and spiritually so distant from that which was known as the "Jewish nature" '.[53] Yet although Redlich was uncomfortably aware of such negative, allegedly Jewish characteristics, and sought to transcend them in himself, he never experienced his Jewishness as the overwhelming, indeed existential, problem it became for Namier. Having grown up in predominantly assimilated Jewish circles, Redlich was never

[46] Ibid. 35.

[47] L. B. Namier, *Conflicts: Studies in Contemporary History* (London, 1942), 172.

[48] Colin Holmes, 'The Tredegar Riots of 1911: Anti-Jewish Disturbances in South Wales', *Welsh History Review*, 11: 2 (1982), 214–225. J. Namier, *Lewis Namier*, 96.

[49] Namier, *Conflicts*, 172.   [50] Rose, *Lewis Namier and Zionism*, 8.

[51] J. Namier, *Lewis Namier*, 110.   [52] Ibid. 54; Namier, *Conflicts*, 128.

[53] RP: Redlich, 'Aus dem alten Oesterreich', 99.

confronted by his own Jewish identity as a thunderbolt out of the blue, in the way that Namier had been.

The men on the train mocked Joseph as 'a Jew more Polish than the Poles—a scion of the northern gentry, if you please'.[54] Arnold Toynbee, who was at Balliol with Namier, recalled that Namier's father's nickname was the 'Count of Jerusalem', that he was unique among the East Galician rural gentry for being Jewish, and that the others did not fully accept them as Polish.[55] In fact, Joseph Niemirowski was not the only Jewish landowner in East Galicia, but it is true that Jewish landowners were rare and that they were not fully accepted as equals by the Polish gentry.[56] Namier's reaction to his family's non-acceptance by the Polish gentry was characteristic—he flaunted his glorious Jewish heritage. One of the first bits of information he imparted to Toynbee was that he was descended from Elijah ben-Solomon, the Gaon of Vilna, the redoubtable enemy of Chassidism.[57]

Yet it would be a mistake to trace Namier's Zionism to pre-war roots, although he did attend a Zionist meeting at the home of Norman Bentwich (1883–1971), a prominent English Zionist and scholar, and attorney-general of the Palestine administration from 1920 to 1931.[58] Despite Namier's attachment to his Jewish past, Toynbee maintained that the pre-war Namier saw international politics with Polish rather than with Jewish eyes,[59] and that Namier pinned his hopes on a resurrected Poland 'administered by socialists with firm liberal intentions'.[60]

The estrangement from religion and radical uncertainty about national identity precipitated by the Jewish revelation left Namier ripe for a new, secular, supranational ideology—socialism. Ironically, it was his parents who unwittingly exposed Namier to an ideology so alien to their own landowning and capitalist interests by hiring Edmond Weissberg as Namier's tutor. Weissberg was the leader of a young socialist group called 'Mlodziez' (Youth), and editor of *Promien*, a political journal. He later changed his name to Wielinski, became the inter-war deputy mayor of Lodz, a wartime hero of the Polish resistance, and ultimately died a violent death at the hands of the Nazis.[61] Through Weissberg, Namier also came to know Marian Kukiel, (later chief of General Staff to Polish prime minister

---

[54] J. Namier, *Lewis Namier*, 54.   [55] Toynbee, *Acquaintances*, 66.
[56] Gąsowski, 'From Austeria to the Manor: Jewish Landowners in Autonomous Galicia', 131–3.
[57] Toynbee, *Acquaintances*, 66.   [58] Rose, *Lewis Namier and Zionism*, 8.
[59] Toynbee, *Acquaintances*, 67.   [60] J. Namier, *Lewis Namier*, 42.
[61] Ibid. 37, 40, 44.

General Sikorski),[62] and himself joined a socialist group, where he was active in collecting subscriptions and in propaganda work.[63] Weissberg's political and economic assumptions were Marxist, but in the absence of a proletariat in non-industrialized Galicia he devoted much attention to agrarian reform. The effect of Namier's exposure to Marxist and agrarian ideas at such an impressionable age was immense:[64] 'Polish socialist preoccupations and problems, as they were in the days of his boyhood, were to colour [Namier's] political outlook for life.'[65] He retained a tendency towards economic determinism in history, and always paid attention to the economic interests of historical actors. More immediately, socialism simultaneously offered Namier a way of rebelling against his father's 'prolix liberalism'[66] and class, and a solution to the problem of national and Jewish identity.

Joseph was part of the Polish generation that had grown up in the aftermath of the failed 1863 revolution, and who had rejected the political activism and sacrifices of their fathers, adopting instead a creed of 'organic work' which sought salvation through self-improvement and abstention from politics.[67] The two most famous products of this movement were the 'Warsaw Positivists' and the 'Cracow Conservatives', who shared a common philosophy of pragmatism and empiricism, and a conciliatory approach towards the occupying power in each partition.[68] The Warsaw-bred Joseph had imbibed much of this pragmatism and conciliation. Namier, however, belonged to that generation that had grown to adulthood at the end of the century, and who found 'organic work' inadequate and sought new answers to social and national problems in nationalism, populism, or socialism.[69]

Namier's adoption of socialism was an outright rejection of his father's worldview. As a child, Namier's constant interaction with Ukrainian servants and his neglect by his parents led to his instinctive sympathy for the Ukrainian peasants in their enmity towards the Polish landlords. Weissberg now added an awareness of political and economic conflicts between the owners of the land (almost exclusively Poles) and the tillers of

    [62] Ibid. 45. Such contacts were to stand Namier in good stead during the Second World War, when he served as an informal adviser on the Polish government-in-exile to the Foreign Office.   [63] J. Namier, *Lewis Namier*, 41, 46.
    [64] Weissberg was Namier's tutor from 1899 to 1903; i.e. from Namier's eleventh to fifteenth years.
    [65] J. Namier, *Lewis Namier*, 40.   [66] Ibid. 98.
    [67] Peter Brock, *Nationalism and Populism in Partitioned Poland: Selected Essays* (London, 1973), 15; Julia Swift Orvis, 'Partitioned Poland, 1795–1914,' in Bernadotte E. Schmitt (ed.), *Poland* (Berkeley and Los Angeles, 1945), 61.
    [68] Brock, *Nationalism and Populism in Partitioned Poland*, 16.
    [69] Orvis, 'Partitioned Poland, 1795–1914', 66.

the soil (almost exclusively Ukrainians) in East Galicia.[70] Weissberg was
passionately concerned with righting the wrongs of the dispossessed native
Ukrainian peasantry, a concern sharpened by outrage at the vast acres
mismanaged by the stewards of absentee landlords.

Weissberg and Namier were by no means unique amongst Polish Jews of
their generation in identifying themselves as socialists and in forging
alliances with the Ukrainians. The Galician Polish Social Democratic party
(PPS), founded in 1892, defended the interests of the Jewish masses, and
opposed the rule of the Polish *Szlachta* and its Jewish establishment allies.
As a result, there was a considerable number of Jews in the PPS, although
many of these Jews, like their counterparts in the Austrian Social
Democratic party, had distanced themselves from their Jewish heritage.[71]
Polish socialist interest in the agrarian question naturally led to a close
community of interests with the Ukrainian radical movement in Galicia.[72]
Zionists also sought out the Ukrainians as political allies—an electoral
alliance between Zionists and Ukrainians led to the election of three Jewish
National candidates from Galicia and the formation of a Jewish Club in the
first Austrian parliament elected through universal suffrage in 1907. This
alliance was anathema to the ruling Polish *Szlachta*, and led to draconian
measures in the 1911 Austrian elections to prevent its recurrence.[73]

Namier, then, was part of a larger movement of Galician Jews question-
ing the traditional social hierarchy in Galicia and the alliance of the small
but influential elite of assimilated 'Poles of the Mosaic tradition' with the
Polish *Szlachta*. During his life he was to take both the socialist and the
Zionist alternatives. At the time, though, Namier seems to have been
attracted by the supranationalism of socialism. In an article on Trotsky
written in 1917, Namier was to write approvingly that the Jewish
'Braunstein-Trotski had no reason to hide his race, which was a matter of
complete indifference to the Socialists among whom he has spent his life'.[74]
Weissberg, himself a Polonized Jew, must have served as a model for
Namier in reconciling Jewish, Polish, and socialist identities.

[70] J. Namier, *Lewis Namier*, 40.
[71] See Robert S. Wistrich, *Socialism and the Jews: The Dilemmas of Assimilation in Germany and Austria-Hungary* (London and Toronto, 1982), 309–22.
[72] John Paul Himka, *Socialism in Galicia: The Emergence of Polish Social Democracy and Ukrainian Radicalism, 1860–1890* (Cambridge, Mass., 1983), 44, 82–5.
[73] See L. Everett, 'The Rise of Jewish National Politics in Galicia, 1905–1907', in A. S. Markovits and F. E. Sysyn (eds.), *Nationbuilding and the Politics of Nationalism: Essays on Austrian Galicia* (Cambridge, Mass., 1982), 149–77.
[74] 'N', 'Trotski', *The New Europe*, 6: 66 (1918), 9. Namier wrote under the pseudonym 'N' in *The New Europe*. See Hugh and Christopher Seton Watson, *The Making of a New Europe: R. W. Seton-Watson and the Last Years of Austria-Hungary* (London, 1981), 282–4.

Even after he became a Zionist, the Galician socialist influence remained discernable. Jewish Galician socialists like Max Zetterbaum had insisted that there was no fundamental difference between philo- and anti-Semitism, since both the Jews and their enemies regarded them as a chosen people and a nation apart. The goal of the Jewish masses ought to be complete solidarity with the international proletariat instead of Jewish separatism.[75] Similarly Namier, even as a Zionist, denied that the Jews were a chosen people or had any transcendent mission to the world. The Jews should aim to be 'neither the chosen race of our own past imaginings, nor the pariahs into which others have persistently tried, and still try, to depress us; but a nation socially and economically complete, with a Mother Country and a Father State of its own, no longer an orphan'.[76] He would praise Masaryk because 'he did not believe Jews to be cleverer than non-Jews; he, for one, did not think us different from other human beings'.[77]

In his new socialist circles Namier naturally came to hear of Józef Piłsudski, leader of the Polish Social Democrats. Namier developed a passionate hero-worship for this romantic revolutionary hero and violent terrorist—a reverence that coexisted paradoxically with a commitment to 'the importance of establishing a democratic legislature by strictly democratic means'.[78] Unlike their counterparts in Russian Poland and in Cracow (where Russian Poles dominated socialist organizations),[79] the Galician socialists based in Lwow (both Polish and Ukrainian) advocated a peaceful and legal transition to socialism, arguing that whilst revolution was indispensable for achieving socialism in a despotic state, parliamentary means were best employed in constitutional Austria.[80] Socialists in Lwow conducted their political activities openly and legally, while those in Cracow adopted Russian-style conspiratorial techniques. Weissberg's and Namier's political affiliations were with socialist parties of Lwow origin. However, the first great wave of Russian Polish students fleeing from Tsarist persecution descended upon Polish universities in Galicia in the 1880s, radicalizing socialist thought throughout Galicia. These Russian Poles urged Galician students, with some success, to embrace more radical social doctrines.[81] Moreover, Japan's defeat of Russia raised hopes of a speedy liberation of at least one part of Poland, giving rise to a ferment of secret political groups and a martial spirit throughout all Polish

75 Wistrich, *Socialism and the Jews*, 312–3.
77 Namier, *Conflicts*, 163.
79 Himka, *Socialism in Galicia*, 176–7.
81 Ibid, 152.

76 Namier, *In the Margin of History*, 73.
78 J. Namier, *Lewis Namier*, 41.
80 Ibid. 78–9.

provinces.[82] This tension between the native Galician inclination towards peaceful means and the Russian advocacy of revolution was reflected in Namier's subsequent political development.

Weissberg's successor as Namier's tutor, Adam Heilpern, was also a socialist, but of a far more retiring disposition. He was a doctoral student at the University of Vienna, and was absorbed in the study of Slavonic languages.[83] Heilpern probably introduced Namier to the linguistic affinities between the different Slav languages. It is likely that Namier's pan-Slavism arose out of this perception of Slav linguistic unity and exposure to the pan-Slavism and pro-Russianism of certain Ukrainian political circles.[84]

Although brought up as a young Polish gentleman, Namier sided with the Ukrainian peasants against their oppressive Polish landlords, thus inducing in him an alienation towards the nation—the Poles—and the class—the gentry—with which his parents identified. However, his background was too different from the Ukrainian peasant whose cause he defended so passionately to identify himself as one of them. Pan-Slavism allowed him to identify with the Slavs, even if he could not and would not identify with one of the individual Slav groups.

In a long lyrical rhapsody to Pan-Slavism, Namier explained that Slavdom was one; that 'in a crude, unreasoned way the Pan-Slav idea is felt by every Slavonic peasant',[85] and that the 'spirit of Slavdom' was to be found 'under the cupolas of the Russian Church . . . in the faith of Dostoievsky and Tolstoi . . . in the gorgeous and yet primitive art of Slav Byzantinism . . . in the life of the Ukrainian steppes and their clustered villages . . . in the long-drawn, melancholy peasant songs'.[86]

Everywhere alike the spirit of Slavdom finds its fullest expression in peasant-life, *and its strongest binding-link it finds in language* [my italics]; every Slav, whatever variation of tongue he may speak, is at least able to understand every other Slav. They call their own wide, racial group by a name derived from the term 'word.' They themselves are 'the worded ones'; their foreign invaders from the West, the German conquerors and oppressors, they all call by a name meaning 'the dumb ones,' 'those incapable of speech.'[87]

In such passages Namier reveals an affinity with the Herderian cultural

---

[82] J. Namier, *Lewis Namier*, 48.
[83] Ibid. 44.
[84] Hans Kohn, *Pan-Slavism: Its History and Ideology*, rev. edn. (New York, 1960).
[85] Namier, *Germany and Eastern Europe*, 37.
[86] Ibid. 38.
[87] Ibid. 38–9.

linguistic nationalism so prevalent in Central and Eastern Europe, a romanticism he would never lose, despite his later fierce criticism of precisely this kind of nationalism. Namier's privileging of the peasants as the original depository of Slavdom stemmed in part from the worship of the *Volk*, as well as the myth of the noble savage which had led other writers, like Tolstoy and Dostoevsky, to revere the unspoiled peasant as the true source of spirituality and morality.

However, like many other worshippers at the altar of the *Volk* and peasantry, Namier did not think much of the intellect of the peasants. Such romanticizing of the simple peasant who cares only about fundamental things like land and food implies a half-unconscious condescension, just as it did for Redlich's father (and to some extent for Redlich). Namier would later dismiss the peasant members of the Polish Club in the Austrian parliament as standing 'mostly on too low an intellectual level to count for much'.[88] Moreover, he despised the Polish peasants for their subservience to Roman Catholicism.[89] The peasants were potentially a great revolutionary force against a rotten social order—but only under the leadership of enlightened socialist leaders. Namier contrasted Napoleon's successful peasant policy with the failure of Louis XVI—the latter tried to consult with the peasants on desired reforms, whereas the former merely gave the peasants what they wanted without asking them to think or vote.[90] Namier's attitude towards the workers was similar. Although the pre-war Namier was a champion of the working classes and of democracy, he praised the English lower classes for understanding that democracy was 'the power given to the average man to choose his ruler, not to rule himself'.[91] He would later quote Otto Bauer's remark, that '[e]very revolution has to protect its march against the masses, which, filled with revolutionary illusions and passions, try to conquer more than can be attained or retained under given historic and social conditions'.[92]

Namier's brand of paternalistic socialism did not prevent him from savouring the joys of landownership—on the contrary, this kind of socialism was related to the paternalist concern for peasant suffering that many progressive landlords displayed. Namier would later argue that the Bohemian aristocrats who spoke German at home yet favoured the Czech

[88] PRO: FO 371/3278/82883, note scribbled by Namier on the folder jacket, 13 May 1918.
[89] PRO: FO 371/3001/92381, Namier memo, 3 May 1917, point 3.
[90] Namier, *Skyscrapers*, 158.
[91] L. B. Naymier [*sic*], 'C'est a l'amour du Vieux Monde . . .', *Blue Book* (Oxford, May 1912), 3.
[92] Namier, *Skyscrapers*, 108.

programme were but one manifestation of the fact that, 'in truly feudal territorial magnates . . . there is a *penchant* towards the people who inhabit their lands'.[93] In 1906 the Niemirowski family moved to an estate of their very own—Koszylowce. Namier spent long hours riding around the grounds, fantasizing about the day when he would own all the land (it would never come). His discovery of prehistoric figurines scattered around the estate added yet another dimension to his love of the land.[94] He organized an archaeological dig there, and later donated the Neolithic remains to the Ashmolean Museum in Oxford.[95]

To his father, Namier's archaeological adventures were yet another proof of an essentially frivolous intellectual disposition. He thought a future landowner needed a minute knowledge of the law, not of archaeology, and put Namier under very heavy pressure to study law. Namier, on the other hand, thought of his parents as 'narrow-minded, self-engrossed provincials, indifferent to all but their immediate present, indifferent even to the vestiges of prehistoric squatters on their land'.[96] The 18-year-old Namier could not withstand his father's pressure, and accordingly went to the University of Lemberg (Lwow) in the autumn of 1906 to study law. He lasted for only one semester. An anti-Semitic encounter with the followers of Roman Dmowski, leader of the right-wing Polish National Democrats, caused Namier to pack his bags and head home.[97]

His father was not as upset as he might otherwise have been, since he had a new pet scheme to improve Namier's health. He decided to send his son to Lausanne, where he could study at the university and benefit from the care of the world-famous lung specialist Dr Demieville.[98] Thus, it was through Joseph's whims rather than Namier's own volition that he left Galicia and Austria, although Namier would later see his exodus from Austria as a deliverance.

Namier's sojourn in Switzerland, though brief, was significant in three ways: his encounter with Pareto, his observations of linguistic nationalism and multinational states, and his first experience of German nationalism. Namier was so impressed with Pareto's lectures that he included him in his 'portrait-gallery of outstanding people'.[99] We do not know exactly what drew Namier to Pareto, but there are astonishing similarities between the

[93] Namier, *1848: Revolution of the Intellectuals*, 101.
[94] J. Namier, *Lewis Namier*, 58–60.   [95] Ibid. 85–6.
[96] Ibid. 61–2.   [97] Ibid. 60–1.
[98] Ibid. 61. See also NP: 1/1a/16, Confirmation of attendance at University of Lausanne, addressed to Julia Namier, 10 May 1961.
[99] J. Namier, *Lewis Namier*, 92.

two men's thought. Originally a liberal with a deep thirst for justice, Pareto had become increasingly disillusioned with society. By the time Namier arrived in Lausanne, Pareto had adopted Nietzsche's distinction of slave morality for the masses and master morality for the few who had risen above the common herd.[100] He saw the masses as forever remaining in the quagmire of superstition, delusion, and ignorance. Pareto's interest in collective psychology and his belief that the masses were motivated by irrational forces rather than reason may have sparked Namier's consuming interest in the same field.[101] Pareto's nihilism and scepticism also found fertile ground in Namier's mind, who, even in this phase of socialist optimism in progress, was noticeable for his 'nihilistic tendencies'.[102]

Namier's stay in Switzerland also impressed him with the power of language and its ability to bind people together. The Swiss university system encouraged free movement of students from university to university. Namier noted that whilst French-speaking students would wander as far afield as France and German-speaking Swiss students to Germany, neither group would attend each other's universities within Switzerland. Perhaps such observations led Namier to believe that a multinational state, consisting of autonomous nationalities speaking different languages, could not truly be successful. In this multinational Switzerland, held up by so many as an example for Austria-Hungary and a federal Europe, Namier perceived the same centrifugal forces (albeit in much milder form) of what he would later call linguistic nationalism at work.

It was also in Switzerland that he first came across extreme German nationalism. A German lecturer at the university, referring to the French character of the place, exhorted German students to always remember that they were in *Feindesland* (enemy country). Even then none of the German nationalist students would be seen in the company of a Jew. 'The essentials of Hitlerism were being developed by the pre-1914 generation, and throughout the world the Germans were already flaunting their "*Deutschtum*" with a provocative arrogance such as only a rare combination of "*Machtbewusstsein*" (consciousness of power) and bad taste can

---

[100] H. Stuart Hughes, *Consciousness and Society: The Reorientation of European Social Thought, 1890–1930* (London, 1959), ch. 7; Peter Roche de Coppens, *Ideal Man in Classical Sociology: The Views of Comte, Durkheim, Pareto, and Weber* (University Park and London, 1976), 77–106.

[101] Robert A. Nye, *The Anti-Democratic Souces of Elite Theory: Pareto, Mosca, Michels* (London, 1977), 21–2.

[102] PRO: PRO 30/57/45, Wingate to Fitzgerald, 28 Sept. 1914.

produce.'[103] These sentences were written thirty-three years later on the eve of the Second World War, but Namier had already developed a violent antipathy for the Germans by the beginning of the Great War.

Where exactly Namier acquired this aversion towards the Germans so early in life is something of a mystery. There were few Germans in Galicia, and the one significant person of German ethnicity in his life was his beloved Moravian nanny Ella, whose duties included teaching Namier and his sister German. Namier had of course inherited a tradition of anti-Germanism from the Niemirowskis, symbolized by the resentment against the imposed Germanized name Bernsztajn which was finally resolved only in 1910, when Joseph succeeded in getting Bernsztajn revoked and the family's original name fully restored to them by Vienna.[104] The Poles had traditionally felt a great affinity with the freedom-loving French, and Namier's childhood bedroom was decorated with a French print, consisting of soldiers in French uniform holding a redoubt against invading Germans.[105] The most important reason, perhaps, was Namier's pan-Slavism, which led him to construe the history of Central and Eastern Europe as a Manichean struggle between Teutons and Slavs.

Unlike the young Redlich, whose Anglophilia can be traced back to Gymnasium days, England scarcely featured in Namier's mental map of Europe at this time. He was Germanophobe, Slavophile, Russophile, and also Francophile. Like many other young intellectuals, he hankered after the 'matchless Sorbonne',[106] and tried to persuade his father to let him continue his studies there. But Joseph, who suspected Namier (wrongly) of conducting an affair with a Parisian actress, vetoed the Sorbonne. A serendipitous visit from a cousin who had just returned from England and who praised the newly founded LSE decided Namier's fate. In the autumn of 1907 Namier enrolled in the London School of Economics.[107]

Namier's first impressions of England were not favourable. His previous experience of rural poverty had not prepared him for the London 'urban wretchedness' which 'revealed a degradation hitherto unsuspected'.[108] Amidst the general gloom of London, the Fabian Society stood out as a bright beacon of hope. Like Redlich ten years before him, Namier soon found himself drawn towards the Fabian circle, where he met Sidney and Beatrice Webb, H. G. Wells, Bernard Shaw, R. H. Tawney, Graham Wallas, and the socialist and suffragette Rachel Barrett. His name appears

---

[103] Namier, *Conflicts*, 37–8.   [104] J. Namier, *Lewis Namier*, 92–3.
[105] Ibid. 16.   [106] Ibid. 63.   [107] Ibid. 66–8.
[108] Ibid. 68.

in the November 1907 issue of the *Fabian News* as a candidate for election, and he attended the Fabian summer school of 1908 in Pen-yr-Allt in North Wales. It is possible that the Fabians' policy of permeation, in which hard-working and dedicated Fabians would advise and influence the people who wielded power in the country, influenced Namier's future mode of political operation.[109] Certainly, Namier always worked behind the scenes in his political career, preparing memoranda and proffering advice to the power-brokers of the Foreign Office, and later of Zionism.

Apart from Halford John Mackinder's geopolitical course, which engendered in Namier a lasting appreciation of geographical factors in the shaping of history,[110] the London School of Economics provided little in the way of intellectual stimulation. Most of the stimulus he received was extracurricular. Graham Wallas's work on mass psychology reinforced Pareto's emphasis on the importance of collective psychology.[111] A remark of H. G. Wells focused Namier's attention for the first time on the English way of managing a nation's life through parliamentary debate. His friend-ship with Frank Reginald Harris, who had been given leave from the Foreign Office to write a life of the fourth earl of Sandwich, introduced Namier to the world of eighteenth-century English history he would later make his own. Harris was so impressed with Namier that he managed to secure an introduction for him to the legendary Balliol senior tutor, A. L. Smith. The immediate rapport between tutor and student earned Namier a place in Balliol College.[112]

Namier's entrance to Balliol in the Michaelmas term of 1908 marked the beginning of a lifelong devotion to the college. 'Balliol taught me to think. All I've done I owe to Balliol. And besides the person who first tried to make a man of me was A. L. [Smith]', a grateful Namier would later reminisce.[113] Namier benefited from a series of outstanding history tutors at Balliol, such as Henry William Carless Davis, who encouraged Namier to go ferreting for facts and details, the Fabian don A. D. Lindsay, who reinforced Namier's tendency to explore the economic bases of political events, L. Francis Fortescue Urquhart ('Sligger'), who awak-ened an appreciation of diaries and memoirs (especially Sainte-Beuve's)

[109] R. C. K. Ensor, 'Permeation', in Margaret Cole (ed.), *The Webbs and their Work* (London, 1949), 57–74.

[110] J. Namier, *Lewis Namier*, 72.

[111] See Namier, 'Human Nature in Politics', in *Personalities and Powers*, 1–7. For Wallas, see Martin J. Wiener, *Between Two Worlds: The Political Thought of Graham Wallas* (Oxford, 1971).

[112] J. Namier, *Lewis Namier*, 70–1.

[113] H. W. Carless Davis, *A History of Balliol College* (Oxford, 1963 edn.), 243.

as sources of history,[114] and of course A. L. Smith. Smith played the role of a father substitute in Namier's life—in his kindness, his concern for the dispossessed, and his enthusiastic support for the Workers' Educational Association, Namier discovered an alternative, quintessentially English role-model.

Armed with new-found models and allegiances, Namier took the first significant steps to break with his past and his family. Although he took his preliminary examinations in Law, in accordance with his father's wishes, he ended up with a first-class degree in Modern History. His growing independence led to much tension on Namier's numerous visits back home (at Christmas, usually Easter, and for the better part of the Long Vacation). Namier refused either to convert to Catholicism or to assume the Niemirowski name along with the rest of the family in 1910. Instead, he changed his name to Lewis Bernstein Naymier by deed poll in Britain in 1910 (he later dropped the 'y' from his name in 1913), explaining that 'Niemirowski' would look far too cumbersome on the title-pages of the English books he would one day write.[115] In other words, by 1910—a mere three years after he had arrived in England—Namier had already decided to integrate into British society by anglicising his name. In 1913 he went a step further and became naturalized as a British subject.[116]

Thus Namier joined a long line of Anglophile Austrian intellectuals, and anticipated those like Karl Popper, Ernst Gombrich, Ernest Gellner, Geoffrey Elton, Nicholas Kaldor, Ludwig Wittgenstein, and Sigmund Freud who would later emigrate to England. Carl Schorske has pointed out that there were two distinct types of Anglophilia prevalent in Austrian intellectual circles, corresponding to the differences between the culture of grace and the culture of law. The first, exemplified by Schnitzler, Hofmannsthal, Herzl, and Loos, emphasized the English combination of bourgeois pragmatism with aristocratic grace. The second drew upon an older, more militant liberal tradition associated with the puritans and with Cromwell. Freud, who named one of his sons Oliver after Cromwell, was the outstanding example of the latter.[117]

Both Namier and Redlich combined these two types of Anglophilia. Redlich praised puritanism as 'the religious counterpart of the democratic conception of the state in the sixteenth and seventeenth centuries',[118] yet revelled in the aristocratic lifestyle of English society. Namier studied English puritanism and Calvinism with great enthusiasm during his time at

---

[114] J. Namier, *Lewis Namier*, 89.
[115] Ibid. 93.   [116] Ibid. 107.
[117] Carl Schorske, *Thinking With History* (Princeton, 1998), 195–6.
[118] J. Redlich, *The Procedure of the House of Commons*, ii. 117.

Balliol, going so far as to take the preliminary examinations in Divinity as well as Law.[119] (At this time Namier first encountered the Authorized Version of the Bible—its cadences left a lasting impact on his prose.) He admired the austerity, intellectual integrity, and doctrine of predestination in Calvinism, which appealed to his own fatalism, and indeed refused Catholic conversion on the grounds that he was a Calvinist.[120] During his stay in America he would be drawn to the study of the New England puritans, 'intellectually the strongest group on the [American] Continent'.[121] Later, on Arnold Toynbee's suggestion, Namier would give a series of lectures on English puritan writers at King's College, London.[122]

Yet Namier simultaneously developed a reverence for the English patrician society which he came to know at Balliol. The Balliol of Namier's day prided itself on its disproportionately large number of alumni in leadership positions in Britain and the empire. The list included imperial proconsuls such as Curzon, Elgin, Lansdowne, and Milner, and statesmen like Herbert Asquith, Sir Edward Grey, and later on Namier's patron, Harold Macmillan. Namier's time at Balliol 'produced in him an almost uncritical admiration for the country's ruling class, and strengthened his belief that a highly gifted and homogeneous oligarchy was the political ideal'.[123] Moreover, Balliol supplied him with his own patrician supporters, who would time and again smooth the path of advancement for him.

Even at that time, when this society was at its seemingly most brilliant and powerful, Namier worried about its survival in the face of the onslaught of the masses. He pointed out that the economic betterment of the lower middle classes, unaccompanied by education, had produced a society and a culture dominated by a spirit of 'noisy indiscretion, of cheap make-believe and unreality'.[124] There had never yet been a democracy like that in contemporary England, 'so rapidly increasing in power and wealth, and still so uncultured. They will change the educated classes into a pageant for their own enjoyment; we or our children, unless we stem the flood, will play the clowns and jesters at the Court of the Sovereign People.'[125] The only way to stem the 'flood of vulgarity' was education—hence Namier's enthusiastic support for the Workers' Educational Association.[126] Towards the end of his life in post-war England Namier believed that his presentiments had come true, and that

[119] Toynbee, *Acquaintances*, 75.   [120] J. Namier, *Lewis Namier*, 93.
[121] L. B. Namier, *England in the Age of the American Revolution*, 2nd edn. (London, 1961), 39.
[122] J. Namier, *Lewis Namier*, 130.   [123] Colley, *Lewis Namier*, 10.
[124] Naymier [*sic*], 'C'est a L'amour du Vieux Monde . . .', 8.   [125] Ibid. 8–9.
[126] Ibid. 10–11; Namier, *Lewis Namier*, 103–4.

he was witnessing the death of the English aristocracy and the old world he loved so much.

Namier's most ardent wish was to join the patrician English society of 'uncontending ease', 'the un-bought grace of life'. The latter phrase occurs for the first time in a 1912 essay,[127] and would become Namier's leitmotif to describe the English culture of grace. 'Anyone can enter English society provided he can live, think, and feel like those who have built up its culture in their freer, easier hours',[128] wrote Namier. Yet despite the porousness of the English upper classes in contrast with the insulated nature of Austrian society, Namier never succeeded in attaining the degree of social success achieved by Redlich. On his death, Namier was commemorated in an obituary as 'the Towering Outsider'.[129]

One reason for his exclusion from the British establishment was no doubt anti-Semitism. Namier was described numerous times by English patricians as a very clever or able Jew, with the spoken or unspoken reservation that he was perhaps too clever—and a Jew. His failure to obtain an All Souls Fellowship in 1911 has been attributed to anti-Semitism,[130] although he himself thought it was because he took the 'Eyre Crowe-Vansittart view of Germany'.[131] He was refused employment by Wickham Steed at *The Times* on the grounds that Jewish journalists were biased.[132] Despite lessons with an elocution expert in New York, he spoke English with a heavy East European accent, although he would achieve a remarkable command of written English. However, it is conceivable that had his personality not been so difficult, he could have won the degree of acceptance by the English establishment enjoyed by Isaiah Berlin, another East European Jewish Anglophile intellectual. Namier lacked social grace and sensitivity. Toynbee, in a generous and affectionate sketch of Namier, nevertheless notes that his psychic radar was 'as inadequate as President Wilson's. His attention was preoccupied by what he himself had to say. He had no psychic energy to spare for picking up what the other person was feeling.' Namier had something of Coleridge's Ancient Mariner about him, and once cornered Toynbee's wife for half an hour in an open draught with

[127] Naymier [sic], 'C'est a L'amour du Vieux Monde . . .', 9.
[128] Namier, *England in the Age of the American Revolution*, 14.
[129] E. H. Carr, 'English History's Towering Outsider', *Times Literary Supplement* (21 May 1971).
[130] J. Namier, *Lewis Namier*, 101.
[131] NP: 1/2/12, Namier to Kingsley Martin, 28 Aug. 1942. Sir Eyre Crowe (1864–1925) and Robert, Baron Vansittart (1881–1957) were both British diplomats who were known for their strong opposition to German militarism.
[132] NP: 1/9/7, John Brooke to Julia Namier, undated letter.

a recital of the original Slav names of many German towns in Eastern Europe.[133] He would also accost strangers at breakfast, a traditionally sacrosanct time of the day, with exuberant observations on the current international political situation.[134] 'In the phylogenetic history of the Englishman the Oxford undergraduate of my own time corresponded to the eighteenth-century man, and with him nearly foremost among social qualifications was that a man should be amusing',[135] wrote Namier. He failed signally, however, in coming across as amusing, and hence in winning acceptance.

Moreover, despite his great desire to be integrated, part of Namier revelled in his local uniqueness. Namier enjoyed regaling his fellows with tales of Eastern Europe and frequently drew attention to his exotic heritage (both Jewish and East European). He was annoyed when his cousin Ehrlich arrived at Oxford, with a head 'still more massive than Lewis's' and 'even more tightly packed with the minutiae of East European lore.' In Toynbee's words: 'One of Lewis's rewards for having trekked so far afield was that, like Odysseus on the last of his wanderings, he had reached a land where he could enjoy the distinction of being unique; and now he had been robbed of this distinction through having been dogged by a relative whose resemblance to him was a caricature.'[136]

It was not merely a wish to stress his own uniqueness which drew attention to Namier's status as outsider, but also his fundamentally contradictory desires to be both spokesman for and critic of English society. On the one hand, the young Namier sprinkled his essays with 'we' and 'our' so insistently as a badge of identification with the English that it prompted G. K. Chesterton's sardonic observation that ' "our" is delightful from a gentleman who has only recently been naturalised'.[137] (In fact, Namier's use of 'we' and 'our' dates back to his first published essay in English in 1912,[138] before he was naturalized.) On the other hand, he would often castigate the English for their lack of seriousness, especially in international relations, noting that the 'school boy mentality of fair play' was not adequate as a principle in dealing with foreign affairs.[139] Thus the principle of fair play, which both Redlich and the English perceived to be the cornerstone of the British parliamentary system, was cavalierly dismissed by Namier. One can imagine

---

[133] Toynbee, *Acquaintances*, 63.
[134] Ibid. 62.
[135] Namier, *England in the Age of the American Revolution*, 14.
[136] Toynbee, *Acquaintances*, 74.
[137] G. K. Chesterton, 'Potash and Perlmutter', *New Witness* (26 Apr. 1918), 586.
[138] Naymier [*sic*], 'C'est a L'amour du Vieux Monde . . .'.
[139] Namier, *Germany and Eastern Europe*, 6–7.

what effect such an attitude towards something so sacrosanct would have had. In fact, this role of being both an insider and outsider, both spokesman and critic, would become typical of Namier, whether he was dealing with the Poles, the English, or later the Jews. No matter how deep his desire to belong, he refused to relinquish the existential role of the grand inquisitor which he shared with his admired Pareto.

At Balliol Namier also discovered the British empire, in the form of Lionel George Curtis and Sir Reginald Wingate, the father of fellow Balliol student Ronald Wingate. Lionel Curtis had served in the Boer War and was a dedicated empire-builder, devoted to the ideal of Commonwealth. Sir Reginald Wingate had been governor-general of the Sudan and sirdar of the Egyptian Army during his son's Oxford days. Namier, invited to stay at the Wingate country house, had several memorable talks with the sirdar, and soon included Wingate alongside Pareto in his personal gallery of great individuals. Namier thought him a man of 'stern independence of mind transfused with a sensitive social conscience';[140] 'the tutelary spirit of a great and good Empire'.[141] He represented 'not imperialism but empire at its very best'.[142] Namier's distinction between imperialism and empire is important. In Namier's lexicon, imperialism meant the strong imposing its will on the weak; empire was a paternalistic concept, a civilizing relationship in which the stronger helped to elevate the level of the weaker. Namier would later point out that while 'the Latin colonial systems follow that of Rome; they Gallicize or Italianize', the British did not, in any way, interfere with the cultural development of their subjects.[143] Whilst he would spend his life combating imperialism of all kinds, he would also spend it promoting empire—even as an ardent Zionist who clashed violently with Colonial Office officials, he wanted Palestine to be the seventh dominion of the British empire.[144]

The awakening of his interest in the British empire necessarily led to a critical look at the empire of which he was a subject—the Austrian. Julia Namier records that his dislike of the 'Austro-Hungarian hugger-mugger' became increasingly purposeful.[145] How much this judgement was free of hindsight must be considered. It is true that in later times his antipathy towards the Austrian empire increased, and that he tried to dissociate himself from it as much as possible. Still, the evidence from the beginning of World War I suggests that Namier looked at the Austrian empire not so

[140] J. Namier, *Lewis Namier*, 95.   [141] Ibid. 92.   [142] Ibid. 91.
[143] Namier, *In the Margin of History*, 88.
[144] Namier, 'Palestine and the British Empire', in ibid. 84–93.
[145] J. Namier, *Lewis Namier*, 92.

much with hostility as with a kind of contemptuous affection. Both Poles and Ukrainians in Galicia enjoyed greater civil liberties than the Poles under German and Russian rule and Ukrainians under Russian and Hungarian rule.[146] Hence, Galician Poles and Ukrainians were relatively pro-Habsburg, although the greater degree of freedom under Austrian rule meant that Galicia became the Piedmont of both Polish and Ukrainian nationalism.[147] Namier's father, although not a native of Galicia, also developed a pro-Viennese orientation.[148]

Namier himself admitted that:

In recent years its [Austria's] rule has seldom been oppressive; even the least favoured nationalities in Austria were still far better off than were the non-German nationalities in Germany, the non-Magyars in Hungary, and most of the non-Russian nationalities in Russia ... the influence and claims of the Austrian Germans were everywhere an irritating nuisance but they nowhere amounted in recent years to downright oppression ...

To many of the other nationalities Austria has been a shelter against storms raging outside, and in future and, let us hope, better ages they will have to think with a certain mixture of sentimental, tolerant sadness of that poor old house in which, after all, they were able to live and to grow.[149]

However—and Namier could well have been describing his own attitude as well as that of the nationalities—'for each of the ten nationalities inhabiting "Austria", the connection to the Austrian government was a marriage of convenience, their affairs of the heart were with those outside the boundary of the Austrian state'.[150] Namier's affairs of the heart were with Pan-Slavism, and with England and the British empire.

The greatest fault of the Austrian empire was that it was not a state, but merely a government.[151] Although 90 per cent of the Austrian population was Roman Catholic, even this did not serve as a bond between the peoples.[152] 'The failure of religion to take the place of nationality implies in Austria the final failure of the State.'[153] Thus, the Austrian state idea, which Redlich was trying so frantically to strengthen, was already dead for

---

[146] Norman Davies, *God's Playground: A History of Poland*, 2 vols. (Oxford, 1981), ii. 156–162; Paul Robert Magocsi, 'A Subordinate or Submerged People: The Ukrainians of Galicia Under Habsburg and Soviet Rule', in Richard L. Rudolph and David F. Good (eds.), *Nationalism and Empire: The Habsburg Monarchy and the Soviet Union* (New York, 1992), 100.

[147] Davies, *God's Playground: A History of Poland*, ii. 160.

[148] J. Namier, *Lewis Namier*, 160–1.

[149] Namier, *Germany and Eastern Europe*, 122–3.

[150] Ibid. 121.   [151] Ibid. 120.

[152] We must assume that Namier is referring only to the population of the non-Hungarian part of the Dual Monarchy.

[153] Namier, *Germany and Eastern Europe*, 123.

Namier. The fact that Redlich identified with the Germans and Namier with the Slavs goes some way to explain the difference between the two. The old idea of Austria being part of the German heritage was alive for Redlich, whereas Austro-Slavism had long lost its attractiveness for many Austrian Slavs as well as for Namier.[154]

Namier did have a great fondness for Vienna, which survived the First World War. He was too perceptive to be taken in by the surface splendour of imperial Vienna and in fact found the city's baroqueness intensely distasteful. Nor was he drawn by the cultural renaissance that we now consider so path-breaking. Neither Namier nor Redlich regarded *fin-de-siècle* Viennese culture as genuinely original and vital. 'Vienna has never produced anything truly great or creative, only a fine blend of a peculiar internationalism with an intensely local colouring.'[155] But he was enchanted by the dreamlike veneer of Vienna, by the way in which '[e]ffervescent wit and song' were 'flung negligently over doom-laden realities' and soon picked up the 'art of laughing off inexpressible calamities'.[156] Yet it was precisely his perception of the apocalypse underlying Viennese gaiety that also made him shun Austria. Namier's own morbid fear of disease and insanity made him recoil from decay and seek out only that which was vital and healthy. Already in boyhood he smelt the 'stench of decay' when considering the political concepts and practices of moribund Austria-Hungary. By contrast, in the British empire he breathed 'the ozonized air of a general predisposition to resurgence'.[157]

We have seen how perceptive Redlich was of the weaknesses of Austria and his predilection to apocalyptic imagination. What distinguishes him from Namier, however, is that Redlich continued to hope for the miracle of rationality and tolerance that would save Austria, until the last days of the empire. Namier, however, suffered from what William Johnston has described as the typically Austrian attitude of therapeutic nihilism[158]—the conviction that diseases defied curing and could only be diagnosed. Namier would later compare history to psychoanalysis, in that it was 'better able to diagnose than to cure: the beneficial therapeutic effects of history have so far been small; and it is in the nature of things that it should be so';[159] whereas Redlich wrote his English political histories with the hope that the

[154] See Andreas Moritsch (ed.), *Der Austroslavismus* (Vienna, 1996).
[155] Namier, *Vanished Supremacies*, 16.
[156] J. Namier, *Lewis Namier*, 51.
[157] Ibid. 297.
[158] Johnston, *The Austrian Mind*, 223–9.
[159] L. B. Namier, *Avenues of History* (London, 1952), 5.

lessons learned could be applied to Austria. Namier's attitude led logically to the belief that Austria was past all curing; hence he averted his face from it.

The British imperial idea could have gone the way of the Austrian state idea during the American Revolution. However, instead of disintegrating, the British empire went from strength to strength in the nineteenth century. This mystery Namier dubbed the phoenix empire. The question, then, confronting Namier was this—what was the British imperial idea, and why did it succeed after nearly failing?

Namier's first addressed the problem in an essay written for the 1912 Beit Essay Prize, for which he was awarded a half-prize along with a Canadian Rhodes scholar. The essay, entitled 'The Imperial Problem at the American Revolution: Imperial Idea or Imperial Spirit?', distinguished two types of plan for a closer union of the empire. The first consisted of colonial representation in the existing parliament at Westminster, modified by various suggestions of intercolonial federation; the second consisted of union in a new national parliament, in the sense of different 'nations' (self-aware communities) being represented in it as 'national' equals. The first would result in small token groups of representatives sent to the great mother country—a proposal rightly rejected by the American colonists as giving them no real say in their own political destiny. The latter, however, implied an empire of equals.[160] Namier's analysis of plans for the closer union of the British empire paralleled debates about empire reform taking place in Austria at the same time.

Namier graduated with a first-class degree in Modern History in 1911. He was burning to write his book on the imperial problem in England at the time of the American Revolution. His father, however, once again had different plans for him. This time Joseph suggested that Namier should go to work for a year in the United States to pay off his gambling debts. Louis N. Hammerling, a former bottle-washer in the distillery owned by Namier's maternal grandfather, had emigrated to the United States, made good, and bought up Joseph's promissory notes, promising to cancel the whole debt if Joseph would send his son to work for him. Outraged at the idea of being 'sold as a bondsman for [his] father's debts',[161] Namier initially refused, but had to accept after his failure to obtain an All Souls Fellowship.

---

[160] J. Namier, *Lewis Namier*, 104–5. See also NP: 1/1a/1 Namier to P. H. Kerr, 11 Aug. 1926.

[161] J. Namier, *Lewis Namier*, 107.

His anger at his father's transaction with Hammerling was mitigated by his eagerness to study American sources, such as the Bancroft Transcripts in the New York City Public Library, and the Ezra Stile Papers at Yale University.[162] In a country where libraries were open late at night and on Sundays, Namier was confident he could work on his own book in addition to his work for Hammerling. During his year in the United States he managed to study several important collections of archival materials and establish influential contacts in the American academic world, one of which, Professor Charles MacAndrew of Yale University, suggested that he should work on the imperial problem from the British rather than the American point of view.[163] Socially his Balliol background stood him in good stead, since it enabled him, through Lord Eustace Percy of the Foreign Office, to make the acquaintance of Sir Cecil Spring-Rice, the British ambassador to the United States.[164]

Namier's glamorous contacts and productive academic work contrasted sharply with the drudgery of his daily working life with Hammerling. Louis N. Hammerling, head of the American Association of Foreign Language Newspapers, controlled almost 400 foreign-language papers which reached 20 million readers in America, thus exerting considerable influence amongst the Central and East European immigrant communities in the United States.[165] During World War I, Hammerling would organize an embargo petition against Allied ships signed by 377 newspapers.[166] Namier soon found he had little patience or talent for the administrative work that Hammerling required of him, but his experiences gave him an invaluable background for propaganda work amongst East European émigrés in America during World War I.

The New World fascinated Namier. It was a fascination that had begun in Galicia, where he had minutely traced the connections binding whole villages economically and emotionally to the United States and Canada through immigration.[167] An immigrant himself, who had been naturalized as a British subject, Namier described with great sensitivity the plight of new immigrants with 'hyphenated identities'—an issue still fashionable in American cultural and political discourse. 'There is sadness at the death of nationality', he wrote; 'the labour of generations is lost, a flame has burnt in

---

[162] J. Namier, *Lewis Namier*, 107, 111–2.   [163] Ibid. 112.
[164] Ibid. 107.   [165] Ibid. 98, 107–8.
[166] PRO: FO 371/2450/43258, Namier, 'Analysis of the Singatures [sic] in the Manifesto', 13 Mar. 1915.
[167] J. Namier, *Lewis Namier*, 75.

vain, a fire has died out without fostering life'.[168] Namier's attitude towards hyphenation was ambivalent. Whilst hyphenation was 'perhaps, still a fruitful way of preserving living values', it could also be a Faustian temptation. 'The human soul turns to something which had formed the deepest meaning of its life, and whispers the fatal words of Faust, "Tarry a while, thou art so fair." '[169] Most importantly, hyphenation did not make for good citizenship—'it is contrary to the union with one's fellow-citizens which is the basis of "community" '.[170] Already Namier was wrestling with the themes of identity, assimilation, citizenship, and community which would preoccupy him all his life.

The modernity of New York, and especially her skyscrapers, intoxicated Namier. Skyscrapers soon became for him an icon of modernity and a symbol of man's ingenuity in transcending limitations of space. Like Adolf Loos, he disliked the sham of the Austrian Neo-baroque, which he condemned as 'elaborate'—a term of deep opprobrium from Namier. Moreover, he also drew parallels between the elaborate Baroque architecture and certain characteristics of his sister, father, and paternal relatives—presumably their hypocrisy and their self-conscious elegance. Thus, the Baroque was not merely an architectural style but an attitude to life.

His preference for the clean lines and functionality of New York skyscrapers over the Baroque architecture of façades is also analogous to his scorn for the smooth flow of rhetoric in Victorian historiography, and his own attempts to strip history of decoration and ornament to reveal its bare bones. Toynbee described Namier's prosopographical historical method as an attempt to 'demythologise' the historical abstractions of nation, state, and public opinion, through a minute, positivist accumulation of facts about the human beings who made up such abstractions.[171] Namier's philosophical stance parallels Redlich's 'positivist revolution' against metaphysical abstractions, and the rigorous assault on façades and duplicity by Kraus, Loos, Schoenberg, and Wittgenstein. Namier felt an affinity with painters who were striving after a new artistic idiom, and was always interested in modern art.[172] His conservatism and nostalgia for the Old World should not obscure the fact that he was also an iconoclast and a heretic. Janus-faced, Namier looked both towards the past and the future, embracing one or the other with more or less enthusiasm during different periods of his life, without ever losing that duality.

---

[168] Namier, *Skyscrapers*, 11. Originally published in *New Statesman* (4 Mar.1916).
[169] Ibid. 11–12.   [170] Ibid. 12.
[171] Toynbee, *Acquaintances*, 81.   [172] Namier, *Lewis Namier*, 165.

Although Namier would later compare the United States and Great Britain to the former's disadvantage, there is no evidence to suggest he had formed a definite preference for one or the other part of the Anglo-Saxon world right before the First World War. It is possible that he would have stayed on in America if war had not broken out. Joseph was once again pushing Namier towards the study of law, and Namier agreed to enter law school in St Louis in the Fall semester of 1914, under the guidance of Charles Nagel, former secretary of Commerce and Labor in the Taft administration, and a close friend of Hammerling's.[173]

But first he sailed to Europe in May 1914 for a short visit. The *American Leader*, a now defunct New York weekly, had commissioned him to write an article on the European situation. Travelling through the Balkans in June, Namier predicted, a fortnight before the assassination of Franz Ferdinand, the imminence of war—in his words, the storm-centre of Europe had shifted East.[174]

---

[173] Yale University Library, Charles Nagel Papers, (Manuscript Group no. 364): Series, I, Box 11, Folder 105, Namier to Nagel, 19 Apr. 1914; Folder 168, Namier to Nagel, 24 May 1914. Namier, *Lewis Namier*, 113.

[174] 'The European Situation', *American Leader* (9 July 1914), reprinted in *Skyscrapers*, 62–72.

3

World War I and the Search for
a New Europe

I hope, that the reasonable democracy of all peoples and the energetic development of the small nations will be the good end result of [this war].[1]

The freedom of all nations in Europe will mean an end to all Imperialisms within it.[2]

The summer of 1914 has entered collective memory and history as the summer of war fever, sweeping across both the Allied countries and the Central Powers, transforming even normally apolitical individuals into fervent nationalists.[3] Not surprisingly, both Redlich and Namier were caught up in the general war hysteria.

To Redlich, the Germans were the 'noblest people in the world', 'caught between the Russian and Asiatic hordes' and 'the devouring envy of weary British decadence', yet heroically striving to fulfill the German mission 'to preserve the true cultural centre of the world—Central Europe'.[4] Redlich's war fervour was such that the authorities suggested he embark upon a propaganda mission to the United States with Count Apponyi (it was later cancelled).[5] We do not have any record of how Namier felt in the

---

[1] Redlich, *Schicksalsjahre Österreichs*, 31 Dec. 1914, I, 295.

[2] Namier, *Germany and Eastern Europe*, 128.

[3] R. J. W. Evans and Harmut Pogge von Strandman (eds.), *The Coming of the First World War* (Oxford, 1988).

[4] WSLB, Handschriftensammlung: I.N.198.655, Redlich to Darkow-Singer, 7 Oct. 1914. See also R. J. W. Evans, 'The Habsburg Monarchy and the Coming of War', in Evans and Pogge von Strandman (eds.), *The Coming of the First World War*, 33–55. Robert A. Kann, 'Trends in Austro-German Literature During World War I: War Hysteria and Patriotism', in Robert A. Kann, Béla K. Király, and Paula S. Fichtner (eds.), *The Habsburg Empire in World War I: Essays on the Intellectual, Military, Political and Economic Aspects of the Habsburg War Effort* (Boulder, Col., 1977), 159–84.

[5] Fritz Fellner, 'The Plan for a Redlich–Apponyi Lecture-Mission in the United States: Origins and Proposals for the Building of an Austro-Hungarian Propaganda Action in Neutral Foreign Countries During WWI', in *Festschrift für Adam Wandruszka zum 60. Geburtstag* (Vienna, Cologne, and Graz, 1974).

summer of 1914. His promptness in volunteering for the British army, however, suggests that his patriotism for his adopted country, his aversion towards the Germans, and his zeal to serve in what he saw as a decisive battle between German and Slav in Eastern Europe was very great indeed.

It would seem, then, that Redlich and Namier started from diametrically opposed viewpoints. Yet underneath the obvious differences was a greater commonality in views. Both shared a burning desire for a new Europe: a fairer and more moral order, especially in Central and Eastern Europe. Both, despite accepting the principle of national self-determination, gradually became alienated from nationalism in the course of the war, and promoted multinational, supranational ideals: Redlich strove to actualize the liberal internationalist interpretation of the Austrian state idea, whilst Namier fought to win British support for the cause of socialism (tinged with Pan-Slavism) in Central and Eastern Europe. In an age of nationalist fervour in Central and Eastern Europe, and of widespread liberal optimism in the West that national self-determination would result in new liberal nation-states, both Redlich and Namier were inevitably isolated.

Redlich's extreme German nationalism proved to be a passing phenomenon. From the beginning of the war, Redlich felt great unease at the manifestations of excessive German nationalism, especially the treatment of the Austrian Slavs. At the end of December 1914 he wrote that the Germans 'must develop their national consciousness to the highest level, and yet at the same time must transcend nationalism. Only then can they lead Europe, when they have won the sympathy of the small Germanic and Slav peoples.'[6] Yet subsequent events in the next two years led him inexorably to the conclusion that, far from overcoming nationalism, the Germans had apotheosized it as their creed; far from winning the sympathy of the smaller nationalities, the Germans were going out of their way to alienate them, and thus had forfeited any moral claim to leadership.

Regarding the Slavs as potential traitors, the German and Austrian military arrested many of the leading Slav politicians and intellectuals. Redlich condemned the military's actions as unconstitutional, and questioned the wisdom of declaring civil war on the empire's Slavs. 'The oppression of those nationalities stigmatized with the charge of high treason is the most horrible harbinger of the coming racial war within the monarchy . . . I see

---

[6] Redlich, *Schicksalsjahre Österreichs*, 31 Dec. 1914, I, 295.

the future as very black',[7] he wrote. Redlich accused the foreign-policy makers in Berlin of calculating success only in terms of battalions and cannons, but of exhibiting absolutely no sympathy towards the other peoples of which Austria-Hungary was comprised, and of their independent brothers across the border. Such a policy lacked both generosity and greatness of soul.[8]

Whilst Redlich tried to help secure the release of a few Slav intellectuals, he recognized that his influence as a member of parliament in a country where parliament had been suspended and which was ruled by a de facto military dictatorship would be very limited.[9] Therefore, he pushed for the recall of parliament, hoping that it would act as a strong civilian counterweight to the military dictatorship.[10]

Redlich found allies both amongst the conservatives and the political left. He was considered as a ministerial candidate by the conservative circles around Count Silva-Tarouca, who had belonged to Archduke Franz Ferdinand's Great Austrian group.[11] Redlich and the Social Democrats also drew closer together.[12] Redlich found an audience as well in the association founded by the Anglophile Viennese Jewish businessman Julius Meinl—the Austrian Political Society. In this forum Redlich argued for peace, for the federalization of Austria, and for the recall of parliament.[13] He was opposed, however, by his colleagues in the German National Union,[14] the majority of whom fully supported the actions of the military. Many did not see any need for the recall of parliament, since the military regime had secured for them what they wanted—German hegemony in Austria.

Far from seeking to redress the injustice against the Slavs, even the historically non-nationalist, German-speaking aristocracy, as well as the German bourgeois politicians regretted that the dynasty had been so 'soft' with them,[15] and expressed admiration for Tisza and the Hungarian policy of ruthless Magyarization.[16] The idea of Austria-Hungary as a German-Magyar state,

---

[7] Redlich to Bahr, 14 Dec. 1914, in Fellner (ed.), *Dichter und Gelehrter*, 102.

[8] Redlich, *Schicksalsjahre Österreichs*, 13 June 1915, II, 45.

[9] Redlich to Bahr, 20 Nov. 1914, in Fellner (ed.), *Dichter und Gelehrter*, 100.

[10] Redlich, *Schicksalsjahre Österreichs*, 6 Jan. 1915, II, 6.

[11] Ibid., 27 July 1916, II, 131–3; 23 Sept. 1917, II, 235; 17 June 1918, II, 281. B. Morgenbrod, *Wiener Grossbürgertum im Ersten Weltkrieg* (Vienna, 1994), 104.

[12] Redlich, *Schicksalsjahre Österreichs*, 26 Sept. 1915, II, 62; 11 May 1917, II, 204.

[13] Morgenbrod, *Wiener Grossbürgertum im Ersten Weltkrieg*.

[14] A loose association of all German middle-class political parties in Austria founded in 1910.

[15] Redlich, *Schicksalsjahre Österreichs*, 19 Dec. 1914, I, 294.

[16] Ibid., 6 May 1915, II, 36.

with the Germans and Magyars as 'master peoples' and the other nationalities as 'servant peoples',[17] gained widespread currency, and was angrily
rejected by Redlich. As pressure to recall mounted, the German National
Union insisted that the necessary precondition for the recall was the guarantee of a permanent German parliamentary majority, and German hegemony in Bohemia. 'The peoples of Austria are young and fresh and healthy,
sick are the "classes", the "parties", the state institutions',[18] Redlich wrote
to his friend Hermann Bahr in disgust.

But the arrest of Karl Kramář, the leader of the Young Czechs and long
a bane of German nationalists, was to show Redlich that national egoism
was pervasive in the population and not just confined to the politicians or
the upper classes. Kramář was arrested in May 1915 on the charge of high
treason, tried by military courts, and sentenced to death in April 1916.
Most Austro-Germans were convinced of Kramář's guilt; Redlich, who
was invited by Kramář to attend his trial, was one of the few who thought
him innocent of high treason. He was shocked at the palpable hatred of the
Germans towards the Czechs, and the exultant rejoicing that accompanied
the announcement of Kramář's death sentence.[19] This was the first time
that Redlich fully grasped the depth of irrational passions and the ugliness
of nationalistic frenzy; the first time he realized that for the Germans the
nationality conflict with the Czechs was seen as a struggle of life and death,
and that no considerations of justice, reason, or tolerance would persuade
them to pass up the opportunity for a final reckoning.

To Bahr, Redlich condemned the 'serious spiritual disease of the
Germans within and outside Austria'—that, 'whether it is the Belgians or
the Czechs, it is always the same fundamental principle—that the Germans
are restrained only by the limits of their power, not by considerations of
law, or humanitarianism, or Christian thought'.[20]

The Germans had put power and self-aggrandisement above justice and
reason. This national egoism manifested itself both domestically and externally. As we have seen, the pre-war Redlich was already critical of German
political culture, especially the German veneration for the authoritarian
state, and the tendency to dismiss parliamentary institutions and parliamentary democracy as a mere varnish to the state. Wartime government in

---

[17] Ibid., 27 July 1916, II, 133.
[18] Redlich to Bahr, 31 Jan. 1915, in Fellner (ed.), *Dichter und Gelehrter*, 105.
[19] Redlich, *Schicksalsjahre Österreichs*, 3 June 1916, ii, 118–19.
[20] Redlich to Bahr, 26 July 1918, in Fellner (ed.), *Dichter und Gelehrter*, 355. The reference
to 'Christian thought' from the non-religious Redlich was partly a bow to Bahr's increasing
religious devoutness.

Austria and Germany confirmed his fears of such an authoritarian state. He would later describe the Austrian war government as a vast machine, 'comprehending and controlling every department of life, and ruthlessly subordinating all alike, men and things, personal services, raw materials, and finished goods, to the iron law of a never ending war'.[21] The Austro-German nationalists had accepted this machine without protest, had in fact been complicit in its construction, and had approved of draconian censorship and arbitrary arrests, for this machine was the means to the end of hegemony within Austria over the other nationalities. Their desire for supremacy had passed beyond all reason.

Internal and external German chauvinism merged in the concept of *Mitteleuropa*, in which Austria-Hungary would be bound to Germany in a permanent alliance, as part of a greater Central European union under German leadership. The German alliance would ensure that the Germans in Austria and Magyars in Hungary reigned supreme,[22] whilst Austria-Hungary would furnish men and material to continue the German imperialist push towards the East.[23] German national egoism had generated a boundless lust for expansion and annexation. At the beginning of the war Redlich had hotly denied that the Germans wanted world domination; they only claimed their rightful place in the sun, denied to them by the envy of Great Britain.[24] His views soon underwent a sea-change. In December 1915 Redlich refused, along with Heinrich Lammasch, to sign a pro-war statement of German-Austrian university teachers.[25] He placed the blame for starting the war squarely on Wilhelm II, who had fanned the flames of aggressive German nationalism.[26] Despite the huge sufferings of the population, the German nationalists had no desire for peace, but insisted on carrying the war to a victorious conclusion.

To Redlich, German imperialist annexationist ambitions, as revealed during the peace negotations at Brest-Litovsk, exposed the moral bankruptcy of German nationalism:

[21] Redlich, *Austrian War Government* (New Haven, Conn., 1925), 127.

[22] Redlich, *Schicksalsjahre Österreichs*, 25 Apr. 1916, II, 111.

[23] Stephan Verosta, 'The German Concept of Mitteleuropa, 1917–1918 and its Contemporary Critics', in Kann, Király, and Fichtner (eds.), *The Habsburg Empire in World War I: Essays on the Intellectual, Military, Political and Economic Aspects of the Habsburg War Effort*, 203–20.

[24] WSLB, Handschriftensammlung: I.N.198.657, Redlich to Dr Darkow, 9 Jan. 1915.

[25] Solomon Wank, 'Josef Redlich', in *Biographical Dictionary of Internationalists* (London, 1983), 603.

[26] Redlich, *Schicksalsjahre Österreichs*, 3 Nov. 1916, II, 153.

First we declare that we want to conclude a peace without annexations and indem-
nities, but then scarcely have the negotiations begun, when Prussia, because it has
promised the Austrian Poles, wants to annex Lithuania, Kurland, and Suwalki. The
whole thing will be passed off under cover of the famous principle of national self-
determination by Czernin and the gentlemen in Berlin. 'Referendums' during the
occupation of our troops! Even the most stupid Bolshevik will see through such a
swindle. Ludendorff and his lot do not want this swindle, but wish simply to annex
even the area around Warsaw![27]

Redlich's criticisms were naturally very unpopular with both the
German National Union and the military. The final severing of ties with
the German National Union came when Redlich publicly declared his
support in 1917 for a negotiated, immediate peace,[28] after which the Union
voted to expel him. Redlich replied defiantly:

I believe myself to be pursuing genuinely German politics if I stand up for the idea
... that the greatest victory is only a means to an end; to the goal of peace, peace
with the whole world; that if the German people is to survive and flourish, it must
work with *the rest of the world* and not against the world.... Finally and conclusively
I believe that I feel and think as a German, when I say that mutual goodwill must
again take the place of this hatred which is destroying the world. Naturally I differentiate my politics sharply from the politics of that small, but immensely wealthy
and influential circle of German industrialists, as well as from the Pan-Germans in
Germany and Austria.[29]

This emphasis on what was 'genuinely' German as opposed to the
Germandom (*Deutschtum*) espoused by the new, base breed of German
chauvinists was a distinction that Redlich, like so many German-speaking
Jews, would continue to make. Yet occasionally he veered towards the radical position of rejecting not only German nationalism but German national
identity as well. 'If to be German means to take such a view [that the
Emperor Karl's amnesty for the imprisoned Slavs was a disaster], then I
must not feel as a German', Redlich declared at a conference on the nationality problem in Austria.[30] He noted in his diary: 'all respect for German
staunchness and German organizational might cannot banish the pain [of
the imminent break up of Austria].'[31]

[27] Ibid., 10 Jan.1918, II, 254.
[28] *Österreich und der Friede: Verständigung unter den Völkern Österreichs. Versammlung vom
17. Juli 1917 in der, ÖPG* (Vienna, 1917).
[29] RP: Redlich to the German National Union, 21 June 1917. See also open letter from
German National Union to Redlich in *Neue Freie Presse*, 13 Oct. 1917, evening edition, p. 2;
and Redlich's answer in the *Neue freie Presse*, 14 Oct. 1917, p. 7.
[30] *Österreich und der Friede*, 34.
[31] Redlich, *Schicksalsjahre Österreichs*, 30 Aug.1917, II, 139.

Redlich's rejection of German nationalism and his sympathy for the oppressed Slavs did not mean, however, that he supported the Slav separatism movements from Austria. Although Redlich accepted the right of national self-determination, he hoped that the political aspirations of the different nations could be satisfied within the framework of a transformed, multinational Austria.

Redlich's acceptance of national self-determination was an extension of the liberal belief in liberty, popular sovereignty and representative government. In the same way that an individual was entitled to liberty and to choose the kind of government he or she wanted, so a people as a collective group should also have this right. The greatest enemy of both individual and national freedom was the authoritarian state. Redlich predicted that 'the twentieth century would see the emancipation of nationalities from the state, just as the period from 1789–1848 accomplished the emancipation of the individual from the state'.[32] The Germans had once been just as oppressed as any of the other peoples in the empire by state absolutism; however, they had made a Faustian bargain with the state, acquiescing in its oppression in exchange for national supremacy in Austria. Hence, they had contributed to the building of a German centralist authoritarian state, which denied civic liberty to both citizens and nations.

The way to emancipation for both individual and nation, however, was not to lead an anarchic existence outside the structure of the state, but to transform the authoritarian state into a 'popular' state—a state of popular sovereignty and self-government. Unlike liberal supporters of national self-determination in the West (including friends and acquaintances such as R. W. Seton-Watson, Wickham Steed, and Louis Eisenmann), who, following in the footsteps of Mill and Gladstone, believed that liberty and democracy were better achieved in national rather than non-national states,[33] Redlich denied that the formation of nation-states would necessarily lessen nationality conflict. He could not share their optimism that the resulting nation-states would be politically liberal, and would willingly surrender part of their newly won national sovereignty to enter into the various federation schemes that the liberal nationalists envisaged. Redlich, situated in Austria, had a much closer acquaintance with Central and East European nationalisms. Moreover, he was very aware that the problem of national minorities would intensify in the proposed new nation-states.

---

[32] Redlich to Bahr, 23 Mar. 1918, in Fellner (ed.), *Dichter und Gelehrter*, 322.
[33] See Harry Hanak, *Great Britain and Austria-Hungary During the First World War: A Study in the Formation of Public Opinion* (London, 1962), 48–55.

Redlich's outlook was fundamentally at odds with the kind of nationalism that had emerged in Central and Eastern Europe under the influence of Herder. This emphasized the nation as a community bound together by blood-ties, sharing a common language, culture, religion, and traditions. Every nation was a natural unit, and had the right to its own state, where it could develop its own unique national character. Such nationalisms were necessarily exclusive and particularist in nature, attaching primary importance to the group rather than the individual. Redlich saw that national self-determination as understood by the nationalists was very different from the liberal understanding of the concept, something which the liberal proponents of national self-determination in the West did not always grasp.[34]

Instead, Redlich belonged to the alternative, anti-nationalist tradition of liberalism most famously associated with Lord Acton.[35] Like Lord Acton, Redlich believed that nationalism tended to subvert liberty; that the goal to attain one's own nation-state was so consuming that other considerations and values tended to become subordinate to it, as illustrated by the example of Germany. 'From nationality to bestiality', he quoted Grillparzer sadly.[36] He originally blamed the war on the jingoist nationalisms of the Balkan nations (fanned by Magyar imperialism).[37] He predicted that 'if the plight of all these great and small states combines with the hatred and insanity of human egoism which finds fertile breeding ground in modern nationalism, there can then be no true progress of culture anymore'.[38]

Redlich was particularly disturbed by Czech nationalism and its hostility to the Austrian state. He thought the Czech romantic yearning for the historical Bohemian state 'not completely healthy'.[39] He cited Milan Hodža, the 'clever leader of the Slovaks', several times regarding the artificiality of the Bohemian state rights idea[40] and Slovakian concern that the Czechs disregarded Slovakian rights and aspirations in their fixation on the Bohemian state. He lamented that a whole generation of Czechs had grown up who had lost all understanding of the Austrian state. But 'how could it be different,' he asked, 'since they have never seen the Austrian government

[34] Thomas D. Musgrave, *Self-Determination and National Minorities* (Oxford, 1997), 2–13.
[35] Lord Acton, *Essays on Freedom and Power* (London 1956), 141–70. Redlich did in fact read Lord Acton. See Redlich, *Schicksalsjahre Österreichs*, 3 Dec. 1916, II, 163; Maitland to Redlich, 5 June 1904, *The Letters of Frederic William Maitland*, 285–6.
[36] Redlich, *Schicksalsjahre Österreichs*, 3 Aug. 1914, I, 242.
[37] Redlich, 'Austria-Hungary and Servia', *Economist*, 25 July, 1914, pp. 179–81 and 1 Aug. 1914, pp. 232–4.
[38] Redlich, *Schicksalsjahre Österreichs*, 5 Feb.1917, II, 189.
[39] *Das Nationale Problem in Österreich* (Vienna, Leipzig, 1917), 5.
[40] Redlich, *Schicksalsjahre Österreichs*, 16 Dec.1915, II, 90.

WWI and the Search for a New Europe

put forward any thought, any principles, any plan, over the course of the past quarter-century to position this state against the autonomist national idea, *to establish it as a higher justice*' [italics mine].[41]
On what basis did the Austrian state embody a higher justice than the national idea? Certainly not on the basis of the Austrian mission to spread German culture to the East, an idea that Redlich had discarded along with German nationalism. Nor was it on the basis of Habsburg dynastic loyalty.[42] Rather, Austria embodied a higher justice because it was a unique historical experiment in the creation of a truly multinational state, and hence was an antidote to the nationalist hatreds that were destroying the world. In the early days of the war Redlich was already defending Austria in the following way:

Austria, whose faults and weaknesses no one knows better than I, has nevertheless attained and created something which has not been achieved anywhere else in the world to such an extent with the exception of Switzerland: namely, this measure of mutual tolerance of languages and peoples . . . Nowhere else in the world, not . . . even in America, has such an attempt been made, to develop the autonomous cultures of eight or nine different peoples simultaneously on a basis of equality. Therefore this venerable state does not deserve the kind of disdainful judgements passed in the crassest ignorance which can be found in the majority of the foreign presses.[43]

This view of Austria, although already a minority opinion at the beginning of the twentieth century, was nevertheless not uncommon. R. W. Seton-Watson and Wickham Steed, for instance, had both begun as defenders of the Monarchy in its role as a successful multinational state and as a European necessity. The spiritual ancestor of such views amongst British liberals was Lord Acton, who had argued that multinational states represented a higher form of political development than nation-states, and had praised Austria in this context.[44] During the war, Redlich's friends Francis W. Hirst and Henry Noel Brailsford continued to defend the Habsburg Monarchy on these lines.[45] One assumption underlying such a

[41] Redlich to Bahr, 4 Aug. 1915, in Fellner (ed.), *Dichter und Gelehrter*, 124.
[42] See Redlich, *Schicksalsjahre Österreichs*, 26 Nov. 1916, II, 161, for his views on monarchy. 'Ist es nicht eine furchtbar-groteske Komödie, was man den "modernen monarchischen Staat" nennt? Ist es nicht seltsam, daß der Träger oberster Entscheidungen schließlich durch den Zufall physiologischer Akte bestimmt wird? . . . Ist das wirklich so, daß die Massen der Menschen noch immer im Fetischismus der Herrschaftsgewalt tief verstrickt sind?'
[43] WSLB, Handschriftensammlung: I.N.198.657, Redlich to Dr Darkow, 9 Jan. 1915.
[44] Hugh Tulloch, *Acton* (London, 1988), 28.
[45] See Hanak, *Great Britain and Austria-Hungary During the First World War*, ch. 6; and Harry Hanak, 'A Lost Cause: The English Radicals and the Habsburg Empire, 1914–1918', *Journal of Central European Affairs*, 23: 2 (July 1963), 166–90.

view was that other factors, like geography, history, economics, and the common cultural ties that had evolved through time, equalled the national idea in importance as a state-organizing principle.

The war disabused Seton-Watson and Wickham Steed of their belief in the Habsburg Monarchy as a viable multinational state. Likewise, Redlich's optimism over the true degree of national tolerance in Austria took a severe battering in the course of the war. In 1916, for instance, when describing a nightmarish vision he had experienced in which he saw Austria disintegrating, he nevertheless wrote: 'In moments of calm thought, I reflect that perhaps the verdict that world history has passed on us is justified, since we have not understood, and have passed up, every opportunity to build a solid structure on the foundation of this splendid land.'[46]

The foundation, then, of Austria was sound, indeed splendid. Unlike other empire reform plans which proposed radical territorial alterations and revolutionary political and social change, Redlich maintained that it was not necessary that the foundation of Austria, which was 'historically, geographically, and ethnically given', be altered.[47] What was rotten was the status quo of Austria, caused by a lack of understanding of the true Austrian state idea. 'This realm has been long in the making, but now millions speak in terms of "deliver us from this evil"! And yet it is indeed the most splendid of realms and only the people, the Austrians, are too incompetent to *understand* it [italics mine]!'[48] Those who had given up on Austria were confusing the present reality with the Austrian idea itself. 'If only the Austrians could truly understand, that the "state" of Herr Biernerth, Stürgkh, and Heinold is not the Austria that we good Austrians have in our minds and hearts, but is instead a historically established straitjacket, that is sometimes portrayed deceptively as the "Fatherland," and at other times imposed with brute force, until none of the limbs can stir freely.'[49]

Disgusted with the Austrian state reality, Redlich nevertheless did not lose faith in the Austrian state *idea*. At the core of the Austrian state idea was its status as a European necessity, not so much in terms of the balance

[46] Redlich, *Schicksalsjahre Österreichs*, 30 Aug. 1916, II, 139.
[47] *SPOR*, XXII, 163: Redlich parliamentary speech, 12 June 1917.
[48] Redlich to Bahr, 9 Jan. 1918, in Fellner (ed.), *Dichter und Gelehrter*, 297.
[49] Ibid., 1 June 1915, 118. See also *SPOR*, XXII, 168: Josef Redlich parliamentary speech, 12 June 1917: 'Wir brauchen eben im modernen Österreich einen Staat, der sich aus diesem Zwangsstaate heraus umbildet in einen Völkerstaat, der darauf beruht, daß alle Völker dieses Staates den Zwang, der um der Einheit willen auf sie ausgeübt werden muß, und die Resignation, die allen Völkern dieser Zwang auferlegt, als ein Ergebnis empfinden, an dem sie mitgewirkt haben.'

of power, but in its all-important role as a multinational state, a bulwark against internecine nationalist strife. Austria was in fact a microcosm of a Europe torn apart by fratricidal war. If Austria could bring about internal peace between her warring nationalities, she would serve as a model for Europe, once again playing the role of civilizing agent that she had in the past. 'We must show the world', Redlich pleaded in parliament, 'that Austria is not what they think, they do not know the Austrian people and that they are committing the greatest injustice against this great and venerable champion of the development of culture, when they come against us with hostile attacks.'[50]

In the last analysis, of course, Redlich's attachment to the Austrian state idea, powerfully supported by liberal internationalist arguments in favour of the multinational state, belongs to the realm of emotional and psychological imponderabilia. After the war Redlich, in a passage ostensibly describing the general Austrian populace, but which surely applied also to himself, wrote: 'Deeply buried, but never forgotten, the sense of the Empire and of the State as a whole persisted. Its positive elements elude analysis, rooted as they are, in the last resort, in the purely emotional life of the individual, and in that part of his thought which can never be rationalized.'[51]

Paralysed by doubt and despair, limited by censorship and the closure of parliament in the first half of the war, Redlich voiced his dissent against prevailing trends only cautiously amongst close friends and acquaintances, and occasionally in the forum of the various political reading groups that had mushroomed at the beginning of the war. The accession of the Emperor Karl in November 1916, the gradual receding of the power of the military in civilian life, and the opening of parliament in May 1917 encouraged Redlich to greater political activism.

To Redlich, who had been pushing for the recall of parliament since the beginning of the war, the emperor's summoning of parliament was in itself a major step towards the salvation of Austria. He did not cease to urge the parliamentarians, however, that they must take parliament seriously, and not revert to their pre-war obstructionist tactics. A strong parliamentary regime was essential to prepare both internal and external peace.[52] Redlich used parliament as the medium through which he tried to get his message across—that national reconciliation and peace were the two most urgent issues facing Austria.

[50] *SPOR*, XXII, 168: Josef Redlich parliamentary speech, 12 June 1917.
[51] Redlich, *Austrian War Government*, 75–6.
[52] Redlich, *Schicksalsjahre Österreichs*, 8 July 1917, II, 219.

Although Redlich had acknowledged privately as early as October 1914 that the old dualism of the Monarchy would need to be replaced by federation,[53] he realized that the prerequisite for the federal reform of Austria was a complete transformation of the atmosphere thick with nationalist hatreds. Hence, he worked hard for national reconciliation between Germans and the other nationalities, arguing that Austrians needed to return to the spirit of the Kremsier constitutional assembly in 1848–9, which was the only time in Austrian history that the peoples of Austria had met in a spirit of mutual tolerance and a readiness to compromise, to try to draw up a new way of living together.

To the Germans, he urged that Austria would be lost unless they altered their fundamental attitude towards the nationality problem. The mood among the non-German nationalities in Austria was such that it might be already too late to reconcile them to Austria. He declared that the Germans must get rid of their belief that the 'State is power, and that power is law',[54] and that they should show more understanding for the dilemmas of the Slavs, forced to fight a war against those they regarded as their brothers. 'Judge not, that ye be not judged', he admonished the Germans, when urging them to accept Emperor Karl's amnesty for the arrested Slavs.[55]

Behind all his attempts to bring about national reconciliation was the fear that the Slavs would be lost forever to the Austrian idea, just as Haynau's regime in Hungary in 1849 had alienated the Hungarians from Austria. In response to Slav grievances towards Austria, he pointed out that the great achievements of the Slavs, in fact the entire modern Slav national renaissance of the past half-century, had been attained within the framework of a unified Austria, and that the Slavs had succeeded in altering the nature of the ruling Austrian bureaucracy through the entrance of large numbers of Slavs into the bureaucratic ranks in the last few decades.[56]

Unlike Aurel Popovici, Karl Renner, and other federalists of the time, Redlich did not work out a detailed programme for the federal reform of Austria. His approach to the problem was characteristic—he decided to study the problem historically, but for the purposes of immediate application.[57] Redlich started work on the first volume of his *Staats- und Reichsproblem* in 1916 and finished it in 1920.[58] In his commentaries on the

[53] Ibid., 13 Oct.1914, I, 282.
[54] *Das Nationale Problem in Österreich*, 3.
[55] *Österreich und der Friede*, 35.
[56] *SPOR*, XXII, 164: Josef Redlich parliamentary speech, 12 June 1917.
[57] Redlich, *Das österreichische Staats- und Reichsproblem*, I, xii.
[58] See Redlich to Bahr, 23 Sept. 1920, in Fellner (ed.), *Dichter und Gelehrter*, 422. It was only published in 1922.

various empire reform schemes put forth in Austria from 1848 onwards, we can discern his own preferences for federal reform.

Federalism was a much-bandied-about term that had not yet acquired a broadly accepted definition. It could mean anything from a personal union of sovereign states with a common monarch on the one hand, to administrative decentralization within a unitary state on the other. The question of the extent of de jure and de facto autonomous powers granted to member states of the federation was one that occasioned much debate amongst the various empire reformers.[59]

Redlich's version of federalism favoured a stronger central power. He rejected any proposal to decentralize the judiciary,[60] and called repeatedly for the preservation of Austria as a strong unitary state (*Einheitsstaat*).[61] Redlich's thoughts on federalism were much influenced by his understanding of the federal structure of the United States. 'I have returned to the "love of my youth", the Anglo-Saxon world, especially to American democracy, which I have been *more* occupied with than anything else. I believe I can still achieve plenty that is useful here, and create more clarity for we Germans over problems that concern us all', wrote Redlich.[62] He expressed regret that not enough had been known about the American example during the Kremsier constitutional assembly in 1848.[63]

Redlich believed that the concept of federation embodied in the American Constitution was 'one of the very few new thoughts which one is able to say have been found or discovered by mankind since the time of Aristotle'.[64] The original confederation of the American colonies was not a new idea—confederations had occurred in later Greek history, and amongst the Swiss cantons in their fight against the Holy Roman Empire. But the Americans had quickly realized that the confederation conferred too little power to the central authority, and hence had replaced it with 'a federal union which, while maintaining the full individuality and autonomy of the thirteen states, at the same time created a national, i.e., central

[59] Rudolf Schlesinger, *Federalism in Central and Eastern Europe* (London, 1945), 38.

[60] Redlich, *Schicksalsjahre Österreichs*, 7 Dec. 1917, II, 248. See also Redlich, *Austrian War Government*, 24, on the significance of the *Verwaltungsgerichtshof* (introduced in 1876), its success in ensuring 'legal and uniform public administration throughout the entire State, and to reduce to the smallest limits the arbitrary element in the functioning of authorities', and its creation of a 'new bond of juridical unity' in the state.

[61] *SPOR*, XXII, 162–3: Josef Redlich parliamentary speech, 12 June 1917; *Das Nationale Problem in Österreich*, 6.

[62] Redlich to Bahr, 31 Jan. 1915, in Fellner (ed.), *Dichter und Gelehrter*, 105.

[63] Redlich, *Das österreichische Staats- und Reichsproblem*, I, 100.

[64] Josef Redlich, 'The World-Wide Influence of the United States Constitution', *Boston University Law Review*, 10: 2 (Apr. 1930), 197.

power'.[65] The Swiss followed the American example when they converted their confederation to a federation in their constitutional reforms of 1848 and 1870.[66] Even in the United States, however, the ultimate question as to whether members of the federation had the right to secede had only been answered by the Civil War.

Redlich pointed out that even František Palacký, leading figure in the mid-nineteenth-century Czech nationalist revival, had realized that a strong central power was necessary for the modern state.[67] He approved the clause in Palacký's constitution which explicitly forbade regional parliaments to unmake a law made by the central parliament.[68] As to whether autonomy in the empire would take an ethnic, historico-territorial, or personal form, Redlich seems on the whole to have preferred the historico-territorial solution. Historico-territorial divisions appealed to his historian's fine sense of, and appreciation for, historical continuity. He reminded parliament of the importance of legal continuity, and advocated that a new federal legal structure be built on the foundation of the old historical rights of the different crownlands, as well as the substantial provisions for regional and municipal autonomy contained in the 1867 Constitution. His great admiration for the political genius of the English stemmed from their ability to pour new wine into old skins, combining 'a pious feeling of conservatism for ancestral forms and ceremonies on the one hand, on the other a political ingenuity which has exercised itself in so differentiating and developing the root principles of the constitution, that the new legislation which it introduces from time to time may not only meet the spirit and needs of the new age, but conform outwardly with the traditions and prescriptions of the old'.[69] Not surprisingly, then, Redlich opted for the path of organic evolution towards a federal state in Austria, building upon elements already present in her structure and her constitution to meet the needs of the new age of nationality.

Redlich had the highest praise for Baron Jozsef Eötvös's empire reform proposals.[70] Eötvös, with his preference for territorial over linguistic nationalism and his appreciation of historical continuity, had also proposed that the empire should be federalized along the existing historico-political-

---

[65] Redlich, 'The World-Wide Influence of the United States Constitution', 197.
[66] Ibid. 199.
[67] Redlich, *Das österreichische Staats- und Reichsproblem*, I, 167.
[68] Ibid., I, 231.
[69] Redlich, *Local Government in England*, i. 7.
[70] Redlich, *Das österreichische Staats- und Reichsproblem*, I, 547–71. See also Kann, *The Multinational Empire*, ii. 93–9, and Gerald Stourzh, 'Die Politischen Ideen Josef von Eötvös und das österreichische Staatsproblem', *Donauraum*, 11: 4 (1966), 204–20.

territories, while retaining a strong central power necessary for the continual existence of Austria as a Great Power.[71] Both Eötvös and Redlich realized that dividing up the empire on linguistic grounds was a proposal fraught with problems, due to the nationally mixed character of the empire's territories.[72] Hence, both believed that claims of linguistic nationalism should be satisfied only on the lower level of *Kreis* and municipal autonomy.[73] Redlich held up Moravia as an example where historical state rights had been reconciled with ethnic autonomy.[74] He also recommended Karl Renner's work on personal autonomy as invaluable for promoting national autonomy and minority rights in nationally mixed areas.[75] Redlich thought that one of the greatest mistakes of the Bach regime had been in abandoning the *Kreise*, and maintained that the *Kreise* could have prevented much of the envenomed power struggles over the linguistic question in the second half of the nineteenth century.[76]

Despite praise for what the framers of the Kremsier Constitution had achieved, he noted characteristically that they had focused too much attention on legislation, and not enough on implementation—in other words, on administration. This neglect had led to a misunderstanding of 'the organic connection between a modern central government and administration with the economic needs of the bourgeoisie and the increasingly capitalist world', an overemphasis on a doctrinaire municipal autonomy as transmitted by Rotteck's teachings, as well as a lack of proper demarcation between the competence of the central versus regional powers.[77] These were the points that Redlich had set out to address in his administrative reform project. Although his political views had since then evolved in a more federalist direction, he did not need to renounce any part of his administrative reform project because of the federal elements in his proposals, elements which now came to the forefront. Significantly, at this crucial time of federalist reform ferment, the Social Democrats, themselves in favour of federalization, chose to draw favourable attention to Redlich's project in the

[71] Eötvös proposed an extremely strong position for the monarch; Redlich would have preferred parliament to be the strong central power.

[72] See Jozsef Eötvös, *Über die Gleichberechtigung der Nationalitäten in Österreich* (Budapest, 1850); id., *Die Garantien der Macht und Einheit Österreichs* (Leipzig, 1859).

[73] *Das Nationale Problem in Österreich*, 6.

[74] *SPOR*, XXII, 166: Josef Redlich parliamentary speech, 12 June 1917. For general background on ethnic autonomy in Moravia, see Kann, *Multinational Empire*, i. 207–9.

[75] *SPOR*, XXII, 166: Josef Redlich parliamentary speech, 12 June 1917.

[76] Redlich, *Das österreichische Staats- und Reichsproblem*, I, 221–322.

[77] Ibid. 231.

94   *WWI and the Search for a New Europe*

Arbeiter Zeitung.[78] Until the end of his life, Redlich viewed the failure of his administrative reform project as a lost opportunity for Austria.[79]

Apart from the crying need for internal national reconciliation, Redlich was aware that the federal reform of Austria was necessary as a basis for a negotiated peace with the allies and the United States. Realizing that a German victory would be very difficult, and would in any case not solve Austria's problems,[80] and that the continuation of war might destroy Austria altogether, Redlich hoped for a negotiated peace with the Allies as the last best chance for Austria. His desire for peace arose not only from the fear of defeat and dismemberment for Austria, but also because of the implications of modern warfare for humanity as a whole. 'Ever since the unchanging evil in human nature gained access to such horrifying weapons through the technology of the nineteenth century, the danger of the suicide of humankind is really at hand',[81] wrote Redlich, an insight confirmed by the startling admission from an Austrian war minister that the generals were on the side of the pacifists, since the technology of modern warfare threatened the existence of the entire world.[82]

Redlich realized that opposition from German policy-makers who still believed in a final German victory reduced the chances for a negotiated peace. He also thought that a separate peace between Austria and the West was almost impossible, since the Germans would never allow it.[83] The very same national egoism that enabled the German politicians to believe in a final victory also blinded them to the need for national reconciliation in Austria. Moreover, the Slavs increasingly wanted full national sovereignty, and Redlich's federal plan held no appeal for them. Redlich's clear-sighted view of all the obstacles to the preservation and salvation of Austria drove him many times to despair, and eventually induced in him a fatalistic resignation.

To those friends, chief amongst them Hermann Bahr, who spoke of his 'political mission' to save Austria,[84] Redlich responded with scepticism, explaining that as a partyless parliamentarian he had very little weight in parliamentary politics; indeed, he could scarcely exert any appreciable moral influence. Moreover, amidst such draconian censorship it was

[78] Redlich, *Schicksalsjahre Österreichs*, 26 Sept. 1915, 62; 'Die Verwaltungsreform voran!' in the *Arbeiter-Zeitung*, 265 (24 Sept. 1915).
[79] Redlich, *Austrian War Government*, 54.   [80] *Österreich und der Friede*, 38.
[81] Redlich, *Schicksalsjahre Österreichs*, 5 Feb. 1917, II, 189.
[82] Ibid., 30 Sept. 1918, II, 294–5.   [83] Ibid., 4 Sept. 1916, II, 140.
[84] Ibid., 19 Feb. 1917, II, 191.

impossible for him to influence public opinion.[85] In the privacy of his diary Redlich was even franker in acknowledging the practical futility of his endeavours, yet the inner necessity which compelled him to persist: 'As long as the Austrians do not learn to hear better, my "speeches" will remain worthless for the masses and their rulers, but they nevertheless remain my innermost and truest spiritual property. And that is ultimately the most important thing, through which I can avoid the only conflict that I fear—the conflict with myself.'[86]

On several occasions, however, it seemed as if Redlich would get the chance to attain power and put his ideas into practice. He expected a ministerial appointment from Koerber in late 1916, but Koerber claimed that the anti-Semitism of the court prevented him from nominating Redlich as finance minister.[87] Twice, in September 1917 and June 1918, his name was mentioned as a ministerial candidate in a cabinet to be formed by Count Silva-Tarouca.[88] His appointment seemed imminent in the summer of 1917, when the Meinl group gained great influence over the young, peace-loving emperor.

The core Meinl group consisted of Meinl himself, the Catholic jurist Heinrich Lammasch, the pacifist F. W. Foerster, and the future inter-war leader of the Christian Socials, Ignaz Seipel, with Redlich sometimes included in the innermost circle.[89] The group conceived of itself as a 'third way' in Austrian politics, between the German nationalist and the Slav separatist movements. The meetings of the Austrian Political Society which Meinl founded were attended by people interested in the preservation of a reformed Austria—pacifists, liberal cosmopolitans, social democrats, some aristocrats, and many prominent representatives of the Viennese high bourgeoisie and intelligentsia.[90] The composition of the society lent some support to Wickham Steed's oft-repeated view that the only people interested in maintaining the Monarchy were financiers, 'society' people, the Catholic Church, and Jews,[91] and indeed, these groups felt acutely that

---

[85] Redlich to Bahr, 13 July 1918, in Fellner (ed.), *Dichter und Gelehrter*, 352. On wartime censorship in Austria, see Kurt Paupie, *Handbuch der österreichischen Pressgeschichte 1848–1959*, Bd. II (Vienna, 1966), 142–7, 161–2; Mark Cornwall, 'News, Rumour and the Control of Information in Austria-Hungary, 1914–1918', *History*, 77 (1992), 50–64.
[86] Redlich, *Schicksalsjahre Österreichs*, 20 Feb. 1917, II, 192.
[87] Ibid., 14 Feb. 1917, II, 190.
[88] Ibid., 23 Sept. 1917, II, 235; 17 June 1918, II, 281.
[89] H. Benedikt, *Die Friedensaktion der Meinlgruppe, 1917/18: die Bemühungen um einen Verständigungsfrieden nach Dokumenten, Aktenstücken und Briefen* (Graz, 1962).
[90] Morgenbrod, *Wiener Grossbürgertum im Ersten Weltkrieg*, 56–70, 181–200.
[91] Hanak, *Great Britain and Austria-Hungary during the First World War*, 135.

96 *WWI and the Search for a New Europe*

the loss of Austria as a great economic unit and a multinational state would be a catastrophe. Hence the urgency with which the society debated empire reform ideas.

Under the influence of the Meinl group, Karl seriously considered either Redlich or Lammasch for minister president to set a new course for Austria, and summoned Redlich twice for personal audiences to explain his programme.[92] However, vociferous German nationalist opposition, opposition by the Prussian military leadership, and (in Redlich's case) anti-Semitism[93] compelled the vacillating young emperor to finally settle on an insignificant bureaucrat instead. Redlich considered the emperor's heart to be in the right place (for instance, in the Sixtus affair), but his personality to be completely unreliable.[94] Therefore, the only thing that sustained him in 1918 was a leap of faith—that the present situation was the health-bringing 'crisis' that would break the fever. 'I have the unshakeable inner certitude, that neither Europe nor Austria are fated to fall prey to the seemingly omnipotent imperialist power insanity of all countries',[95] he confided to Bahr.

Yet impending signs of Austria's doom crowded upon him from both within and outside the empire. When, for the first time, Redlich read through a copy of the *New Europe* that Meinl had procured, he found his old friends Wickham Steed, Seton-Watson, and Louis Eisenmann all vigorously pushing for the dismemberment of the empire. His many Czech contacts told him that they did not need Austria. The Czechs did not even bother to attend the Austrian parliamentary sessions anymore.[96] Viktor Adler, leader of the Social Democrats, likewise no longer believed in the empire's preservation, and looked forward to the task of constructing a new republic after the catastrophe.[97]

Kann, *The Multinational Empire*, ii. 242–3; Morgenbrod, *Wiener Grossbürgertum im Ersten Weltkrieg*, 120–4. See also Redlich, *Schicksalsjahre Österreichs*, 5 July 1917, II, 212–6; 6 July 1917, II, 216–8.
Redlich, *Schicksalsjahre Österreichs*, 12 July 1917, II, 221.
Ibid., 20 Apr. 1918, II, 268. Emperor Karl dispatched his brother-in-law, Prince Sixtus of Bourbon-Parma, to a secret meeting with the French president Poincaré in February 1917 for preliminary peace negotiations. French premier Clemenceau revealed these dealings in April 1918, causing Karl great political embarrassment both with his German allies and with his Austro-German subjects.
Redlich to Bahr, 3 May 1918, in Fellner (ed.), *Dichter und Gelehrter*, 337.
Redlich, *Schicksalsjahre Österreichs*, 6 Oct. 1918, II, 296–7.
Ibid., 2 Oct. 1918, II, 295. On the gradual dissolution of the bonds between the dynasty and its peoples, see Z. A. B. Zeman, *The Break-Up of the Habsburg Empire 1914–1918* (London 1961); Manfried Rauchensteiner, *Der Tod des Doppeladlers. Österreich-Ungarn und der Erste Weltkrieg* (Graz, 1993).

As Redlich had prophesied in early 1915, he was called upon to be minister only when Austria was on the brink of the abyss.[98] On 25 October 1918 Emperor Karl, hoping that the international reputations of Heinrich Lammasch and Redlich would rescue the day, appointed Lammasch as minister president and Redlich as finance minister. But there was little anyone could do. In the words of Namier: 'During the Lisbon earthquake of 1755 a man hawked anti-earthquake pills, in October 1918 the Emperor Charles changed his ministers.' Redlich's 'old deserving ambition' was 'realized in a Cabinet posthumous to the State. From the outset the new government was described as *ein Liquidierungskabinett*, liquidators of a bankrupt concern. They were to assist in the transfer of administration to the national governments, and try to preserve a place for the Habsburgs and a central government. But even for liquidation they were not wanted: the State was breaking up of itself.'[99] The last imperial ministry endured for only eighteen days. Redlich resigned, along with his ministerial colleagues, on 11 November 1918, the day the empire came to an end.[100]

Unlike Redlich, Lewis Namier had ceased to believe in the Austrian state idea by the beginning of World War I. As we have seen, any allegiance to Austria that Namier might have felt had been supplanted by socialism, Pan-Slavism, and more recently British patriotism. Hence, he had no compunction in volunteering for the British army in a war against Austria. Moreover, his antipathy towards the Germans was yet another incentive to join the British war effort. 'Even the cruelty of a Tartar does not approach that of a German; the German beats the Mongol in being dispassionate, systematic, and scientific.'[101]

Ironically, given his animosity towards the Germans, Namier's friends worried that he would be mistaken for a German because of his name (Bernstein) and his accent, and that he might be shot by someone from the British side in the confusion of war. Moreover, they thought his talents were wasted as a mere private in the army.[102] Hence Namier was discharged from the army and joined the propaganda agency directed by Charles

---

[98] Redlich, *Schicksalsjahre Österreichs*, 20 Jan. 1915, II, 10.
[99] Namier, 'The Downfall of the Habsburg Monarchy', in H. W. V. Temperley (ed.), *A History of the Peace Conference of Paris*, vol. iv, part 3, p. 110.
[100] See Redlich, *Austrian War Government*, 163–6, for Redlich's analysis of the last days, and his argument that the Lammasch ministry ensured the peaceful and orderly disintegration of the empire.
[101] Namier, *Germany and Eastern Europe*, 17, n. 1.
[102] J. Namier, *Lewis Namier*, 117, 119–21.

Francis Masterman at Wellington House in early 1915.[103] In 1917 he was transferred to the new intelligence bureau of the Department of Information, which in turn was merged into the Foreign Office in early 1918 as the Political Intelligence Department (PID).[104] Namier found himself working closely with liberal historians such as R. W. Seton-Watson, James Headlam-Morley, Arnold Toynbee, E. H. Carr, A. E. Zimmern, and Allen and Reginald Leeper, as well as with the group associated with the *New Europe*, the journal inspired by Thomas Masaryk and founded by R. W. Seton-Watson.[105] He agreed with many of the key views of the *New Europe* group, such as the necessity to destroy German militarism and German imperialism in Central and Eastern Europe; national self-determination for the Czechs, the Slovaks, the South Slavs, Romanians, and other oppressed nationalities; and the need for the dismemberment of Austria-Hungary.

However, there were important differences between Namier's views and those of the *New Europe* group. Their support for national self-determination grew out of a century-long British tradition of sympathy for oppressed or partitioned nations fighting for their freedom, whether it be enthusiasm for Kossuth's Hungary, sympathy for *Risorgimento* Italy, or for the liberation of Greece. In portraying the subject nationalities of the Habsburg empire as freedom-loving nations fighting against tyranny and autocracy, there are more than a few echoes of the Whig vision of British history as a series of hard-fought battles against monarchical absolutism, resulting in the establishment of religious toleration, cabinet government, the two-party system, and constitutional monarchy.

Namier, although equally convinced that he was fighting against oppression and injustice, understood the oppression in Marxist economic terms rather than political ones. He never wearied of explaining that the national conflicts in Central and Eastern Europe were really class struggles—the age-old struggle of land-hungry peasants against landowners, and of workers against their capitalist exploiters. His support for the principle of national

[103] K. J. Calder, *Britain and the Origins of the New Europe 1914–1918* (Cambridge,1976), 55–7; Hanak, *Great Britain and Austria-Hungary During the First World War*, 85–93.

[104] For details of Namier's political career during the First World War, see K. J. Calder, *Britain and the Origins of the New Europe 1914–1918*; Alan Sharp, 'Some Relevant Historians—the Political Intelligence Department of the Foreign Office, 1918–1920', *Australian Journal of Politics and History*, 34: 3 (1988), 359–68. See too James Wycliffe Headlam-Morley, *A Memoir of the Paris Peace Conference, 1919* (London, 1972), pp. xx–xxxi.

[105] See Hanak, *Great Britain and Austria-Hungary*, and Hugh and Christopher Seton-Watson, *The Making of a New Europe*.

self-determination was conditioned and ultimately limited by his allegiance to socialism and Pan-Slavism.

In 1915 and 1916 Namier was hampered by the difficulties of reconciling Pan-Slavism, socialism, and his duty as a British civil servant, although he exercised considerable ingenuity in surmounting the contradictions. Like the members of the *New Europe* group, Namier sought to convince the British policy-makers that national self-determination of the Slavs in Eastern Europe and the dismemberment of Austria-Hungary were vital to a lasting peace after victory. Contrary to those who saw the primary causes of the war in the recent naval and commercial competition between Great Britain and Germany, Namier maintained that the origins of the war and its chief problems lay in Eastern Europe. He contended that the war was caused by the oppression of the Slavs by the Germans—a centuries-old injustice which had originated with the migration of the different Teutonic Knightly Orders along the Baltic Coast almost up to the Gulf of Finland, 'exterminating or enslaving the native Slavonic and Lithuanian races'.[106] Successive waves of German emigration had resulted in scattered German settlements throughout the area between Germany and Russia.

The advent of Pan-Germanism and modern German imperialism represented a new danger to the Slavs, since the acknowledgement of the brotherhood of all Germans meant that German settlers had the power of the German empire behind them in their struggles against the surrounding Slavs. Moreover, these German settlers to the East were seen as the forefront of a new wave of German colonization. Modern Germany keenly felt its lack of an empire outside of Europe for colonization or trade. Austria-Hungary was thus a very valuable asset for German imperialism, since it opened up the possibility of an overland route to Turkey and Asia. For many years now, Austria-Hungary in foreign-policy terms had become a mere 'branch institution'[107] of Germany.

Namier argued that 'the elimination of German influence from Eastern Europe forms an indispensable preliminary of free development in those regions'.[108] The only way to check German influence was the emergence of an effective Pan-Slavic bloc. Hence it was in the interests of the British to support the Slavs in their struggles against the Germans.

Namier's eloquent flow of rhetoric, however, could not sweep away the two obstacles to his recommendations—first, Russian autocracy, and not

[106] Namier, *Germany and Eastern Europe*, 12.
[107] Ibid. 90.
[108] Ibid. 127.

German imperialism, was felt by many Slavs to be their chief oppressor; secondly, Britain, as Russia's ally, could not openly proclaim the principle of national self-determination as a right, since this principle would have dire consequences for the Russian empire. Britain had to be especially careful about Poland, since Russia treated Poland strictly as an internal affair.[109]

Namier tried to explain away the first obstacle by arguing that Russian autocracy was not of Slavonic creation, but a result of her Germanized bureaucracy. The descendants of the Teutonic Knightly Orders included both the Prussian Junkers and the Baltic gentry. In time, these Baltic Germans came to rule Russia through her Germanized bureaucracy. However, 'Russia is ruled by the Russian Germans, and still the people hate them . . . They have no understanding for, and still less sympathy with, the Russian Nationalists and the Pan-Slav movement.'[110] Nor was the partition of Poland the work of Slavonic statesmen, 'who would have preferred not to take an inch of Polish territory rather than to partition a Slavonic country with German States'. Rather, it was Catherine II, '*née* Princess of Anhalt-Zerbst', who perpetrated this crime.[111] Later, German influence had always strengthened the forces of autocracy in Russia and had prevented Russia from reaching an understanding with her Slavs, most notably in 1863 with the suppression of the Poles, and again in 1905. Hence, 'whilst they consider *the entire German nation to be the enemy of the Poles*, they do not profess any hostility against the Russian nation but only against the Russian government'.[112]

As for the principle of national self-determination, Namier was careful only to apply the principle to the Slavs of Austria-Hungary and not those of Russia. He also scrupulously observed the British policy that Poland was an internal issue of Russia, and merely expressed the hope that an autonomous, united Poland could quickly emerge under Russian sovereignty.

In the case of Poland, Namier was not only restrained by British determination not to offend Russian sensibilities, but more importantly by the fact that the Polish socialists, led by his boyhood hero General Piłsudski, had chosen to side with the Central Powers against Russian autocracy. As a result, Namier barely mentioned socialism in his documents of 1915 and 1916, although he could not resist stating, in an outburst remarkable for a

[109] For general background on Poland during World War I, see Norman Davies, *God's Playground: A History of Poland*, ii. 381–92.
[110] Namier, *Skyscrapers*, 65–6.
[111] Namier, *Germany and Eastern Europe*, 13–4.
[112] PRO: FO 371/2450/29614, Namier Preliminary Report, 12 Mar. 1915.

civil servant of a country allied with Russia, that '[i]n Austrian and Russian Poland the anti-Russian movement is now being conducted almost entirely by extremists and socialists; its leaders include some of the finest and greatest men from among the Poles'.[113]

Namier also lent covert support to the Polish Information Committee, which was led by August Zaleski, a close friend of Namier's from the London School of Economics, and Piłsudski's representative in England.[114] He ensured that the only Polish organization with which Wellington House dealt was the Polish Information Committee. The arrival in London of Roman Dmowski in November 1915, though, caused great difficulties for Namier. Dmowski, leader of the anti-Semitic, ultra-nationalist National Democrats, quickly gained ascendancy over Zaleski in the eyes of the Foreign Office, since he had been a leader of the Polish members of the second Duma and hence was known to be pro-Russian.

Although Namier could not openly side with the left-wing Poles against Dmowski, he rather ingeniously suggested that no support or encouragement should be given to any Polish politicians or organizations whatsoever, because all of them violated Russian policy by advocating Polish independence and by attempting to internationalize the Polish question.[115] He also managed to obtain proof that Dmowski, contrary to his protestations that he treated Poland as an internal matter for Russia, had agreed to internationalize the Polish issue in a conference of Polish émigrés in Lausanne in March 1916.[116] He paid heavily for publicizing this fact, in the form of a vicious press and personal campaign that Dmowski and his friends waged against him.[117] Namier's efforts to discredit Dmowski and reinstate Zaleski were paralleled by Lucien Wolf's activities to the same end. Although Wolf, director of the Conjoint Foreign Committee of British Jews, differed radically from Namier on the subject of the Habsburg empire (Wolf argued for its preservation), both agreed that the anti-Semitic Dmowski had to be stopped at all cost. Wolf too proposed that Britain should support Zaleski and left-wing Polish leader Alexander Lednicki rather than Dmowski,[118] and may have helped scotch insinuations by Dmowski that Namier and Rex Leeper were pro-German.[119]

[113] Ibid.

[114] Calder, *Britain and the Origins of the New Europe 1914–1918*, 87.

[115] PRO: FO 395/26/255781, Namier to Gower, 15 Dec. 1916.

[116] PRO: FO 395/26/249429. See also Tadeusz Piszczkowski, *Anglia a Polska 1914–1939 w świetle dokumentów Brytyjskich* (London, 1975), 51–2, for a pro-Dmowski account of Namier's role in this affair.

[117] Calder, *Britain and the Origins of the New Europe 1914–1918*, 93; Namier, *Lewis Namier*, 124–7.

[118] See Mark Levene, *War, Jews, and the New Europe: The Diplomacy of Lucien Wolf 1914–1919* (Oxford, 1992), ch. 10.   [119] Ibid. 195.

The Russian revolutions of 1917 freed Namier from most of the constraints he had had to observe previously. The fall of Russian absolutism removed the greatest obstacle to the Pan-Slav cause.[120] The ascendancy of the Cadets and their left-wing allies also meant that Namier now felt free to advocate socialism as a progressive, pro-Entente force. The declaration by the Provisional Government on 29 March 1917 that 'free Russia' would not dominate or conquer other nations, would seek 'a durable peace on the basis of the right of nations to decide their own destinies', and that it recognized Polish independence within her ethnic boundaries, made it possible now for the Allies to consider adopting national self-determination as an official principle.[121] Polish independence was no longer a pro-Austrian platform.[122]

With the change of government, Dmowski and his National Democrats lost influence in Russian official circles, to be replaced by Lednicki and the Polish Democrat Club. The condition that independent Poland must arise only within her ethnic boundaries gave Namier another weapon against Dmowski, since Dmowski laid claim to areas where Poles were in the numerical minority but where they owned most of the land.[123]

In his battle against Dmowski's imperialist pretensions to lands ethnically Ukrainian, White Russian, and Lithuanian, Namier had the wholehearted support of the *New Europe* group.[124] Like Namier, the *New Europe* group, indeed most of liberal British opinion, welcomed the Russian Revolution of February 1917. The combination of the Provisional Government's support for national self-determination, its concern with political and constitutional reform, and last but most importantly its commitment to continuing the war to a victorious end, endeared it to the British public.

Namier was almost alone, however, in his ardour for the Bolsheviks. It is a testimony to Seton-Watson's fair-mindedness and willingness to allow every viewpoint to be heard that he included Namier's article 'Trotski' in

---

[120] See T. G. Masaryk, 'Austria Infelix', *The New Europe*, 3: 29 (1917), 76–82: 'A free and democratic Russia is the gravest possible threat to Austrian and German absolutism; the Slavs of Austria-Hungary, like the Italians and Roumanians, never loved Russian absolutism; but they could not successfully fight Austrian absolutism so long as the greatest Slav country itself was absolutist. Tsarism was for the Slavs the heel of Achilles; free Russia is the end of Austrian absolutism, and that means the death of Habsburg Austria.'
[121] Musgrave, *Self-Determination and National Minorities*, 17.
[122] PRO: CAB 24/17/1142, Namier, 'Weekly Report on Poland VI', 22 June 1917, 3.
[123] PRO: FO 371/3016/194676, Dmowski memo, 26 Mar. 1917.
[124] Hugh and Christopher Seton-Watson, *The Making of a New Europe*, 158–160; and Calder, *Britain and the Origins of the New Europe 1914–1918*, 87–92.

New Europe, albeit with a note that the article did not necessarily represent the journal's point of view. Headlam-Morley, one of Namier's staunchest supporters, also begged to differ from him on the subject of Bolshevism, attributing their differences to 'ultimate causes and our whole attitude of mind towards political affairs'.[125] Despite his background as a socialist of gradualist rather than revolutionary convictions, Namier always possessed a militant side, to which Piłsudski's terrorist acts had appealed. The pressure of war had radicalized Namier to such an extent that he concluded that revolution must take place before evolutionary reform could be achieved. 'Evolution comes after revolution to eliminate the moribund forms by a gradual process. That is why systems survive revolutions and yet cannot be killed apart from revolution.'[126]

The greatest ground for bitterness against the Bolsheviks in Britain was their decision to seek a separate peace with the Central Powers instead of fighting to the bitter end. Namier, however, argued that the logic of ideas and the moral force inherent in the Bolshevik programme would be an effective force against the Central Powers, since the Bolshevik 'demands complete self-determination for all nationalities throughout the world— which implies . . . the end of German imperialism, the disruption of the Habsburg Monarchy and the Turkish Empire'. The example of a free Russia which did not oppress her nationalities would work like a ferment amongst the oppressed nationalities of the reactionary empires, which would surely lead to revolution, since 'revolution results from the logic of ideas'.[127]

In an appreciative article on Trotsky, Namier tried to show that his way to victory had been through ideas and not material weapons, that he knew 'how to capture the man behind the machine gun instead of countering the two in their own kind'. In 1905 Trotsky had fought Russian autocracy and succumbed, since the Russian army remained with the Tsar. Twelve years later this army went over to the revolution. In July 1917 he had fought Kerensky and succumbed again; the army was with his rival. However, 'in November he won without having raised or armed new forces. He is now trying the same game on Germany; nay, on the entire world—each man has only one method of acting, just as he has only one face. Can Trotski win this time? He will undoubtedly succumb again, but the seed will have been sown.'[128] Confronted with the forces of revolution, the Germans were 'in

[125] Headlam-Morley to Namier, 27 Feb. 1919, in Headlam-Morley, *A Memoir of the Paris Peace Conference, 1919*, 36.
[126] 'N' [Namier], 'Trotski', *The New Europe*, 6: 66 (1918), 14–5.
[127] Ibid. 10.   [128] Ibid.

the position of the mediaeval knight, playing a weird game of chess with supernatural powers'.[129]

The fact that Russia, the greatest Slav country, was now in the grip of a socialist revolution made it very easy for Namier to construct a grand synthesis of socialism and Pan-Slavism, with national self-determination as the tool serving both causes. According to Namier, there were only two dominant interests left in Central and Eastern Europe—the conservative, supported by German militarism, and the revolutionary, represented by Russia and the other revolutionary Slavs. (Namier tended to ignore the non-German, non-Slav peoples such as the Baltic nationalities and the Romanians.) The struggle now was between landlords and capitalists, who were either German or were supported by the Germans, and the revolutionary Slav peasantries and workers. National self-determination was both the path to social justice and the instrument that would break the German system.

Socialism in essence was an international doctrine. However, various socialist groups had tried to reconcile socialism with nationalism. By reason of Galicia's position, Galician socialists were exposed both to Austro-Marxism as well as to the more radical currents coming out of Russia.[130] The Austro-Marxist Otto Bauer argued that what Engels called nations without history represented the proletariat, while Germans and Hungarians represented middle-class capitalists. Hence, the national struggles in Austria-Hungary were actually disguised class conflicts. Karl Renner refined the analysis by distinguishing between the nobility and bourgeoisie, contending that whilst the nobility favoured historic provinces, and the bourgeoisie championed a centralized state in order better to exploit labour, it was the proletariat that desired national-cultural autonomy.[131] Galician socialists had used this line of reasoning to maintain that the exploitation of undeveloped Galicia by developed Western Austria could be understood in terms of class conflict.[132]

In the absence of a proletariat in Galicia, Galician socialists had focused on the plight of the peasant instead. Namier's socialism, too, was tinged with strong agrarian sympathies. He tended to classify both the middle-class capitalists and the nobility/landowning gentry under the heading of 'conservative/reactionary', and the peasants/workers under the label

[129] 'N' [Namier], 'Trotski', *The New Europe*, 6: 66 (1918), 16.
[130] J. Himka, *Socialism in Galicia*, 77–85.
[131] See Hans Mommsen, *Die Sozialdemokratie und die Nationalitätenfrage im habsburgischen Vielvölkerstaat* (Vienna, 1963).
[132] Himka, *Socialism in Galicia*, 82.

'revolutionary'. In his reports, Namier repeatedly stated that the national conflicts in Central and Eastern Europe were really class struggles, and that class interests took precedence over nationality, using press clippings, statistics, and even popular songs to illustrate his point.[133] In arguing against Polish imperialist ambitions on her eastern borders, he explained that 'the Little Russians, White Russians and Lithuanians of these provinces hate the Poles with a truly fanatical hatred; it is the hatred of a land-hungry peasantry against alien landlords'.[134] One of his favourite techniques was the extensive use of statistics to bolster his case. For instance, he noted that '39.8% of the entire area of Lithuania and the Ukraine belongs to a few thousand Polish "noble" families; just as in Courland most of the land belongs to the notorious German barons who have ruled and poisoned Russia'.[135] Similarly, he attributed the intensity of the Slovene national movement against the Germans to the fact that 'in Carniola, where only about 5 per cent of the population are Germans, one fourth of the land, all the mines and most of the industrial establishments are owned by German capitalists'.[136] National self-determination meant first and foremost the recovery of land by peasants and the means of production by the Slav workers.

National self-determination was also the crucial instrument to dismantle the German imperialist system. The creation of a Central European Union under German auspices required as its pivot an Austria-Hungary consolidated as a German-Magyar hegemony over the other nationalities. Hence, as Redlich too realized, 'not even the very modest measure of national self-government such as was allowed to them [the non-German nationalities] in Austria before the war, will be tolerated anywhere in "MittelEuropa", once they have been an issue in an armed conflict'.[137]

---

[133] In PRO: FO 371/3278/148264, Namier, 'The Settlement of Polish Affairs', 28 Aug. 1918, 3, n. (x), he quotes 'a popular song sung in some districts of Posnania by German colonists, i.e. by men expressly brought as a guard for German Nationalist interests', to illustrate the extent to which 'the Agrarian interest takes precedence with the peasant before nationality:

> Michel sagt zu seinem Sohne:
> Hol' der Teufel die Barone,
> Ob sie Deutsche oder Polen,
> Soll sie all' der Teufel holen.'

[134] PRO: FO 371/3016/194676, Namier memo, 14 Sept. 1917, 2–3.
[135] Ibid. 14.
[136] PRO: FO 371/3135/116831, Namier to Tyrell, 24 June 1918, p. 4.
[137] L. B. Namier, *The Case of Bohemia* (London, 1917), 4–5.

He scoffed at those socialists and liberals who wanted to preserve the Habsburg Monarchy as a reformed, multinational state. Unlike Redlich, Namier believed that the empire was too vested in reactionary conservative interests, and too dependent on Germany ever to become the Switzerland of Central Europe. For daring to hope for the reformation of Austria, he labelled the two moderate socialist leaders Karl Renner and Engelbert Pernerstorfer an 'Austrian imperialist' and 'German nationalist' respectively. He championed the left-wing forces headed by Otto Bauer and Friedrich Adler for endorsing the separatist movements of their Slav colleagues, and exulted at the growth of support for the Bolsheviks within the Austro-German socialist movement.[138] As for the British socialists and radicals associated with the Union of Democratic Control, he exclaimed in exasperation: 'One has to come to England to find socialists or "democrats" who from sheer controversial perversity become champions of such dynasty [*sic*] creations.'[139]

He argued:

Austria cannot continue on its present basis, but it is not within the power either of the Emperor or of any Austrian Government to satisfy the demands for change. Those of the non-German nationalities go beyond the frontiers of Austria, those of the Austrian-German Socialists beyond the limits of capitalist society. These two groups have together a majority in the Austrian Parliament, and the Socialist doctrine of complete national self-determination supplies a link between them, not for opposition alone, but also for action.

Hence, 'irredentist nationalisms, Socialism among the industrial working classes, and the agrarian movement stimulated by the example of Russia and the Ukraine . . . are working in the same direction'.[140]

Mitteleuropa extended far beyond Austria-Hungary, and the system that Germany would construct to manage its new empire could be seen at work in the peace negotiations at Brest-Litovsk. Like Redlich, Namier regarded German lip-service to the principle of national self-determination as a device to claim Russian land. The Germans proposed to carve out new states in defiance of the principle of nationality, so that each state would either contain only part of a nationality with an *irredenta* population across the border, or would itself contain a resentful national minority, hence leading to constant feuding between neighbours. Moreover, the Germans would support the big landowning interests and bourgeoisie of

---

[138] 'N' [Namier], 'Revolutionary Forces in Austria', *The New Europe*, 7: 27, (1918), 15–6.
[139] 'N', 'Trotski', 14.
[140] 'N', 'Revolutionary Forces in Austria', 14.

each country against their socialist peasantry. 'From the Baltic to the Black Sea and the Aegean a series of small States would extend, nationalist though not national, conservative and in constant fear of revolution, each of them involved in feuds with its neighbours, and every one dependent on Germany.'[141]

In the Baltic Provinces, Germany would partition the Estonians and Letts between three separate states controlled by the Baltic barons of German nationality. It would distribute White Russian areas between Lithuania, Poland, and the Ukraine. It would divide and conquer by simultaneously protecting the conservative social interest of the Polish landowners in Lithuania and the Ukraine, whilst at the same time stimulating Lithuanian and Ukrainian nationalism. There was only one way of cutting through this Gordian knot. 'The nature of the German system indicates the means for combating it. It rests on violence against nationality, on feuds engendered by it and on social reaction. National self-determination and social justice are the only weapons which can break it.'[142]

It will be clear by now that Namier detested nationalism divorced from the quest for social justice. He believed that nationalism could be both a progressive and a reactionary force. Nationalism was progressive if it worked against reactionary states like Austria and Germany. Nationalism was reactionary if it was used as a pretext by the aristocracy or bourgeoisie to perpetuate economic oppression or by imperialists for forcible annexations. Namier was prepared to support the national struggles of oppressed nationalities against the imperialism of stronger nations—hence, he supported the Ukrainians against Polish imperialism; the Slovaks, Serbs, and Croats against Magyar imperialism; the Czechs against Austro-German imperialism; the Poles against Prussian imperialism; and the Lithuanians, White Russians, Latvians, and Estonians against the oppression of the Baltic barons of German extraction. He showed no mercy towards what he regarded as reactionary nationalisms.

Of all the Slav nationalisms, Namier displayed the greatest ambivalence towards that of the Poles. As might be expected, he framed this ambivalence in both Pan-Slav and socialist terms. The Poles were alone amongst the non-Russian Slav nations in retaining its aristocracy and gentry classes. These powerful classes exploited the labour of the oppressed peasant, and hence lived in constant fear of peasant revolutions against them. Since Namier thought that the spirit of Slavdom found its most genuine expression in the

---

[141] 'N', 'Germany and Her Vassals', *The New Europe*, 6: 74 (1918), 277.
[142] Ibid. 277.

peasant,[143] the Poles, with their highly stratified society, were necessarily the one Slav nation most alienated from Slavdom. Although they had briefly joined forces with other Slavs in the liberal, linguistic-based Pan-Slavism of 1848, 'they have long thrown behind them the Pan-Slav ideas which they embraced for a while in 1848, and have never in recent times shown any feeling for their humbler and more democratic Slav brethren'.[144] The Austrian Poles, through a parliamentary alliance with the Germans, had abandoned the Czechs and Yugoslavs to German rule.

Without the Poles, however, whose country lay between the Czechs and the Russians, Pan-Slavism could not possibly grow into an effective power on Germany's Eastern flank.[145] Hence, Namier's untiring focus on Poland in his reports and memos—he hoped that the British would choose to support the true interests of the Polish people, embodied in the Polish socialist programme, over the Polish imperialists, thereby saving Poland from herself and for Slavdom.

Namier distinguished between Polish imperialism to the East, in which the Poles laid claim to predominantly Ukrainian, Lithuanian, and White Russian lands on the basis of history and landownership, from the just aspirations of the Poles for national self-determination in the West or South, where the Polish workmen, miners, peasants, and fisherman formed the majority of the population, although the area was controlled by the German landlords, mine-owners, and manufacturers: 'Poland is like a photographic plate with two impressions on it: there is one Poland, the country of the Polish people, and there is another, the country of the Polish land-owning gentry, and more often than not the two do not coincide.'[146]

By differentiating between the Polish people and the Polish nationalism of the upper classes, we see the germ already of Namier's later denunciation of ideological nationalism as a product of the middle-class intelligentsia. Such a divergence between the true interests of the people and the distortions of the nationalists was not unique to Poland. Deeply disgusted by the Lithuanian and Ukrainian nationalist demands at the Brest-Litovsk peace negotiations, Namier made the same distinction between the 'nationalists' and the 'people'. 'Lithuanian nationalism is the creed of a small group of intelligentsia of peasant extraction, of the lower ranks of the Roman Catholic clergy and of a very restricted petit bourgeoisie; Ukrainian

[143] Namier, *Germany and Eastern Europe*, 38–9.
[144] Namier, *The Case of Bohemia*, 1.
[145] Namier, *Germany and Eastern Europe*, 46–7.
[146] *Manchester Guardian*, 21 Apr. 1919.

nationalism has not even the support of the clergy, which is Great Russian in its tendencies.'[147] Therefore, when the Agrarian movement in the Ukraine threatened to merge in the All-Russian peasant movement, the Ukrainian nationalists had to call in the Germans to maintain their own position.[148] The negotiations at Brest-Litovsk made Namier realize that the nationalism of oppressed nations and classes had the same potential to turn imperialistic as the nationalism of the Germans, Magyars, and Poles.

The Lithuanian imperialists claimed land that was ethnically Belorussian. Since Namier regarded the Belorussians and the Ukrainians as the two south-western branches of Russia,[149] he thought the imperialist claims of Lithuania at the expense of the Belorussians and Ukrainians especially egregious. Namier believed that the geopolitical configurations of Central and Eastern Europe meant that the various East European nationalist movements had to align themselves with one of the only two dominant forces left in Eastern Europe, Russian revolution or Germany militarism.[150] In a discussion of Poland that could apply equally to the other nations between Russia and Germany, Namier wrote:

Poland's position is such that, as long as international politics are discussed in terms of power and not of law, she cannot be truly independent. When the independence of a nation is not secured by its own strength, it needs to be safeguarded by a favourable geographical position . . .

The Poles inhabit the centre of a vast, open plain; in contiguous settlement number less than 20 millions; have for neighbours the two most numerous nations of Europe—the Germans and the Russians—and are strategically a land-locked nation. In time of war the Baltic is closed to all Great Powers except the two which also by land border on Poland, and outside help could, therefore, reach her practically by no other way than through Germany or through Russia. In the days of *Realpolitik* Poland must, therefore move either in the Russian or in the German orbit.[151]

The Poles and the other nationalists demanded land that rightfully belonged to Russia. If they succeeded, they would stand in natural permanent antagonism to Russia. Since they could never be equal in strength to either Russia or Germany, still less superior to both, any aggrandisement at the expense of Russia therefore implied dependence on German protection.[152] In

[147] PRO: FO 371/3278/148264, Namier, 'Settlement of Polish affairs', 28 Aug. 1918, 2.
[148] Ibid. 3.
[149] PRO: FO 371/3016/194676, Namier memo, 14 Sept. 1917, p. 2.
[150] 'N', 'Revolutionary Forces in Austria', 17.
[151] 'N' [Namier], 'Poland and Brest-Litovsk', *The New Europe*, 6: 71 (1918), 181–2.
[152] PRO: CAB 24/46/GT4016, Namier, 'Weekly Report on Poland', 21 Mar. 1918.

other words, they had to choose 'between scheming aggrandisement under the wings of the Central Powers and fighting for principles at the side of the Russian Revolution'.[153]

Namier warned that, despite the enticing promises of the Central Powers, a policy of co-operation with the Germans would ultimately lead to both moral and political bankruptcy. The conservative Poles had expected the Central Powers to uphold their claims to Ukrainian land in the East; however, they were dealt a rude shock by the Treaty of Brest-Litovsk, when the Germans, hoping to secure the Ukrainian grain supply for themselves, promised the Ukrainians a strip of genuine Polish territory in Western Cholm and the district of Biala.

[The peace treaty with the Ukraine] marks the utter bankruptcy of the Realpolitik of the Polish upper classes, which meant compromise with the strong and menace to the weak . . . The Polish cause has once more become linked to the course of revolution . . . For it requires now elemental forces, which are not respecters of men, to free Poland from her grave clothes. A mighty wind has risen out of the north; it has put out small lights, but fans big flames into a conflagration. The Poles must go whither it leads.[154]

Namier's distinction between progressive and reactionary nationalisms had much in common with Redlich's loathing of nationalism yet respect for the national consciousness of a people and the nation's struggle for justice. Moreover, whilst acknowledging and even preaching the principle of national self-determination, Namier, like Redlich, believed in the multinational state. Unlike Redlich, however, Namier pinned his hopes not on a reformed Austria but on the new Federative Republic of Russia.

During the first half of the war Namier often mentioned his hopes for the formation of nation-states in place of Austria-Hungary and the Ottoman empire. Behind his words lay the unspoken assumption that the formation of nation-states from the corpses of anachronistic, dynastic empires was an inevitability conforming to the forward march of history. This assumption underlay both liberal nationalist and socialist attitudes, since both shared the belief in history as a linear progression. Lenin, for instance, believed that nationalism was a phenomenon of the capitalist era and would disappear with capitalism itself. However, the formation of nation-states was vital in the historical evolution towards the socialist society, since historically the creation of the nation-state resulted in the

---

[153] 'N', 'Poland and Brest-Litovsk', 181.
[154] Ibid. 183.

triumph of bourgeois democracy over feudal autocracy. Hence, the formation of nation-states was a progressive step in feudal Eastern Europe.[155]

Before the Russian revolutions hardly anyone expected the socialist revolution to happen first in backward Russia or Eastern Europe. Given the impossibility of an immediate socialist revolution, the best outcome would be the formation of liberal nation-states. Here Namier, like so many of the British liberal nationalists, held up the Czechs as a shining example of the 'best spirit of a modern democracy'.[156] He praised Masaryk for his 'extraordinarily high moral character', and predicted that he 'would survive longest of all Czech bourgeois politicians'.[157]

However, the Russian revolutions in 1917 and the victories of the Russian left seemed to suggest that, just as it was possible to pass from the feudal stage directly to the socialist state, so it would also be possible to leapfrog the nation-state and immediately form a socialist federation. Since the socialist state had already been established, the formation of independent nation-states had lost much of its socialist *raison d'être*. Hence, Namier proposed that even non-Slav countries such as Lithuania should remain joined to Russia. After citing the Russian promise to Lithuania and to 'all other territories in Russia inhabited by different nationalities' of 'the most far-reaching autonomy, especially regarding language, religion, schools, administration and extensive rights of decision in local matters', Namier added, with utter disregard of the Lithuanian viewpoint: 'These are words to which certainly every honest Russian without any difference of politics will subscribe.'[158]

Propelled by his revolutionary zeal, Namier, despite priding himself on his own understanding of *Realpolitik*, succumbed completely to utopianism when he hoped that the British would support and help actualize his vision of the new Europe. To be sure, Namier's programme seems to have succeeded far better than Redlich's—after all, Namier was fighting for the winning side. National self-determination did become one of the official war aims; Austria-Hungary and the Ottoman empire were dismembered, and Germany defeated. However, what succeeded in winning over Woodrow Wilson and with him, somewhat grudgingly, the Allies, was not

[155] Helmut Konrad, 'Between "Little International" and Great Power Politics: Austro-Marxism and Stalinism on the National Question', in Richard L. Rudolph and David F. Good (ed.), *Nationalism and Empire: The Habsburg Monarchy and the Soviet Union*, (New York, 1992), 269–94.

[156] L. B. Namier, *The Czecho-Slovaks: An Oppressed Nationality* (London, 1917), 24.

[157] PRO: FO 371/3135/127473, Namier to Tyrrell, 23 July 1918.

[158] PRO: FO 371/3016/206035, Namier, 'Report on the Occupied Russian Provinces', 25 Oct. 1917, p. 4.

Namier's socialist and Pan-Slav programme, but the liberal version of national self-determination as propounded by the *New Europe* group. Moreover, official British sympathy for liberal goals of national self-determination had come about not so much because of ideological conviction as for strategic reasons.[159] The difference between the various historians who pushed for national self-determination and those in power was stark: 'The Political Intelligence Department wanted to formulate ideal goals and then fight till these were attained; other departments adapted war aims to fit realistic assessments of British power.'[160] This limited the political efficacy of the historians in the Political Intelligence Department, a weakness which became overwhelmingly obvious during the Paris Peace Conference.

Namier certainly failed to change the direction of policy in his own specialist field—Poland. Although the Russian revolutions of 1917 seemed to present an opportunity for Namier to finally shake the Foreign Office's trust in Dmowski, the latter's position was too secure for Namier to make much of a dent.[161] His attack on Dmowski was two-pronged, focusing on the question of Poland's eastern borders[162] as well as the inevitable rapprochement between the National Democrats and the Central Powers. Although the question of the Polish eastern borders was a burning issue for Namier, the Foreign Office and the War Cabinet had matters of more immediate concern to worry about during the difficult year of 1917 than the future territorial dimensions of Poland.[163] Namier's second point, that Dmowski's party would veer towards the Central Powers, impinged much more immediately upon British interests. Recognizing this, Namier did not let an opportunity pass to remind the Foreign Office and War Cabinet that the Russian Revolution had profoundly changed the entire situation, so that the old party divisions, though not the personal and party feuds, had vanished to a very large extent.[164]

He argued that a natural symbiosis existed between the Polish conservative elements and the Central Powers, for the 'Polish gentry and bourgeoisie require the help of the Central Powers to ban the spectre of a Polish social revolution', whilst the 'Central Powers require Poland as an insulator against the revolutionary movement from the east'.[165] Hence, he warned

[159] Calder, *Britain and the Origins of the New Europe 1914–1918*, 11.
[160] Ibid. 9.   [161] Ibid. 154.
[162] Marek Baumgart, *Wielka Brytania a Odrodzona Polska 1918–1933* (Szczecin, 1985), 44.
[163] Calder, *Britain and the Origins of the New Europe 1914–1918*, 168.
[164] PRO: CAB 24/15/GT968, Namier, 'Weekly Report on Poland IV', 7 June 1917, p. 2.
[165] PRO: FO 371/3281/8026, Namier, 'Weekly Report on Poland XXIII', p.3.

that the creation of a Polish army under the auspices of the National Democrats would turn against Russia and the Allied cause.

Instead, he urged support for the left-wing forces of Poland, excusing their former support of the Central Powers by explaining that 'they were not led by devotion to the Habsburgs but by hostility to the Russian autocracy'.[166] He pointed to the mounting evidence of estrangement between the Polish left wing and the Central Powers, culminating in Piłsudski's arrest in July 1917, as well as to signs that the National Democrats had gradually begun to co-operate with the Council of State, the right-leaning Polish Council established by the Central Powers in January 1917.

Namier's warnings were ignored. The British Government, whilst aware of the changes in Polish politics in Russia, did not seem to understand the situation in Poland.[167] Hence, Dmowski's proposal for the formation of a Polish army was looked upon favourably. By August 1917 the Entente had agreed to finance a Polish army, which was later recruited by the Poles in North America, trained by the Canadians, transported by the British, and commanded by the French. The Polish army was exclusively associated with the National Democrats, who also argued that the creation of such an army necessitated some form of complementary political organization. In August 1917 the Polish National Committee was created under Dmowski's presidency in Lausanne, and was subsequently recognized by France and Britain. In Russia, despite the opposition of the Provisional Government, Russian military authorities, in collusion with the National Democrats, created the Polish corps under General Jozef Dowbor-Musnicki in August 1917.[168] After the Bolshevik Revolution of November 1917, and the clear signs that Russia intended to negotiate a separate peace, the Allies decided to use Polish, Czechoslovak, Cossack, and Romanian troops on the Eastern Front, and thus began to finance the Polish corps.

Dmowski had many supporters in the British Government, including Sir Eric Drummond, private secretary to the foreign secretary Sir Edward Grey, and Sir Arthur Nicolson, permanent undersecretary of state. As Dmowski's star rose throughout 1916 and 1917 at the Foreign Office, Namier came increasingly to be viewed as a biased, untrustworthy authority on Polish affairs. For instance, George Clerk, senior clerk in the war department of the Foreign Office, lamented that '[t]here is no one from whom we can derive information as to the cross currents of Polish politics

---

[166] PRO: CAB 24/17/1142, Namier, 'Weekly Report on Poland VI', 22 June 1917, p. 2.
[167] Calder, *Britain and the Origins of the New Europe*, 184.
[168] Ibid. 166. See also Norman Davies, *God's Playground*, ii. 388.

and the underlying aims of Polish political leaders, as for instance Dr. Seton-Watson has enabled us to do in the case of the Jugoslavs'.[169] In reference to the Dmowski–Namier conflict, Sir Eric Drummond wrote: 'I regard him [Namier] with considerable suspicion. I disagree with a great deal of what he writes . . . his attack on Dmowski and other Poles is, in spite of what he says, purely personal and quite unjust.'[170] The historian C. W. C. Oman, who advised the Foreign Office on Polish affairs and who had tutored Namier at Oxford, wrote of him: 'He is quite sincere, but very self-centred and disputatious: he used to consider himself as the only authority in England on the Ruthenian question, and to resent any one having independent views upon it . . . In my opinion Mr. Namier's criticism of "The Problems of Central Europe" [Dmowski's memorandum] is written in a spirit of exaggerated hostility, making the worst of the Polish case whenever it is possible to do so.'[171]

Some of this distrust stemmed from Namier's extreme rhetoric, which caused even Wickham Steed, a fellow-supporter of national self-determination, to reject an article written by him on the Polish problem. 'I have read Namier's article with great care, but I do not think we can publish it . . . though the facts are pretty nearly as he has stated them', wrote Steed to Seton-Watson; 'the Poles will need to be called to order, but I do not think that the best way of calling them to order is to write with the animus which Namier displays.'[172]

Namier also evinced a degree of revolutionary enthusiasm that must have been highly unsettling to the officials he dealt with, coming as they did mostly from the patrician elite classes of English society. Bolshevism was popularly perceived at the time to be a Jewish movement. By his open sympathy with the Bolsheviks, Namier must have seemed like a menacing troublemaker, yet another Jewish revolutionary intent on sabotaging the foundations of a stable and law-abiding society.

Moreover, Namier was the victim of a clever and unscrupulous campaign by Dmowski and his friends and followers, who played on British anti-Semitism and xenophobia to tarnish Namier's reputation. 'It is ridiculous even to imagine a Jew as champion of Ukraine, White Russian, or Lithuanian nationalism', snorted G. K. Chesterton; 'it is not fitting that an East-European Jew should conduct an anonymous propaganda in the

[169] PRO: FO 371/3012/133576, Clerk minute, 18 July 1917.
[170] PRO: FO 800/384, Drummond to Kerr, 6 Apr. 1917.
[171] PRO: FO 371/3016/194676, Oman to Balfour, 27 Sept. 1917.
[172] SEES, R. W. Seton-Watson Papers: SEW/17/26/6, Steed to Seton-Watson, 28 Mar. 1920.

British Press against Poland and the Polish National Committee, a body officially recognised by our own and by all Allied Governments'.[173] 'I cannot help thinking that in his paragraphs about the religious dissentions of the Roman-Catholic Poles + [*sic*] Lithuanians, his personal feelings against those of an alien religion to his own are peeping out',[174] wrote C. W. C. Oman.

Some of these suspicions about Namier's objectivity and accuracy were well founded. He was not above distorting facts and mixing subjective speculation with objective reportage in order to prove his points.[175] In a remarkable fit of historical amnesia, for instance, Namier wrote: 'For the last 100 years the Conservative elements in Poland have been opposed to "maximalist" or revolutionary tactics with regard to the partitioning Powers; having much at stake they disliked a policy of adventure and preferred to gain some measure of power and freedom by a show of loyalty to their rulers (moreover they naturally disliked revolution of any kind).'[176] Since 'Conservative' in Namier's lexicon at the time always referred to the aristocracy, gentry, and bourgeoisie, he at one stroke erased the aristocracy- and gentry-led Polish uprisings of 1830, 1845–6, and 1863 from his version of Polish history.

Namier's reports are also strewn with instances where he freely mixed speculation with reportage, so as to present the right in the worst possible light. Two examples will suffice:

On May 16 [1917] the Polish Club decided to pass into opposition, this being since 1867 the first time in the Parliamentary history of Austria that the Poles have taken up such an attitude. The decision was carried by the votes of the Socialists, the Democrats and the Peasants' Party, the Conservatives abstaining from voting. *It seems that strenuous attempts were subsequently made by the Conservatives to reverse the decision—the general situation remains unclear.* [Italics mine.][177]

Meantime the Provisional Council of State makes pathetic efforts to clear itself in the eyes of the public; it protests to the Germans against . . . the arrest of Piłsudski, whom they now try to clear of accusations *which originally had been probably suggested to the Germans by the adherents of the Council.* [Italics mine.][178]

Notwithstanding Namier's passionate bias, however, he was far more perceptive than most observers on Polish politics. True to Namier's predictions,

[173] G. K. Chesterton, 'Potash and Perlmutter', *The New Witness* (26 Apr. 1918), 587.

[174] PRO: FO 371/3016/194676, Oman to Balfour, 27 Sept. 1917.

[175] Namier would later practise selective use of evidence even in his works on English history. See Colley, *Lewis Namier*, 62–3.

[176] PRO: CAB 24/17/1142, Namier, 'Weekly Report on Poland VI', 22 June 1917, p. 1.

[177] PRO: CAB 24/15/GT968, Namier, 'Weekly Report on Poland IV', 7 June 1917, p. 5.

[178] PRO: CAB 24/22/GT1669, Namier, 'Weekly Report on Poland XII', 10 Aug. 1917, p. 2.

Dowbor-Musnicki's army devoted itself to defending the Polish landlords'
rights against the Bolsheviks rather than to fighting the Central Powers,
and on 25 February 1918 signed an agreement with the Germans to cease
attacks on the Central Powers.

After the Dowbor-Musnicki defection, there is more than a hint of satisfaction in Namier's reports, where he argued that such a result could have
been predicted all along:

> Nature takes its course, politics have their iron laws no less than physics. The Polish
> National Democrats stand for social Conservatism and Polish imperialism. Since
> the Russian Revolution Germany has been the stronghold of social Conservatism in
> Eastern Europe, and conquests at the expense of Russia can obviously never be
> made otherwise than with German help. The National Democrats when forming
> the Polish Army in Russia loudly professed anti-German sentiments and views. *But
> sentiments and views in politics are merely momentary equations; interests and tempera-
> ment are the permanent factors* . . . Considering the interests for which the Polish
> Army stood and was meant to stand by its organisers, the compromise which they
> have concluded with Germany must be described as the logic, and not as an irony, of
> history. [Italics mine.][179]

Instead, 'the real aims of the promoters of the Polish Army was [*sic*], by
creating such an Army, to compel the governments of the Entente to extend
to them some official recognition and thereby to pledge themselves in case
of victory to endeavour to impose these men as a government on Poland,
whether they are agreeable to the Polish nation or not'.[180]

The Dowbor-Musnicki incident forced British policy-makers to
reassess their trust in Dmowski. Meanwhile, the intelligence bureau of the
Department of Information was transferred to the Foreign Office in
February 1918, and became the Political Intelligence Department (PID)
under the leadership of Sir William Tyrrell and the historian James
Headlam-Morley. Namier, as a member of the Foreign Office, was now
better protected against Dmowski's attacks.[181] Moreover, Tyrrell and
Headlam-Morley supported Namier in his attempts to rehabilitate Zaleski
and the Polish Information Committee. This resulted in the establishment
of contact between the Foreign Office and the Bureau Polonais de Presse in

[179] PRO: CAB 24/46/GT4016, Namier, 'Weekly Report on Poland, XXVII', 21 Mar. 1918,
p. 2.
[180] PRO: FO 371/4359/PID72, Namier memo, 26 Apr. 1918, p. 3.
[181] PRO: FO 371/4363/PID137, Namier memo, 15 May 1918; Hardinge to Drummond,
16 May 1918. PRO: FO 800/329 Drummond to Dmowski, 17 May 1918.

Berne, in opposition to Dmowski's Agence Polonaise Centrale.[182] Namier was further vindicated by the naval intelligence report of June 1918, which pointed out that the National Democrats in Poland were co-operating with the enemy and that the Socialists were the only group in Polish politics firmly opposed to the Central Powers.[183]

The year 1918, then, was one of partial triumph and vindication for Namier personally. It was also, of course, the year of the Allies' victory. On 11 November 1918 Namier danced the night away with a euphoric crowd in London, unaware that his multinational dreams would prove just as elusive as Redlich's internationalist Austrian state idea, and that the greatest battles were still to be fought, and lost, at the Paris Peace Conference.

[182] Calder, *Britain and the Origins of the New Europe*, 197.

[183] PRO: FO 371/3279/169676, 'Present Condition of Political Parties in the Kingdom of Poland', 25 June 1918.

4

Lost Worlds, Present Dangers

I dwell ever more on the old German fairytale of Vineta—the seaside city of Vineta, which was submerged by the sea but whose church bells can still be heard on calm days by the lonely wanderer on the coast. Austria is such a Vineta, Vienna more so than any other Austrian city. Many, however, are still alive that once knew Vineta before it was sacrificed to the raging elements. I am one of those survivors, and I can still summon, from the ringing church bells, the old melodies of Austrian life and essence from the past, so as to set them down in these pages.[1]

A wood once destroyed cannot grow up again in the Russian steppes unless carefully protected; the exuberant growth of grass and weeds keeps the sun and air from the young trees in spring, and the drought kills them in summer or the storms in winter. But grass can be destroyed and will always come up again with the returning season. The trees are the superstructure of society and the grass is the peasantry, closer to the earth, dense, invincible and indestructible in its numbers.[2]

The break-up of Austria-Hungary devastated Redlich. To him, whose life, identity, and political activities had been so closely woven with the Habsburg Monarchy, its dissolution was tantamount to the 'collapse of the world'. Despite his best efforts to rebuild his life after 'that unholy day of 12 November 1918', he never truly adjusted to the new Europe of the inter-war years.[3] Already by January 1919 Redlich was grieved and astonished that he regarded himself as being part of history, although he was not yet old either in years (he was 49) nor in nature (*Wesen*).[4] His feeling that life after the break-up of the empire was merely a coda to the lost world was to intensify throughout the remainder of his life.

[1] Redlich, *Aus dem alten Oesterreich*, 5.
[2] Namier, *Skyscrapers*, 160.
[3] Redlich to Schober, 15 Dec. 1926, in Fritz Fellner (ed), 'Johann Schober and Josef Redlich: Aus den Tagebüchern und Briefwechsel', *Zeitgeschichte*, 9–10 (1977), 315.
[4] Redlich, *Schicksalsjahre Österreichs*, 1 Feb. 1919, II, 332.

'The lost world', 'the world of yesterday', 'the golden age'—such phrases abounded amongst those whose lives had been disrupted and displaced by the chaos of inter-war Europe.[5] To Redlich, the lost world meant the loss of his 'great fatherland'; the marginaliation of Vienna, transformed from a great capital to a provincial city; and the loss of political vocation. It also meant the loss of culture and civilization submerged by a wave of barbarization, a catastrophe which both Redlich and Namier regarded as not merely local to Central and Eastern Europe but a wider phenomenon that threatened western civilization.

The break-up of the empire confronted Redlich immediately with the problem of allegiance—whether to seek Czechoslovakian or Austrian citizenship.[6] He opted for Czechoslovakian citizenship, but continued to live in Vienna.[7] In 1919 and 1920 Masaryk considered Redlich for the post of German *Landesminister* or finance minister in Czechoslovakia[8]—an idea stillborn because of ferocious German nationalist opposition.[9] Simultaneously, however, Johann Schober, chancellor at various times in inter-war Austria, tried to nominate Redlich for the post of finance minister in Austria, a proposal once again shot down by German nationalist opposition.[10] It is a sign of the confusion of the times that Redlich could be considered for ministerial posts in two successor states simultaneously. His nomination to the World Court in 1929 was supported by both Austria and Czechoslovakia, as well as by influential friends in the United States.

More immediately pressing even than questions of national and civic allegiance, however, was the problem of economic survival. Famine, starvation, disease, and economic collapse were all features of life in post-war Vienna.[11] The death of Redlich's brother Fritz in 1921, quite apart from its shattering emotional impact, was also an economic blow, since Fritz had supported Josef throughout his adult life, providing him with that

[5] Claudio Magris, *Der habsburgische Mythos in der österreichischen Literatur* (Salzburg, 1966).
[6] See Edward Timms, 'Citizenship and "Heimatrecht" after the Treaty of St. Germain', in Ritchie Robertson and Edward Timms (eds.), *The Habsburg Legacy: National Identity in Historical Perspective*, Austrian Studies, 5 (Edinburgh, 1994), 158–68.
[7] See Redlich to Bahr, 9 Nov. 1919, in Fellner (ed.), *Dichter und Gelehrter*, 383; WSLB, Handschriftensammlung: I.N.198.661, Redlich to Darkow-Singer, 30 Oct. 1919.
[8] Redlich, *Schicksalsjahre Österreichs*, 20 Apr. 1919, II, 341; 4 July 1919, II, 344; 15 July 1919, II, 344.
[9] Ibid., 9 Sept. 1919, II, 347, 352.
[10] Redlich to Schober, 15 Dec. 1926 in Fellner (ed.), 'Johann Schober and Josef Redlich: Aus den Tagebüchern und Briefwechsel', *Zeitgeschichte*, 9–10 (1977), 307–8.
[11] Harvard University, Houghton Library: FMS Ger 145.2, Josef Redlich, 'The Food Situation in Austria' (1921).

much-treasured independence from the vicissitudes of political life and academic employment. For the first time Redlich had to worry about his own financial future, a position exacerbated by the industrial and unemployment crisis in Czechoslovakia, the location of the bulk of the Redlich family's enterprises. By 1926 Redlich's finances were in desperate straits, and he found himself increasingly hard-pressed to support his wife and two young daughters, as well as his musician son. He received the summons to a professorship at Harvard Law School in 1926 with joy, not least because it solved his immediate financial quandaries.

Redlich felt marginalized, not only in time but in space. 'I feel removed from the real great life of our age, sitting in that metropolis of one of the largest empires of Europe until 1918, now the capital of a small state of not quite seven millions of people.'[12] Cut off from the mainstream of the life of the world, Redlich thirsted after news from the wider world, immersing himself in American and British diplomatic circles in Vienna, and resuming his extensive correspondence with American and British friends. Redlich was profoundly moved as visitors and letters arrived from British, American, and French friends, assuring him of their unchanged friendship after the years of war. His acceptance of German responsibility for the war enabled him to bear no malice towards old friends like Seton-Watson, Steed, and Louis Eisenmann, who had worked so much for the break-up of Austria-Hungary. On the eve of his departure to England in 1920 for a month-long visit, Redlich wrote joyously: 'This is the first time in seven years that I am escaping the Austrian jail!'[13]

Redlich's own political vocation was so inextricably linked to the old Austria that he felt little inclined to take part in post-war politics. Although he sometimes complained querulously that in Austria not much had changed, since he was still eternally a minister-in-waiting,[14] his will to be involved in politics had gone. Redlich greeted the collapse of ministerial hopes for himself with relief. Yet despite his disavowal of the new Austrian republic in the 1920s—'this republican Austria was *never* my homeland'[15]—he could not completely ignore her call.[16] The republican

---

[12] HLS, Charles C. Burlingham Papers: Box 15, Redlich to Burlingham, 10 Dec. 1923.
[13] Redlich to Bahr, 23 Sept. 1920, in Fellner (ed.), *Dichter und Gelehrter*, 422.
[14] Redlich to Bahr, 13 Jan. 1924, in ibid. 516.
[15] Redlich to Bahr, 21 Feb. 1927, in ibid. 556
[16] For the vexed question of post-Habsburg Austrian identity, see William T. Bluhm, *Building an Austrian Nation* (New Haven 1973), ch. 1; Kurt Skalnik, 'Auf der Suche nach der Identität', in Erika Weinzierl and Kurt Skalnik (eds.), *Österreich 1918–1938*, Bd. I (Graz 1983), 11–24.

Austria was, despite everything, still 'a part of my inheritance'.[17] He was sent on a mission to the United States in 1921 to beg aid for Austria.[18] Nevertheless, Redlich steadfastly refused Schober's pressing invitation to become finance minister in 1929, finally acquiescing only for a month in 1931 to contain the damage done by the collapse of the Austrian *Creditanstalt*.[19] Instead, Redlich devoted much of the remainder of his life to scholarship.

He had started *Das österreichische Staats- und Reichsproblem* in the middle of the war and worked on it obsessively until the second volume appeared in 1926, refusing invitations to leave Vienna for long periods of time because of his archival work in the Haus, Hof- und Staatsarchiv. He credited the writing of the *Staats- und Reichsproblem* with the salvation of his sanity, his armour against the pressures of the disintegration of his world.[20] Hofmannsthal once asked Redlich how he could possibly bring himself to write about the collapse of Austria, a subject upon which Hofmannsthal himself, precisely because it meant the break-up of his world, could only remain silent.[21] 'A certain rationalist streak in my being', explained Redlich, 'means that a cause-and-effect understanding of historical events leads me to an inner calmness.'[22]

However, neither rational post-mortem nor the emotional need to build a mausoleum for the Austrian empire could replace the old sense of mission Redlich felt previously in his pursuit of scholarship. In the past, his various studies had the immediate purpose of contributing to the 'future development of Austria, and the betterment of her public life and her institutions'.[23] Now, although he bravely declared that the collapse of 1918 had not rendered these studies worthless but had deflected them to the purely scholarly goal of research and presentation, he could not shake off a sense of malaise and superfluity. He felt unappreciated and forgotten by Austria. Redlich resented being passed over for the position of professor of Constitutional Law at the University of Vienna in favour of Hans Kelsen,

---

[17] Redlich to Schober, 15 Dec. 1926 in Fellner (ed.), 'Johann Schober and Josef Redlich: Aus den Tagebüchern und Briefwechsel', *Zeitgeschichte*, 9–10 (1977), 315.

[18] Harvard University, Houghton Library: FMS Ger 145.1 'Bericht des o. Univ. Prof. Dr. Josef Redlich, Ministers a.D. an den Herrn Bundeskanzler Dr. Michael Mayr über seinen Aufenthalt in den Vereinigten Staaten von Amerika in den Monaten Marz und April 1921.'

[19] Redlich, *Schicksalsjahre Österreichs*, II, 356. See also HLS, Sheldon Glueck Papers: Box 59, Folder 6, Redlich to Glueck, 21, Jan. 1932.

[20] HLS, Roscoe Pound Papers: Box 80, Folder 22, Redlich to Pound, 12 Dec. 1920.

[21] Hofmannsthal to Redlich, 28 Nov. 1928, in Fußgänger (ed.), *Briefwechsel*, 116.

[22] Redlich to Hofmannsthal, 14 Dec. 1928, in ibid. 118.

[23] Redlich, 'Aus dem alten Oesterreich', 1.

fifteen years younger than himself, whose work, moreover, in drafting the new Austrian Constitution Redlich held in very little esteem.[24] 'I cannot achieve much in this country, will also no longer try to achieve anything here', wrote Redlich.[25] More and more, he looked upon his work on Austrian history as a debt he owed to the past. After its completion, he would be free to leave.

Given Namier's enthusiasm for radical causes and solutions during World War I, he should have been happy with the New Europe. Yet his reactions were very similar to Redlich's. As we have seen, Namier had strong social conservative tendencies from childhood onwards. This conservative side now came to the forefront, as reports regarding the destruction wrought by agrarianism, socialism, and nationalism flowed in from Central and Eastern Europe onto Namier's desk at the Foreign Office. Piłsudski, Namier's hero since boyhood, invaded the Ukraine and Lithuania in an attempt to unite them to Poland by force. Whilst he tried to excuse Piłsudski by describing him as a broken man after imprisonment in Magdeburg, leaving him open to manipulation by Dmowski's National Democrats, Namier had to admit that 'in international politics Polish Socialists do not differ much from Berlin Junkers or stock-jobbers'.[26]

His three-year sojourn in Central and Eastern Europe from 1921 to 1924 confirmed Namier in his suspicion of the new order. To accumulate enough capital for a prolonged period of writing, Namier became a representative of certain British cotton interests in Czechoslovakia and a special correspondent for the *Manchester Guardian* and the *Manchester Guardian Commercial*.[27] Using Vienna as a base, where he engaged a room in the Hotel Sacher for three years, Namier journeyed extensively through Central and Eastern Europe.[28]

He found that impoverishment and barbarization were already universal throughout the region. During the war Namier had lumped agrarianism and socialism together as progressive forces. Now, however, as he surveyed the scene of the peasants triumphant, seizing land from the landowners

---

[24] Redlich to Bahr, 16 Nov. 1920, in Fellner (ed.), *Dichter und Gelehrter*, 435.
[25] WSLB, Handschriftensammlung: I.N. 185.205, Redlich to Michael Holzmann, 3 Sept. 1927.
[26] PRO: FO 371/4384/PID722, Namier, 'The Problem of East-Galica', 30 Dec. 1918, p. 2. See L. B. Namier, 'Marshal Piłsudski. Liberator of Poland: Socialist Turned Dictator', *Manchester Guardian*, 13 May 1935, for a measured assessment of Piłsudski.
[27] J. Namier, *Lewis Namier*, 167–8. See too MGA: A/N2/2, Namier to C. P. Scott, 23 June 1919, and A/N2/4a, A. E. Zimmern to C. P. Scott, 13 June 1919.
[28] J. Namier, *Lewis Namier*, 170.

under the rubric of land reform, Namier became convinced that agrarian revolutions were detrimental to progress. 'Socialist production would require a higher degree of organisation than now exists', whereas '[a]grarian revolutions . . . mark a descent to lower, well-known forms of production—when they break up big agrarian enterprises, highly organised on a capitalist basis, and hand over the land to peasants who will work it in ways known since time immemorial'.[29] He would later describe the Soviet policy of collectivization, despite the 'excessive zeal and ruthlessness in certain officials' and the 'tragedies and losses on quite a serious scale', as on the whole justified and successful: 'it has produced a new type of agriculture with far greater prospects for the future than small-holdings offer, especially in the production of cereals.'[30]

Namier also regarded the parliamentary triumph of the peasants in the Polish elections of 1919 with dismay. 'The atmosphere of the Polish Parliament will be that of an East-European third-class railway-carriage',[31] he wrote. Interestingly, Namier defended the choice of Biliński as finance minister to Seton-Watson, who was worried by Biliński's intimate associations with the Habsburg empire. 'I consider his appointment not merely justifiable, but even good', wrote Namier, and called for Seton-Watson to 'view past Hapsburgite [*sic*] leanings with equanimity'.[32] After all, the only people of any intellectual standing and 'up to the standard of European Parliaments' were the Galician Polish conservatives who had been members of the Austrian parliament.[33] They were the only remnants left of the old ruling class in the new 'peasant parliament',[34] which Namier regarded as more truly 'Bolshevik' than if it had been dominated by socialists. 'One should not take too narrow a view of Bolshevism. The essence of Bolshevism is class struggle, a suspicion on the part of the lower classes against the upper classes and the educated people and the belief among the lower classes that they can best run the government themselves.'[35]

Even at the height of Namier's enthusiasm for Bolshevism, he had realized that 'it is not democracy which the Bolseviks [*sic*] aim at, but a "turn of the wheel"—the rule of the down-trodden'.[36] Now, the unfolding events in

[29] Namier, *Skyscrapers*, 147–8.
[30] L.B. Namier, *Facing East* (New York, 1966), 128.
[31] PRO: FO 371/3897/30573, 27 Feb. 1919, Namier, 'The Polish Elections', 4.
[32] SSEES, Seton-Watson Papers: SEW/17/18/7, Namier to Seton-Watson, 14 Aug. 1919.
[33] PRO: FO 371/3907/122897, 10 Sept. 1919, p.349.
[34] PRO: FO 371/3897/30573, 27 Feb. 1919, Namier, 'The Polish Elections', p. 5.
[35] Ibid. 3.
[36] 'N', 'Trotski', 10–11.

Russia and Eastern Europe, combined with Namier's long talks with Masaryk about the Russian Revolution, forced him to the conclusion that Bolshevism had not really established the constructive social revolution envisaged by Marx.[37] Still, Namier's attitude towards Bolshevism remained ambivalent, which led to misunderstandings between himself and politically aware English friends. 'Too benevolent towards Russia for the more banal propagandists on the Right, he was too clear-sighted about Bolshevism for the more banal propagandists on the Left. Where they admired or detested an entity, he discerned two, in conflict more often than not.'[38] Despite his second marriage to a Russian émigré who had suffered greatly in the gulag in 1947, Namier always retained a certain affection for Bolshevism, inextricably linked to his lingering Pan-Slav sympathies and a lifelong love of Russia (both his first and second wives were Russian). In a commemorative article on the twenty-fifth anniversary of the Russian Revolution, he praised the results of collective farming, and industrial and city planning. 'True, it was done at a terrible sacrifice, but the readiness of the peoples of the U.S.S.R. to make yet greater sacrifices in this war shows that they have found themselves in their new Fatherland and that moral and educational progress has been achieved since 1917.'[39]

Namier might have been in awe of the constructive achievements of Bolshevism, but he fiercely condemned its impulse to wipe out the ruling classes and elevate the lower classes to the position of rulers—an impulse he regarded as not only confined to Russia but widespread throughout the East European peasantry. Despite inveighing against the conservatives and gentry during the war, Namier showed no joy at their passing. He now differentiated between the conservative gentry and the National Democrats, whom he continued to detest for the rest of his life. The National Democrats were the servants of the gentry, but were made up chiefly of the petite bourgeoisie. Dmowski, their leader, was 'a child of the Warsaw riverside and reproduced its type in the arena of international politics'. 'Unscrupulous in the choice of means, he did what the indolent but fundamentally honourable Polish nobleman would never have done.'[40] These indolent but honourable noblemen were now on the path to extinction. 'The old ruling classes have practically disappeared on the European continent: they perished mostly because they were not equal to their task;

[37] J. Namier, *Lewis Namier*, 171; Namier, *Skyscrapers*, 119.
[38] J. Namier, *Lewis Namier*, 172.
[39] Namier, 'The Russian Revolution: 1917–1942', *Manchester Guardian*, 7 Nov. 1942.
[40] Namier, 'Obituary: Dr. Roman Dmowski', *Manchester Guardian*, 3 Jan. 1939.

but even so their countries are the poorer.'[41] The triumph of the peasant would lead to the sinking of economic and intellectual culture,[42] since there would be 'no room for a leisured class of independent means and of independent spirit' in a peasant republic.[43] Moreover, the elevation of the peasant to the status of ruler was not merely destructive to the upper classes, but also to the peasants themselves. '[B]ig peasants are infinitely harder taskmasters for the village labourers than the average squire.'[44] 'It suffices for a man to rise one rung off the ground, and to put on an official uniform, even that of a gendarme, to create the contrast of rulers and ruled; and the position is not improved by the "ruler" being brutish and new to the pleasures of wielding authority.'[45]

Namier was no less moved and distraught by the plight of Vienna, impoverished and disoriented, its population debased into paupers or speculators. Most disastrously, Vienna's food supply was threatened both by the disruption of the empire which placed Hungarian, Galician, and Moravian grain behind high tariff walls, and by the Austrian peasants' suspicion of 'red Vienna' and their reluctance to trade food with the capital.[46] 'There is a state in the retrograde development known as general paralysis, when only by a supreme effort the human being still manages to walk on two legs, and there is a stage in social paralysis when all the efforts of the community have to be concentrated once more on securing its indispensable food-supply',[47] wrote Namier. The shortage of food-supply increased the power of the peasants at the expense of the old ruling classes.

Namier's pound-sterling income ensured that he was far less vulnerable to the economic crisis than Redlich. However, his capital dwindled under the twin impact of family demands and his expensive new passion for psychoanalysis. Koszylowce, the family estate, had been sacked and burned by marauding Ukrainian peasants.[48] Namier, out of a sense of guilt and obligation, undertook to pay off the debts from the estate as well as his

---

[41] Namier, *Facing East*, 65.   [42] Namier, *Skyscraper*, 151.
[43] Ibid. 155.   [44] Ibid. 152.
[45] Namier, *Facing East*, 63–4.   [46] J. Namier, *Lewis Namier*, 162–3.
[47] Namier, *Skyscrapers*, 146.
[48] SSEES, Seton-Watson Papers: SEW/17/18/7 Namier to Seton-Watson, 14 Aug. 1919: 'Your brother-in-law Luttman-Johnson has taken very energetic action on behalf of my people, and only because of insuperable difficulties he was unable to reach them at the moment of their worst need. I am sorry to say that they have been very badly treated by an Ukrainian military detachment, but in spite of most outrageous treatment and sufferings have survived it and are now perfectly safe.' Despite the privations suffered by his family, Namier excused the Ukrainians on the grounds that they could not be expected to feel friendly towards his father, who had been 'always on the Polish side and known to be closely involved with the Polish nobility'. See J. Namier, *Lewis Namier*, 144.

father's gambling debts. Torn apart by the conflicting pull between the new Polish national state and Vienna, his *ville lumière*, Joseph Niemirowski was gambling, and losing, as never before. Namier was appointed by his family as Joseph's guardian on the latter's fund-raising trips to Vienna. Responsible for restraining Joseph from gambling, Namier's role further increased the enmity between father and son.

Namier's reunion with his family had not been a happy one. His family accused him of making their lives miserable, for he was now known amongst Poles, thanks to Dmowski's efforts, as an anti-Pole Ukrainian-lover and in Vienna as a spy for the Entente.[49] His father forbade Namier to visit Koszylowce, since local sentiment against him was too strong.[50]

There was no bridging the gap between Namier and his family. His parents identified themselves as Austrian Poles. Any residual identity as a Pole for Namier, however, had disappeared as a result of Polish depredations against Ukrainians and Jews alike. The struggle to secure East Galicia for the Ukrainians, and the struggle to protect the rights of Polish Jews as a national minority absorbed most of his time and efforts during his post-war employment at the Political Intelligence Department.[51] Namier's hatred of Polish imperialism and anti-Semitism caused him to cast Poland in the role of arch-villain in place of prostrate Germany, to the extent that Sir James Headlam-Morley had to remind him that 'the Poles have no special monopoly of vice'.[52] '[Y]ou are charged with Polish affairs and what people look to you for is not merely criticisms of Poland, but sympathetic advice as to how the Poles can best be helped',[53] wrote Headlam-Morley to Namier, but Namier was too much in the grip of therapeutic nihilism to think that the Poles could be helped.

He stoutly defended both Ukrainians and Jews against Polish calumnies. He particularly questioned Polish allegations that the Ukrainians had committed atrocities against the Jews, believing that these were 'less serious than those proved to have been committed by the Poles against the Jews.'[54] To Polish charges that the Jews were collaborating with the Bolsheviks and

[49] J. Namier, *Lewis Namier*, 160.
[50] Ibid. 164.
[51] Taras Hunczak, 'Sir Lewis Namier and the Struggle for Eastern Galicia, 1918–20', *Harvard Ukrainian Studies*, 1 (1977).
[52] Headlam-Morley to Namier, 12 Feb. 1919, in Headlam-Morley, *A Memoir of the Paris Peace Conference, 1919*, 28.
[53] Headlam-Morley to Namier, 3 Feb. 1919, in ibid. 20.
[54] FO 371/3907/86258, Namier to Tyrrell, 13 June 1919, p. 179. See Henry Abramson, *A Prayer for the Government: Ukrainians and Jews in Revolutionary Times, 1917–1920* (Cambridge, Mass., 1999).

the Ukrainians in East Galicia, Namier noted tersely: 'As neither the Ukrainians nor the Bolsheviks put such indignities on the Jews and ill-treat or oppress them as the Poles do, it is but natural that the Jews should welcome them—in fact the Jews would welcome the Martians if these merely freed them from the Polish insults and oppression.'[55] 'The Prussian rule in Poland was mild and constitutional compared to the present Polish regime in White Russia',[56] he wrote. Namier even defended the Germans against Polish allegations of German attack at Babimost and Kargova X, pointing out that these places, 'generally known as Bmost and Unruhstadt . . . lie in overwhelmingly German territory where the Germans may reasonably claim to have been fighting in self-defence'.[57] Namier's antagonism towards the new Polish national state was such that he opposed Poland's entry into the League of Nations Council in 1926. He made his peace with Poland only during World War II, acting as an informal liaison between the British Foreign Office and the Polish émigré leaders, many of whom were lifelong friends like Stanisław Kot, Marian Kukiel, and August Zaleski,[58] with whom he agreed to disagree over the question of Poland's eastern boundaries.[59] Once again, he tried to impress upon both the Foreign Office and the Polish leaders the necessity for co-operation with the Soviet Union against Germany.[60] Still, this was no resurgence of any emotional identification with the Poles. Namier collaborated with the Poles mainly because he hoped to obtain their help on

[55] PRO: FO 371/3907/109220, Namier to Tyrrell, 1 Aug. 1919, 290. Namier argued that the Poles were far more anti-Semitic than the Ukrainians. For a less rosy picture of Ukrainian–Jewish relations, see John Paul Himka, 'Ukrainian–Jewish Antagonism in the Galician Countryside during the Late Nineteenth Century', in Peter J. Potichnyj and Howard Aster (eds.), *Ukrainian–Jewish Relations in Historical Perspective* (Edmonton, 1988), 111–49.

[56] PRO: FO 371/4384/PID691, Namier, 'Memorandum on Eastern Frontier of Poland', 5 Dec. 1919, p. 282.

[57] PRO: FO 371/4377/146, Namier to Tilley, 20 Feb. 1919, p. 255.

[58] A delicate task since Zaleski and Kot were at logger-heads with each other. See FO 371/24474/ C7639, J. M. Roberts note, 19 July 1940, p. 280. On the whole, Namier took Kot's side because he regarded Kot and Sikorski as having far more of a mandate from the population of Poland than did Zaleski.

[59] MGA, B/N8A/355, Namier to A. Wadsworth (undated). 'Kukiel was C-in-C. of the Polish Army in Scotland, and Minister of War in Sikorski's Cabinet; he is an awfully good fellow, & I am very fond of him, but when with him refuse to talk, or listen, about the "Eastern Borderlands." '

[60] FO 371/23153/C19384, Namier memo to R. A. Butler on impressions on Polish émigré leaders, 28 Nov. 1939, pp. 66–69; FO 371/24474/ C7639, J. M. Roberts note, 19 July 1940, p. 280; FO 371/24482/C8027, Report from Naval Intelligence Department Admiralty, Major General E. G. Beaumont-Nesbitt, CVC., MC., 24 July 1940, p. 278.

behalf of the Jews.[61] From this more dispassionate viewpoint, Namier could finally bring himself to see that the Poles were neither 'paladins of liberty' or 'reactionaries' but 'a case *sui generis*, as is every nation, though more complex owing to the complexities of their position'.[62])

His father was appalled not only by Namier's anti-Polish crusades, but also by his son's growing concern with Zionism. The depth of estrangement was only made clear a few months after Joseph's death in 1922 in Merano, when Namier learnt that he had been disinherited by his father's will, and that the whole of Koszylowce had passed to his sister.[63] Namier's rage and disappointment knew no bounds. In later life he attributed his right hand's deteriorating functionality to his dispossession by his father. Throughout his absence from Koszylowce, he had dreamed of returning to the well-loved land, where, 'with a very special joy—he would once again ride out to *his* Neolithic *obuz* (tumulus), and organise on *his* land shoots of wild boar and other game. His right hand having symbolically become of no pleasurable use to him, he had let it die.'[64] He never saw his mother or sister again, nor did he visit Koszylowce. His disinheritance broke the final major link to his East European past. It also signified the end of the dream of being rooted in his own soil. Despite his passionate identification as both a British subject and a Jew, and the overwhelming importance he attached to landownership for psychological ease and social status, Namier always lived in rented houses and apartments, and never tried to purchase any land in Palestine.

Namier began to make preparations for returning to Britain and historical work. Despite the demands on his capital, he managed to amass enough money to secure several years of undisturbed historical writing, in large part due to shrewd currency speculation in Central Europe, under the tutelage of no less than Dr Rašín, the Czechoslovakian finance minister.[65] His funds were also augmented unusually by research grants from the Rhodes Trust.[66]

---

[61] See MGA, B/N8A/23, Namier to Crozier, 4 July 1941, in which Namier wrote about the need to refrain from embarrassing the Poles in public because he needed to be on good terms with them so as to protect Jewish interests. See also MGA, B/N8A/209, Namier to Crozier, 15 Apr. 1943, in which he described the Polish and Czech governments' efforts to help Jewish children of their nationality migrate to Palestine.

[62] Namier, *1848: Revolution of the Intellectuals*, 14.   [63] J. Namier, *Lewis Namier*, 182.

[64] Ibid. 182.   [65] Ibid. 173.

[66] NP: 1/1a/1, correspondence between Namier, the Secretary of the Rhodes Trust P. H. Kerr, H. A. L. Fisher, H. E. Egerton, and Lionel Curtis about two grants of £300 each awarded to Namier by the Rhodes Trust.

After his return to London in 1925 Namier saw signs everywhere that the loved old world was on the retreat even in England. 'The disenchantment of victory is far more paralysing than the bitterness of defeat',[67] he wrote, explaining that it was this disenchantment, rather than a literal 'missing generation', that caused the lowering of political, social, and artistic culture in the western democracies. 'It is not a generation which seems to have perished in the last war, but an atmosphere, an inspiration, *un élan vital*—and their loss has deadened the living.'[68] 'Eagles and lions' were out of place in inter-war England, led, as Namier saw it, by middle-class mediocrities who had replaced the traditional ruling classes.[69]

From present-day England, Namier took refuge in the past. Led to the study of eighteenth-century English history through his interest in the mystery of the 'Phoenix Empire', Namier became more and more engrossed in the era for its own sake. The tidal wave threatening the patrician, landowning society led him to study the era of the pure blossoming of English aristocratic and gentry society. Research into archival holdings in different manorial houses also gave him a good excuse to associate with their descendants. 'There is something very peculiar about that period [the eighteenth century] in the way it affects us who work in it; when [the historian Romney] Sedgwick and I meet, we talk eighteenth-century gossip, and tell each other funny stories about the Duke of Newcastle, and laugh at the old man whom, somewhere at the bottom of our hearts, we both love.'[70] Namier needed the comic relief.

Despite their conviction that German nationalism had been responsible for the war, Redlich and Namier directed their anger in the immediate post-war years towards the victors for destroying what remained of the loved old world. Redlich complained bitterly that Austria had been ruined more by the 'so-called Peace of St. Germain' than by the war and its immediate consequences. 'Though I had some doubts concerning President Wilson's informations [*sic*] on European things, I trusted him entirely when he stepped in and proclaimed his great principles . . . What he has done in the last twelve months was for me, as for all truly liberal men here and in Germany who fought against Prussian militarism, the severest disillusionment.'[71] Namier, in the euphoria of impending victory, wanted to right

---

[67] Namier, *Conflicts*, 76. [68] Ibid. 74–5.
[69] Ibid. 75. [70] Namier, *In the Margin of History*, 132.
[71] Columbia University Library, Munroe Smith Papers: Redlich to Munroe Smith, 12 Dec. 1919.

centuries-old injustices and create a New Europe. The outcome of the Paris Peace Conference disillusioned him equally severely.[72]

Both thought the reparations policy of the victors disastrous for Central and Eastern Europe, inspired mostly by the French thirst for revenge.[73] Although far from a German nationalist, Redlich referred to the Treaty of Versailles and of St Germain as 'Diktatfrieden'.[74] Moreover, he was extremely bitter that the promise of help and aid for reconstruction of Austrian economic and financial life had not been forthcoming until Seipel's bold political blackmail.[75] Namier, too, believed that generous aid should be forthcoming from the western powers for reconstruction in Central and Eastern Europe, and helped organize the hugely influential 'Reconstruction in Europe' issues of the *Manchester Guardian Commercial*, in which articles by him and by Redlich appeared.[76]

Altogether, Namier is more benevolent towards Germany than Redlich at this period—a fact worth stressing, given Namier's later reputation as a fire-eating German-hater. He praised the defeated Germans for their 'indomitable self-respect and a proper sense of human dignity, good to see in a great nation when down'.[77] He even went so far as to praise the Germans, alongside the Czechs, as 'the most civilised, one is almost tempted to say the only civilised nations in East-Central Europe'.[78] Redlich, however, was sceptical about the new republican Germany from

---

[72] Of the vast literature on the Paris Peace Conference, the most comprehensive is still Harold Temperley (ed.), *A History of the Peace Conference of Paris* (London, 1920–4), to which Namier contributed.

[73] HLS, Charles C. Burlingham Papers: Box 15, Redlich to Burlingham, 16 Sept. 1922: 'The collapse of German money is the result both of the French reparation policy and of the financial policy of the real leaders of the German people, its industrial captains.' Special correspondent [anonymous, but internal stylistic evidence points to Namier's authorship], *Manchester Guardian Commercial*, 24 Aug. 1922, p. 201: 'one wonders what will happen should French policy complete the work of economic destruction so successfully furthered by the ill-fated decision of the League of Nations with regard to Upper Silesia.'

[74] Houghton Library, Harvard University: FMS Ger 145.1, Redlich, 'Report to Chancellor Mayr', 1921.

[75] Seipel's successive visits to Italy, Germany, and Czechoslovakia in 1922 succeeded in arousing enough fear to spur the Conference of Allies to grant Austria a huge loan at Geneva. Both Redlich and Namier much admired this political gamble. Josef Redlich, 'Austria and Central Europe', *Yale Review*, 12 (1923), 338–9; L. B. Namier, 'Ignaz Seipel Obituary', *Manchester Guardian*, 3 Aug. 1932.

[76] J. Namier, *Lewis Namier*, 180.

[77] Namier quoted lines from Goethe's 'Prometheus' to describe the German attitude to the Peace Conference: 'You must still leave me my earth standing, and my hut which you did not build, and my hearth for whose warm glow you envy me.' See J. Namier, *Lewis Namier*, 141.

[78] L. B. Namier, 'The Problem of East-Central Europe', *Round Table* (June 1923), 572. This article appears anonymously but is identified as Namier's in his biography. See J. Namier, *Lewis Namier*, 180.

the start. 'The republican persuasion of the masses is in many cases only a manifestation of the anger against having been swindled by the Wilhelminian-Ludendorf regime. Fundamentally, however, all of them believe in the miraculous powers of the strong man.'[79] He understood that democracy, introduced or imposed by the western powers in the wake of the World War, would be connected in Germany with that 'terrible feeling of defeat',[80] and would hence be unpopular. He distrusted the new Germany so much, he proposed that German Austria should be reorganized according to a federal and cantonal constitution, and should constitute with Switzerland a neutral ring both against the South as well as against the East 'that would preclude every German *revanche* policy.'[81] Redlich, however, bitterly opposed the Great Powers' prohibition on Austria joining with Germany, seeing this as a matter for self-determination by the Austrian people themselves.

Living in what was arguably the most wretched victim of the Paris Peace Settlement, the new republic of Austria that no one wanted, Redlich also resented the selective application of the principle of self-determination. He believed that the independent existence enforced on German Austria was fatal, and that Austro-Germans should have been allowed to decide through referendum if they wanted to join Switzerland or Germany.[82] He pointed out that even Masaryk, who denied the right of national self-determination to the 4 million Germans within Czechoslovakia's borders, 'expressly reserved to the Germans of Austria proper . . . their right to join Germany, to which they had always belonged in one form or another until 1866'.[83]

For Namier, Great Power commitment to the principle of national self-determination was exposed as a sham through the way the victors handled the conflict between Poland and the newly founded Western Ukrainian People's Republic. To Namier, this was a vitally important problem for several reasons: first, his personal attachment to the Ukrainians of East Galicia (or Western Ukraine); secondly, sheer numerical weight, as the fate of 4 million Ukrainians was at stake—ten times the size of the population

---

[79] Redlich, *Schicksalsjahre Österreichs*, 4 July 1919, II, 344.

[80] *The Decline of Parliamentary Government, Discussed by Harold J. Laski & Dr Josef Redlich, March 28, 1931 . . . New York Luncheon Discussion* (New York: Foreign Policy Association, 1931), 18.

[81] Redlich, *Schicksalsjahre Österreichs*, 13 Jan. 1919, 330.

[82] Bruce Pauley, 'The Social and Economic Background of Austria's Lebensunfähigkeit', in Anson Rabinbach (ed.), *The Austrian Social Experiment* (Boulder, Col., 1985), 21–37.

[83] Josef Redlich, 'Reconstruction in the Danube Countries', *Foreign Affairs*, 1: 1 (1922), 78.

of Fiume and the parts of the Dalmatian coast disputed between Yugoslavia and Italy;[84] and thirdly, Russian (both White and Red) intolerance of Ukrainian subjection to Poland,[85] a factor the western powers ignored at their peril, despite Russia's temporary eclipse.

Namier believed that Poland had no right to East Galicia, where the ratio of Ukrainian to Pole was more than three to one. However, his proposal that East Galicia should become a self-governing state under the League of Nations mandate was defeated. Instead, with French and American backing, East Galicia was put under Polish control, albeit with the caveat that it should be autonomous, and subject to a referendum at a later date. That there existed such a caveat at all was due to protest by Great Britain, whose pro-Galician policy has been partially attributed to Namier's influence.[86] Namier's immediate superior, Sir James Headlam-Morley, was much impressed with his work. He managed to convey the substance of Namier's proposals while moderating their expression, thus making them more palatable to the British decision-makers.[87]

Namier regarded the Austrian issue more dispassionately than Redlich, but agreed that Austria should have been granted the right to self-determination and *Anschluss*. 'Austria lacks both the moral and the material conditions of an independent existence' was Namier's succinct summary of the Austrian dilemma.[88] Both Redlich and Namier regarded Austria as a European, not merely a provincial, problem. Redlich argued that the dissolution of Austria could set off war between Hungary, Czechoslovakia, Italy, and Yugoslavia for territory,[89] whilst Namier pointed out that Austria, by allying with either the Hungarians or Czechoslovakia, could 'close the ring of the Little Entente round the Magyars, or alternatively establish the

---

[84] PRO: FO 371/4384/PID725, Namier note to Headlam-Morley, 1 Jan. 1920, p. 236.

[85] FO 371/3907/134198, Namier note to Sir John Tilley, 29 Sept. 1919, p. 482.

[86] Taras Hunczak, 'Sir Lewis Namier and the Struggle for Eastern Galicia, 1918–20', *Harvard Ukrainian Studies*, 1: 2 (1977), 198–210. Certainly, Namier seems to have credited British hostility towards Polish ambitions regarding their eastern boundaries to Namier, lamenting that 'such a little Galician Jew could play such an important role in the Polish question'. Roman Dmowski, *Polityka polska i odbudowanie panstwa* (Warsaw, 1925), 226, quoted in Hunczak, 210. Dmowski's views are echoed by other Polish historians as well. See Baumgart, *Wielka Brytania a Odrodzona Polska 1918–1933*, 108; Piszczkowski, *Anglia a Polska 1914–1939 w świetle dokumentów Brytyjskich*, 146; Maria Nowak-Kiełbikowa, *Polska–Wielka Brytania w latach 1918–1923* (Warsaw, 1975), 60.

[87] Alan Sharp: 'Some Relevant Historians in the Political Intelligence Department'; Headlam-Morley, *A Memoir of the Paris Peace Conference, 1919*.

[88] Namier, 'The Problem of East-Central Europe', 582; Josef Redlich, 'The problem of the Republic of Austria', *Quarterly Review*, 464 (July 1920), 216: 'Seven little provinces cannot stand alone in Europe.'

[89] Redlich, 'Austria and Central Europe', 339–40.

connection between them and Italy'.[90] Most importantly, Austria's attitude would determine the direction of German policy in Central and Eastern Europe. Redlich expressed the hope that 'Austria could finally accept a national destiny of her own—to be the German middleman between the great stock of her race and her neighbour States and nations',[91] Namier declared:

[I]t is in Austria and through Austria that German policy in South-Eastern Europe will declare itself. Will this German outpost seek friendly co-operation with its Slav neighbours, or, when it feels Germany's renewed strength behind it, will it aim once more at supremacy, encouraged by, and in turn encouraging, Magyar ambitions? The choice will rest with the Austrian Germans at least as much as with Germany; even clear interests of the vast majority of a nation do not always prevail against the will and the passions of the exposed and directly interested minority.[92]

Ultimately, Redlich and Namier believed that the problems with the New Europe created by the Paris Peace Conference extended far beyond the punitive reparations policy or miscarriages of justice with regard to national self-determination. That the principle of national self-determination was privileged above other criteria of state-formation was itself an error.

Redlich argued passionately that the work of dissolution alone of a big empire like Austria-Hungary, 'though in many parts antiquated and vicious',[93] could not be regarded as a constructive act for the future peace and prosperity of Europe.[94] The different nationalities of Austria, although increasingly drawn into fierce conflict with each other, were linked together by ties that had grown up on the basis of history and geography—by industrial and economic ties, by 'a well devised system of railways', by 'thousands of common habits, interests and ways of life', 'thousands of cases of international or inter-racial family ties, which had impressed on Austrian society a character of its own and knitted all these nations together'.[95] The erection of nation-states on the corpse of Austria-Hungary, without ensuring that these ties remained in place through confederation or at least a permanent economic association, had been detrimental to the entire region.

---

[90] Namier, 'The Problem of East-Central Europe', 574.
[91] Josef Redlich, 'The Destiny of Austria', *Reconstruction in Europe, The Manchester Guardian Commercial* (4 Jan. 1923), 732.
[92] Namier, 'The Problem of East-Central Europe', 574.
[93] Redlich, 'Reconstruction in the Danube Countries', 79.
[94] Ibid. 74.
[95] Ibid. 80.

Namier agreed that Western Austria 'had grown up on a genuine geographical basis and numerous economic and cultural bonds encompassed it, across territories of divers language'.[96] The problem with applying the principle of national self-determination to this area was that '[g]eographic and national unity clash in the countries which face the middle Danube'.[97] One of the most pernicious effects of the collapse of Austria-Hungary was the break-up of the large free-trade zone and the erecting of tariff barriers between formally complementary components. Vienna had been the commercial centre, Bohemia and Moravia the workshop, and the South Slav areas and Galicia the bread-basket of the former empire. High tariff barriers were detrimental to all alike. Redlich and Namier regarded the mercantilist economic policies of the new nation-states, dictated as they were by political concerns and national egoism rather than sound economic principles, with the gravest concern.

Their advocacy for some sort of federation or confederation in Central and Eastern Europe was by no means unique.[98] British and American liberal supporters of national self-determination in Central and Eastern Europe had also envisaged these newly created nation-states in some sort of federal arrangement after the war.[99] Redlich and Namier differed, however, from these liberal nationalists in that both doubted the validity of privileging language as a criterion to delineate the political units. Seton-Watson, bitterly disappointed as he was by the illiberality of the new nation-states and the absence of any federation or association between them, nonetheless never wavered from his linguistic definition of Central and Eastern European nations—hence, his history of Czechoslovakia instead of Bohemia and Moravia;[100] of the Romanians instead of Romania or Transylvania.[101] Redlich had always stressed history and geography as the state-building factors; now Namier too, formerly so enthusiastic an adherent of 'linguistic pan-Slavism',[102] began to see that linguistic nationalism could be a very destructive state-building principle:

[96] Namier, 'The Problem of East-Central Europe', 569.   [97] Ibid. 570.

[98] Rudolf Wierer, *Der Föderalismus im Donauraum* (Graz, 1960), ch. 9; Karl R. Stadler, *The Birth of the Austrian Republic 1918–1921* (Leiden, 1966), ch. 13; Peter M. R. Stirk, 'Ideas of Economic Integration in Interwar Mitteleuropa', in ibid. (ed.), *Mitteleuropa: History and Prospects* (Edinburgh, 1994), 86–222.

[99] Hugh and Christopher Seton-Watson, *The Making of a New Europe*; Hanak, *Great Britain and Austria-Hungary During the First World War*–182; Headlam-Morley, *A Memoir of the Paris Peace Conference, 1919*, p.xxvii.

[100] R. W. Seton-Watson, *A History of the Czechs and Slovaks* (London, 1943).

[101] R. W. Seton-Watson, *A History of the Roumanians: From Roman Times to the Completion of Unity* (London, 1934).

[102] Namier, *Germany and Eastern Europe*, 35–7.

The politics of East-Central Europe are now dominated by an uncompromising linguistic and racial nationalism which, well suited to nomadic conditions, causes deep disturbances when applied to settled communities and would-be States. Each nation asserts its own unity, and tries to gather in even its small, scattered minorities, regardless of the rights of its neighbour; the more iniquitous a conquest, the harsher is as a rule the treatment meted out to the 'alien' majority. Regional patriotism is practically non-existent; every frontier district is an object of dispute.[103]

Here we see the kernel of Namier's later famous argument that linguistic nationalism was detrimental to state building and civic development.

Despite the clear economic advantages of economic union amongst the former successor states, Redlich and Namier were rather pessimistic about the chances of any such union coming into existence in the near future. 'The creation of anything like a United States of Central Europe in an economic sense is impossible until a complete intellectual, moral and sentimental disarmament has taken place among them as well as throughout the German nation',[104] wrote Redlich. Moreover, despite all liberal hopes, the different nations, 'on a honeymoon with sovereignty',[105] were more nationalistic than ever before. Nationalism, distrust, and the recent, too recent, memory of oppression carried far more weight than any economic argument. Both men applauded the efforts of the Czechs to act as peacemaker in the region, and to seek closer economic ties with Austria and Yugoslavia. 'Yet even with the Czechs nationality by far outweighs all economic considerations, and they would not think of a political federation with other States unless Prague were to be its capital',[106] wrote Namier. It was self-evident to Namier that 'naturally the centre of such a federation would have to be Vienna or Budapest—ominous cities, not to be reinstated as capitals by the recently subject, now victorious nations',[107] whereas Redlich always believed, not merely for sentimental reasons, that any federation of the successor states should come under Austrian leadership.[108]

Both were bitterly disappointed that the western powers had failed to provide for a replacement association amongst the successor states to take the place of the vanished empire. 'The principle of non-interference in the internal affairs of other states, that "antiquated and insincere diplomatic rule," as Masaryk says in his memoir, has been rigorously applied by

---

[103] Namier, 'The Problem of East-Central Europe', 572.
[104] Redlich, 'Reconstruction in the Danube Countries', 84.
[105] Namier, 'The Problem of East-Central Europe', 573.
[106] Ibid. 573.
[107] Ibid.
[108] RP: Redlich to Dr Friedrich Funder, 6 Nov. 1935 (draft).

France, Great Britain, the United States and Italy toward the new states, which could never have been born without their help and assent',[109] wrote Redlich. Namier, too, deplored the fact that '[n]o mentor of down-trodden nations had emerged to guide them up crags of self-discipline to the dignity of a new, shared freedom'.[110]

What they both especially regretted was the withdrawal of the Anglo-Saxon powers from the affairs of Central and Eastern Europe. To Redlich, the United States, '[r]espected by all, loved by many of those smaller nations of Central Europe and the Near East', was naturally suited to carry out the work of reintegration in Central and Eastern Europe, especially because it also represented 'the possibility of liberal material aid and support in the work of economic and financial reconstruction of Europe'.[111] He believed that the unanimous support of the Great Powers for a scheme of an economic federation 'would overcome strong forces arrayed against it in both Austria and Hungary and in Slav States', and would also restore to the world-policy of the Allied Powers 'elements of the ideal conception of European order proclaimed by Wilson and endorsed by the allies'.[112]

Namier thought that even the more limited regional association between Austria and the Little Entente could only be realized under Anglo-American auspices. '[T]he first step towards such co-operation would probably have to be the handing over of the railways of all the three countries, Czechoslovakia, Austria and Yugo-Slavia to one single Anglo-American railway concern which would eliminate bureaucratic waste and political jealousies, and thus provide good and cheap transport.'[113]

Neither shared the pious hopes of certain optimistic liberal internationalists that any international federation could come about merely because of good will without regard to power relationships. As practical politicians, they realized that French hegemony in Europe, based as it was on an artificial eclipse of Germany and Russia and the withdrawal of Anglo-Saxon powers, was unsustainable.[114] Hence, French patronage of the Little

---

[109] Redlich, 'Reconstruction in the Danube Countries', 79.
[110] J. Namier, *Lewis Namier*, 151.
[111] Redlich, 'Reconstruction in the Danube Countries', 84.
[112] Redlich, 'The Problem of the Republic of Austria', 220.
[113] Namier, 'The Problem of East-Central Europe', 590.
[114] HLS, Charles C. Burlingham papers: Box 15, Redlich to Burlingham, 10 Dec. 1923: 'You cannot overlook the absolute instability of the present European center. The equation of forces, working on this continent, contains . . . the two indefinable quantities of Russia and Germany.' Namier, 'The Problem of East-Central Europe', 572: 'Whilst the artificial eclipse continues of the two greatest Continental Powers, Germany and Russia, it is difficult to fore-

Entente was dangerous to the latter, especially French encouragement of Beneš's anti-German policy, since German–Czech reconciliation was vital to peace.[115] By the same token, they thought the League of Nations idea, although commendable, was unworkable since it was deprived of true Anglo-American support. 'Insularity, not internationalism, was the life-breath of the League idea . . . the will to do good and the wish to have it cheap',[116] charged Namier. As it stood, the League of Nations had a written constitution without the moral basis of true acceptance or backing of force—'the burden of legalism without the advantages of law'.[117] The 'Pax Anglo-Saxonica, to be effective, required Anglo-Saxon world police; in fact, world dominion exercised by America and British Empire'.[118] 'League of Nations principles, seriously held, are incompatible with the blind, unconditional pacifism which swelled the following of the League ideal.'[119]

Redlich has been described as an internationalist and an enthusiastic supporter of the League of Nations and of various projects for the union of Europe.[120] Certainly in public Redlich would uphold the League of Nations as uniquely important for Austria, quoting Lammasch that the choice now was between a true society of nations (League of Nations) or the physical and moral suicide of nations.[121] Privately, however, he resolved 'not to be a part of this nonsense [the Austrian League of Nations committee]'.[122] 'Today Hofrat Grünhat . . . tried to interest me in a German-Austrian-Italian league—I refused even as I had yesterday Meinl's suggestion of a "League for free economy". Every day a new idea, and none of much worth!'[123]

Actually, Meinl's reconstruction proposals were remarkably similar to Redlich's. Meinl also believed that the basic error of the Peace Treaty was the failure to establish an economic union in place of the former Monarchy.[124] The difference between Meinl and Redlich lay chiefly in that

cast political developments in Europe; most difficult of all in East-Central Europe, their natural sphere of interests and influence.'

[115] J. Namier, *Lewis Namier*, 172–3; Redlich, 'Reconstruction in the Danube Countries', 83.
[116] Namier, *Conflicts*, 29. [117] Ibid. 29.
[118] Ibid. 27–8. [119] Ibid. 30.
[120] Dr Constantin Dumba, 'Persönliches über Josef Redlich', *Neue Freie Presse*, 22 Nov. 1936.
[121] Josef Redlich, 'Heinrich Lammasch', in *World Unity: Non-Partisan Discussion of International Movements* 273.
[122] Redlich, *Schicksalsjahre Österreichs*, 5 Feb. 1919, II, 332.
[123] Ibid., 23 Mar. 1919, II, 338.
[124] FO 371/4385/785, Julius Meinl memo, 'The Reconstruction of Austria', Feb. 1920, pp. 319–23.

Meinl still believed in political activism, whereas Redlich had given up hope of achieving anything through political efforts. From the beginning of his political career Redlich had frequently struggled with dilemmas of political expediency versus conviction. During World War I, he had come to realize that, despite the practical futility of his actions, he could not compromise any longer with the dominant political trends of the age. Redlich pleaded in parliament in 1917 that he would like to speak as a professor and not a politician on the great problem in Bohemia. 'The professor knows that someone else could write about the same issues and prove him wrong. A politician, however, will not accept being proved wrong, otherwise he fears that he would not be elected again', said Redlich, adding that only 'the politician, the chauvinist, and the nationalist' would consider reconciliation impossible in Bohemia.[125] After the war he resolved to give up politics for pure scholarship. How disillusioned Redlich was with politics can be seen in the unsolicited advice he sent to his friend Felix Frankfurter, advising him against taking up the position of solicitor-general in the new Roosevelt administration since it would be impossible to maintain his independence in government.[126]

The invitation to the United States gave Redlich a new lease of life. 'This call [to Harvard] means so much to me . . . How full my heart is with satisfaction, full of hope',[127] he wrote. 'I see always new synthesis of solutions to old problems related to my decades long study of law and the state . . . America has given me more raw material for mentally creative activity . . . As long as I am here, I have no anxiety over material things. The political, financial, and also moral misery of Vienna does not affect me directly.'[128]

Redlich had always been somewhat ambivalent about America, disliking her materialism but loving the air of freedom and prosperity there.[129] 'I find your book most valuable for each who wants to know what has gone on over there in the last hundred years,' wrote Redlich to Jaszi on receiving his *Dissolution of the Habsburg Empire*;[130] But do they really want to know? I doubt it. Statistics show that the increase in number of visitors to stadiums is quite out of proportion to the growth of the sale of good books on Europe

[125] *SPOR*, XXII, 166: Redlich parliamentary speech, 12 June 1917.
[126] HLS, Felix Frankfurter Papers: Box 197, Folder 21, Redlich to Frankfurter, 12 Mar. 1933.
[127] HLS, Charles C. Burlingham Papers: Box 15, Redlich to Burlingham, 23 June 1926.
[128] Redlich to Hofmannsthal, 22 Feb. 1928, in Fußgänger (ed.), *Briefwechsel*, 923.
[129] HLS, Charles C. Burlingham Papers: Box 15, Redlich to Burlingham, 10 Dec. 1923.
[130] Oskar Jaszi, *The Dissolution of the Habsburg Empire* (Chicago, 1929).

in this country [the United States].'[131] The part of America closest to his heart was Harvard and New England, where he treasured the moral legacy of puritanical rectitude. The same puritanism of Cambridge and Boston depressed his wife greatly, however, to the extent that she decided to return with their two young daughters to live in Vienna after two years in America. Redlich had left for America with an open mind about the possibility of settling there. His wife's decision forced him to maintain his house in Vienna, and condemned him to a lonely existence in a hotel for the remainder of his tenure at Harvard. Even if his family had adjusted to American life, however, it is doubtful if Redlich, by then in his fifties, would have been able to forge an American identity and wholly settle in the United States. The more time he spent in the States, the more aware he became of how 'European' he really was. 'I am about to leave my house and Vienna without any corresponding warmth for America,' he wrote in 1928. 'Oh no, I am not in the least tired of Europe. But perhaps I will move to Switzerland or to North Italy.'[132]

Nor could he rid himself of his Austrian past or Austrian history, despite his eagerness to plunge into new fields of labour—a projected book on Woodrow Wilson[133] and another one on Queen Victoria and her statesmen came to nothing. 'I live here in the land of the Puritans, but cannot get away from Franz Joseph. I fear, that I must write a little book about him before I can be rid of him', wrote Redlich, and accordingly, a rather more substantial biography of Franz Joseph that the self-described 'little book' appeared in 1928.[134] Yet after his forced retirement from the Harvard Law School in 1935[135] Redlich found it very difficult to readjust to life in Vienna, and suffered from a great 'homesickness' for America.[136]

---

[131] Columbia University Library, Oskar Jaszi Papers: Redlich to Jaszi, 6 Dec. 1929.
[132] WSLB, Handschriftensammlung: I.N.198.685, Redlich to Darkow-Singer, 17 Mar. 1928.
[133] RP: four pages exist of a plan for a projected book on Woodrow Wilson.
[134] Redlich to H. Bahr, 28 Oct. 1926, in Fellner (ed.), *Dichter und Gelehrter*, 552.
[135] The ostensible reason given by the Harvard President for Redlich's departure was that Redlich had exceeded the age limit. Redlich felt unjustly singled out, however, since the age limit had never been applied before in the Harvard Law School. Despite the support of Roscoe Pound (Dean of the Law School), Felix Frankfurter, and Charles C. Burlingham (at the time President of the Harvard Alumni Association), Redlich was requested to leave, although granted Professor Emeritus status and a pension. See LOC, Felix Frankfurter papers: Box 92, report on conversation between Pound and Frankfurter, 7 Nov. 1934; Redlich to President James B. Conant, 12 Mar. 1935; Redlich to President James B. Conant, 4 Apr. 1935.
[136] WSLB, Handschriftensammlung: I.N.198.636, Redlich to Darkow-Singer, 11 Dec. 1935.

Life back in Vienna was overshadowed by the rise of Nazism in
Germany, and the constant threat that Nazism posed to Austria, intensifying Redlich's never entirely suppressed concern even for the truncated
Austria. Despite his distaste for the dictatorial regime of Dollfuss and his
Heimwehr troops,[137] he was grateful to Dollfuss for his steadfast resistance
against Germany.[138] 'I am tortured by anxiety . . . What should be the
future of this poor country?' exclaimed Redlich in great agitation after the
assassination of Dollfuss.[139] He had the deepest misgivings about the
friendship pact between Austria and Germany.[140] Still, he was spared the
Anschluss. One month before his death, Redlich would write that Austria 'is
continuing bravely to maintain the spirit of the specific Austrian patriotism
against the crude radicalism and mad nationalism which rules Germany.
That repudiation of Nazism is the main reason that makes life in Vienna to
me possible and to a certain extent satisfactory.'[141]

Unlike many other contemporaries, Redlich did not underestimate
Hitler, nor did he dismiss Nazism as a passing phenomenon. 'The repudiation of Hitlerism is not only an Austrian vital interest, but also a European
interest: everything depends on whether France and England will remain
committed to repulsing the plans of Hitler's regime at any price.'[142] 'The
dreadful spiritual and mental chaos of the German people lies like a shroud
over the whole of Europe.'[143] Like Namier, Redlich believed that Nazism
had deep roots in German history.[144] He had never been taken in by the
democratic façade of the Weimar Republic. 'Germany has not learned
anything of the code of the "Democratic comity of nations" ',[145] he noted.
The 'dream of *Anschluss*' to Germany could only arise in those Austrians
with 'a complete misunderstanding of German history and out of a strange
self-delusion about conditions created by the Weimar constitution in
Germany.'[146]

[137] Ibid., I.N.198.715, Redlich to Darkow-Singer, 15 Oct. 1933.
[138] Ibid., I.N.198.723, Redlich to Darkow-Singer, 30 July 1934.
[139] LOC, Felix Frankfurter Papers: Box 91, Redlich to Frankfurter, 1 Aug. 1934.
[140] WSLB, Handschriftensammlung: I.N.198.742, Redlich to Darkow-Singer, 27 Aug.
1936.
[141] HLS, Roscoe Pound Papers, Box 80, Folder 22: Redlich to Pound, 14 Oct. 1936.
[142] WSLB, Handschriftensammlung: I.N.198.714, Redlich to Darkow-Singer, 23 Aug.
1933.
[143] Ibid., I.N.198.715, Redlich to Darkow-Singer, 15 Oct. 1933.
[144] *The Decline of Parliamentary Government, Discussed by Harold J. Laski and Dr Josef
Redlich, March 28, 1931 . . . New York Luncheon Discussion*, (New York: Foreign Policy
Association, 1931), 23.
[145] HLS, Charles C. Burlingham Papers: Box 15, Redlich to Burlingham, 13 Mar. 1928.
[146] Redlich to Hofmannsthal, 20 June 1928, in Fußgänger (ed.), *Briefwechsel*, 103.

Namier had read *Mein Kampf* on its publication, and unlike most of his contemporaries in Britain, was convinced that it should be taken literally.[147] Throughout the 1930s, Namier sought to awaken the British public to the Hitler danger. 'In this century the German menace has placed Britain's frontier on the Rhine, and America's at Dover',[148] he wrote. The rise of totalitarianism and dictatorships throughout Europe reinforced both men's perception of the sharp contrast between British freedoms and continental despotisms. Namier's intensive study of English parliamentary history in the 1920s had been inspired, in part, by the need to defend the 'Mother of Parliaments' against the 'crude simplicities of totalitarianism or dictatorship' which were captivating people's imagination even in Britain.[149] Felix Frankfurter spoke of an almost 'religious' experience with Redlich, when the latter, catching sight of the towers of the Houses of Parliament after a year's absence, exclaimed: 'Raise your hat. In a Europe fast being devoured by dictators, she is still the mother of parliaments.'[150] 'Democracy is on trial in this continent [Europe]',[151] wrote Redlich in 1932.

This seemingly simple statement—that democracy was on trial—could be taken in two ways. European democracy was certainly being threatened by totalitarianism and dictatorships; however, democracy itself as an institution was also on trial with regard to its merits and defects. The track-record of democracies in Central and Eastern Europe was dismal. 'Democracy is there [in America] and here [Europe] on its trial: people are so stupid, too self-absorbed, and much too malicious to be considered ripe for democracy',[152] wrote Redlich. Both Redlich and Namier were very conscious that the nationalist dictatorships now the norm in most of Europe had arisen out of democracies. Moreover, Hitler himself had been elected by the German masses through parliamentary means, only to dismantle the parliamentary apparatus once in power. They concluded that democracy was not synonymous with either parliamentary government or with political liberty.

The pre-war Redlich had already been aware of the tension between representative self-government and democracy, when he warned that mass democratic nationalist movements could very well turn out to be the worst

---

[147] Berlin, 'Lewis Namier', 219.   [148] Namier, *Facing East*, 100.
[149] J. Namier, *Lewis Namier*, 185–6.
[150] Frankfurter, 'Josef Redlich—Obituary', 389.
[151] HLS, Sheldon Glueck Papers: Box 59, Folder 6, Redlich to Glueck, 21 Jan. 1932.
[152] WSLB, Handschriftensammlung: I.N.198.673, Redlich to Darkow-Singer, 13 Aug. 1923.

enemy of parliamentary government.[153] Redlich's post-war critique of democracy centred upon the oppression of minorities in a democracy, thus continuing a long eighteenth- and nineteenth-century tradition warning about the need to safeguard liberty and minorities against the 'tyranny of the masses'.[154] Like Acton and Eötvös, Redlich was especially concerned about the oppression of national minorities by a national majority. Redlich cited Temperley approvingly that '*it is not always an autocratic Government which is the greatest enemy of justice and equality; even in a democratic State popular passion may claim for itself legal forms, and the tyranny of racial antagonism may become the worst form of oppression.*'[155]

Redlich argued that those democracies which had adopted Rousseau's doctrine of 'the sovereignty of the people' were especially prone to this danger. Rousseau had assumed that society should be governed by the 'will of the people', that the 'people' was homogeneous, that therefore the 'will of the people' could be ascertained by the will of the majority, and that the will of the majority should rule supreme. This line of argument suffered from two major problems. First, most of Europe consisted of multinational states, not national ones with an ethnically homogeneous population; secondly, Redlich was uncomfortable with any kind of absolute sovereignty, whether it was monarchical, bureaucratic, or popular.[156] Redlich's own conception of liberty was far closer to the Burkean concept of limited sovereignty—that liberty was freedom from coercion and arbitrary power, and hence, that sovereignty needed checks and balances upon it.[157] He would have agreed with Lord Acton that power tends to corrupt, and that absolute power corrupts absolutely. Redlich praised the independence of the British judiciary as a healthy limitation on the doctrine of popular sovereignty, since it ensured that the people should remain law-abiding as well as law-making, and that minorities would have a haven in law against popular passions directed against them.[158]

---

[153] Redlich, *The Procedure of the House of Commons*, vol. I, p. xxiv.

[154] To name just a few: Tocqueville, Guizot, C. de Montalembert, Acton, John Stuart Mill, Thomas Jefferson, Alexander Hamilton, James Madison, József Eötvös.

[155] Josef Redlich, 'Sovereignty, Democracy, and the Rights of Minorities', in Joseph H. Beale (ed.), *Harvard Legal Essays* (Cambridge Mass., 1934), 392. Italics in original citation.

[156] Ibid. 377–97.

[157] Quentin Skinner, 'The Idea of Negative Liberty: Philosophical and Historical Perspectives', in Richard Rorty, J.B. Schneewind and Quentin Skinner (eds.), *Philosophy in History: Essays on the Historiography of Philosophy* (Cambridge, 1984), 193–221; Berlin, 'Two Concepts of Liberty', in *Four Essays on Liberty*, 118–72.

[158] Redlich, *Local Government in England*, i. 216.

However, Redlich was no anti-democrat. Like Tocqueville and John Stuart Mill, he believed that the only cure for the ills of democracy was more democracy, which can alone educate a sufficient number of individuals to independence, resistance, and strength.[159] We have seen throughout that Redlich had no sanguine Enlightenment faith in progress or the perfectibility of human nature. Nevertheless, he continued to believe that one could appeal to the rationality in human nature against its worst instincts, with the obvious correlation that human beings were not just prey to instincts and primal passions but could be educated. He applauded local government in Great Britain, not so much because it was a bulwark of freedom against a central authoritarian state, but because local government was the best political education for the population, thus elevating the political culture of the masses to the extent that they could responsibly participate in the political life of their state.[160]

Democracy presented a challenge to parliamentary government and to the multinational state, but it was a challenge that had to be met and surmounted, since the stability of the state could only be secured by participation of all its citizens in the common life of the state.[161] 'Modern democracy has risen above other theories—systems of thought on the desirable form and substance of rules and principles—as the specific theory which gives the best guarantee of preserving, at the same time, the liberty of the individual citizen and the prosperity, power, and growth of the national body',[162] wrote Redlich, in the same spirit in which Winston Churchill famously once said that democracy was a terrible form of government, but that all the others were even worse.

Namier fully concurred with Redlich's analysis that modern democracy could give rise to far worse oppressions than monarchical absolutism. Whilst the advance of democracy 'tended to remove barriers raised by caste or wealth, it merely aggravated those of race, religion, or language: the rule of a *Staats-Nation* or a *Herrenvolk* is harder and more galling than that of a dynasty or of a feudal aristocracy'.[163] 'The sovereignty of the people merely substitutes the proprietary claims of nations for those of princes, because States are still based on territories and not on "sovereign" hordes: and the conflicts grow fiercer.'[164]

---

[159] Berlin, 'John Stuart Mill and the Ends of Life', in *Four Essays on Liberty*, 196.
[160] Redlich, *Local Government in England*, i. 163.
[161] Ibid. 215.
[162] Redlich, 'Sovereignty, Democracy, and the Rights of Minorities', 378.
[163] NP: 1/1b/1, Creighton Lectures, 3.
[164] Namier, *1848: Revolution of the Intellectuals*, 27.

However, Namier's attack on democracy was more fundamental than Redlich's, for he argued that democracy, in the sense of the levelling of class distinctions, was incompatible with liberty. Parliamentary government was dependent on oligarchy,[165] and '[l]iberty . . . is in its origin an aristocratic idea'.[166] In this, Namier was merely echoing the familiar nineteenth-century liberal argument that free institutions were more compatible with oligarchy than with popular government. Namier's insistence on the proprietary nature of parliamentary government in Britain strikingly parallels Benjamin Constant's argument that the ability to vote depended upon enlightenment, that enlightenment derived from leisure, and leisure was only possible through the possession of property.[167]

Democracy in the sense of the levelling of society swept away the old ruling classes, leaving a political and moral vacuum which 'plebiscitarian Caesarism', claiming to speak in the name of the masses, could fill. The result: 'disregard of legality in spite of professed guardianship of law and order; contempt of political parties and the parliamentary system, of the educated classes and their values; blandishments and vague, contradictory promises for all and sundry; militarism; gigantic, blatant displays and shady corruption.'[168] It had occurred when the first French parliament elected by universal suffrage voted for Louis Napoleon; it had happened again when the German parliament voted for Hitler. Both had then dismantled parliament, thus realizing Machiavelli's precept, 'to acquire power while men believe in them, so as to be able to enforce the faith after it is gone'.[169]

Nazism was the victory of the petite-bourgeoisie over the old ruling classes. 'The raving hatred and contempt which the Nazis feel for Liberal and Socialist intellectualism made certain types of Conservatives mistake them for allies. In reality Fascism expresses the egalitarianism and conceit of the half-educated',[170] wrote Namier. To Namier, it was no accident that the core Nazi supporters consisted of Austrians, Bavarians, and Rhinelanders, with a noticeable absence of members of the former Prussian ruling class, and that the army general conspirators against Hitler came from the Prussian Junker class.[171]

[165] Ibid. 11.
[166] Namier, *Vanished Supremacies*, 37–8.
[167] J. R. Jennings, 'Conceptions of England and its Constitution in Nineteenth-Century French Political Thought', *Historical Journal*, 29: 1 (1986), 72.
[168] Namier, *Facing East*, 10.
[169] Namier, *Skyscrapers*, 43.
[170] Namier, *Conflicts*, 195–6.
[171] L. B. Namier, *Europe in Decay: A Study in Disintegration 1936–1940* (London, 1950), 234.

Such themes were not new to Namier—as we have seen, he had expressed very similar fears of the petit bourgeois flood (albeit in the sphere of culture rather than politics) in his very first published essay back in 1912. At the time he had placed his faith in projects like the Workers' Educational Association to hold back the vulgar tide.[172] Now, however, he denied that the masses could be educated at all. Namier argued that mass democracy as political doctrine and reality was the result of a fundamental error in Enlightenment thought: optimism in 'the light of human reason, the omnipotence of human thought, and the infinite perfectibility of human nature'.[173] Such optimism had survived in liberalism and Marxism, and had led to the pernicious doctrine that the masses could be educated, and hence were entitled to equal participation in the political process. These intellectuals had set out to replace the authority of 'tradition and prescription' with reason. However, they 'who had seen themselves as the rational leaders of mankind set free by their thought, were to find that the disintegration of spiritual values—their work to some extent—had released demoniac forces, beyond control by reason'.[174] 'The *Volksgeist* of mass-movements replaced the *Zeitgeist* of the intellectuals and came to be worshipped by the modern *clercs*.'[175] The irrational masses, free of traditional restraints and politically empowered, now threatened to destroy European civilization. 'Hitler and the Third Reich were the gruesome and incongruous consummation of an age which, as none other, believed in progress and felt assured that it was being achieved.'[176] Such theories show Namier to be a member of the 'irrationalist' generation or the 'revolt against positivism', which included Pareto, Sorel, Mosca, Michels, Nietzsche, and Freud, all of whom denied the primacy of human rationality and regarded the inscrutable masses as fundamentally irrational.[177]

To Namier, British and French appeasement could also be explained by the European-wide process of decay and takeover by the lower classes. The reader may recall Namier's lament that 'eagles and lions' were out of place in inter-war Europe. Namier's use of the word 'lions' may be a conscious or unconscious echo of Pareto's distinction between 'lions' and 'foxes'. Pareto

---

[172] J. Namier, *Lewis Namier*, 103–4.   [173] Namier, *Conflicts*, 195.
[174] Namier, *Vanished Supremacies*, 176.
[175] Namier, *1848: Revolution of the Intellectuals*, 73.
[176] Namier, *Vanished Supremacies*, 176.
[177] Hughes, *Consciousness and Society*, esp. ch. 2. The terminology 'revolt against positivism' is of course not strictly accurate, since people like Freud and Namier shared a positivist urge to accumulate facts despite a depreciation of reason. See also Philip Rieff, 'The Origins of Freud's Political Psychology', in W. Warren Wagar (ed.), *European Intellectual History Since Darwin and Marx* (New York, 1967), 89–109.

famously theorized that societal elites alternated between the 'lions'—the conservative elites, upholders of traditional values and defenders of national honour, and the 'foxes'—progressive, manipulative, innovative, suffering from over-intellectualization and a timidity in the use of force, usually covered by false humanitarianism. Despite his acknowledgement that both were necessary to society, Pareto's preferences, like Namier's, leant hugely towards the lions.

Namier's analysis of British and French foreign policy parallels almost exactly Pareto's analysis of lions and foxes in the conduct of foreign affairs. According to Pareto, 'foxes' in foreign affairs usually opt for negotiations and compromise even in dangerous situations, with commercial advantages foremost in mind. Such a policy may succeed for a while, but the final result is usually disastrous, for the enemy strikes the lethal blow just when the foxes have been lulled into false security. Lions, however, with their native common sense, do not suffer from the delusion that reason and money are mightier than the sword.[178] Namier believed the conduct of foreign affairs should be left to an elite of trained experts and diplomats, that diplomacy should be conducted in secret, and that intervention even by the House of Commons in foreign policy was dangerous.[179]

To Namier, Churchill, the Cecils, Viscount Cranborne, and Anthony Eden, having never lost the moral fibre and the sense of reality of the ruling classes in England, were lions committed to opposing Hitler; Chamberlain and company were foxes.[180] 'The official "Conservative" leaders of 1938–1939 were mostly ex- or semi-Liberals of middle-class Non-conformist extraction, whose Liberalism had gone rancid—anxious business men lacking imagination and understanding even in business, and in foreign politics lay preachers full of goodwill *à bon marché*',[181] wrote Namier. Even his old friend Beneš was described as 'the man who tried to survive by being reasonable (and plausible) in an age when reason had ceased to count: a Victorian in twentieth-century Central Europe . . . A democrat, both in faith and by nature, he did not tower over other men, but tried to conciliate them, even too readily and too anxiously . . . he was no match for the dictators.'[182] Once again, Namier's ideological beliefs led to a drastic simplification of a complex situation, leading him to ignore patrician appeasers like Lothian, Halifax, Londonderry, Buccleuch, Bedford, and some of the Mitfords.[183]

[178] Hughes, *Consciousness and Society*, ch. 7.
[179] Namier, 'Diplomacy, Secret and Open', in *In the Margin of History*, 3–20.
[180] Berlin, 'Lewis Namier', 219.   [181] Namier, *Europe in Decay*, 147–8.
[182] Namier, *In the Nazi Era* (London, 1952), 135.
[183] Colley, *Lewis Namier*, 42.

Unlike Namier, Redlich considered the general unease in inter-war Britain as a manifestation of transition rather than decline,[184] noting that '[e]very generation in England found that the former political generation had been much better',[185] and pronounced himself 'an optimist for the future of British parliamentary government and its traditions'.[186] Since Redlich did not share Namier's view that the British parliament was contingent on an aristocratic oligarchy, he saw nothing to fear from the accession to power of the Labour party. 'And this is England's glory; abdications of classes and of institutions in England have never been the product of revolutions and of a sudden collapse of the historic classes ruling the nation. They have been made by a piecemeal process, peacefully, step by step',[187] wrote Redlich. Indeed, the British parliament was proof to Redlich that democratization need not endanger parliamentary government, and that the masses could be educated in parliamentary traditions and a respect for the constitution. Despite Redlich's social desire to ingratiate himself with the Austrian aristocracy before World War I, he never valued the aristocracy as a political force, pointing out that neither the 'old, powerful bureaucracy accustomed to mastery or the splendid high and court aristocracy' had participated in the greatest reform plan in the modern history of the Habsburg Monarchy—the Kremsier Constitution.[188] Significantly, Redlich had condemned the eighteenth-century English *ancien régime* as a one-class tyranny whereas Namier defended the entire system, rotten boroughs and all.[189]

Redlich pinned his hopes on the political left rather than the political right in Britain and America for the end of Anglo-American isolationism from European affairs.[190] He greeted the election of Ramsay MacDonald and the Labour Government in 1924 with relief, hoping that his many old

---

[184] *The Decline of Parliamentary Government, Discussed by Harold J. Laski and Dr. Josef Redlich*, 13.

[185] Ibid. 15.   [186] Ibid. 16.   [187] Ibid. 14.

[188] Redlich, *Das österreichische Staats- und Reichsproblem*, I., 92.

[189] Redlich, *Local Government in England*, i. 49–61; Namier, *England in the Age of the American Revolution*, 4–5.

[190] HLS, Charles C. Burlingham Papers: Box 15, Redlich to Burlingham, 25 Mar.1923: 'President Harding's policy fails everywhere, most perhaps in respect to the problem of the connection of the United States with Europe, particularly of its economic interests with the recovery of Europe as a whole. Indeed I think it most improbable, that any new policy towards Europe will be laid down in Washington as long as the Republic party and President Harding remain in the saddle.' See also Harvard University, Houghton Library: FMS Ger 145.1, Josef Redlich, 'Report to Chancellor Mayr', for a perceptive analysis of different American political constellations and what this meant for American attitudes towards Europe, European reconstruction, and the League of Nations.

friends in the Labour Government, with their interest in international affairs, would end British isolation from continental affairs.[191] He thought American isolationism could be broken by the demise of the Republican regime, which he held responsible for an 'American "nationalism" against the whole of Europe',[192] and the return to power of the Democrats under Franklin D. Roosevelt's leadership, a leader for whom he had great respect.[193]

'The little bit of hope, that I still have for the world, is bound up with the hope that I have always preserved for America and England.'[194] Even that little bit of hope was almost eclipsed by appeasement and the frankly pro-Hitler circles in the United States and Great Britain. Writing on 18 July 1935, the day of the Anglo-German Naval Agreement, Redlich wrote sadly, '[t]hat influential capitalist circles in London have worked for a long time for Hitler and his regime is very difficult to understand'.[195] Moreover, Redlich thought that some of the policies of Roosevelt, whom he otherwise admired greatly, were too similar to Bolshevik or Fascist state-socialist measures for comfort. Redlich had witnessed during the war how the hunger blockade imposed by the Allies necessitated state control over the economy and the distribution of food stuffs, resulting in a 'war state social-ism' which in turn reinforced and consolidated the conception of the sovereign, authoritarian state and the 'Super-State' ideology in Germany and Austria.[196] He now worried that a similar result might come about from Roosevelt's economic policies. 'I am very anxious about the fascist move-ments throughout the Anglo-Saxon world, not least in the Bolshevik idea disguised as a planned economy which has emerged in America. The moral credit of American finance people and great capitalists seem to me to be fully destroyed.'[197] 'This state-socialism . . . shocks me. . . . I fear, that Roosevelt leads—without wanting to—a kind of giant American Hitlerism here.'[198]

---

[191] HLS, Charles C. Burlingham Papers: Box 15, Redlich to Burlingham, 29 Feb. 1924: 'Things in Europe are decidedly better, since the Labour Government has become the Director of British policy: I know many of them since long and they are, in my opinion, a lot of good men, who will show the world another lesson of the wonderful political temper and the reasonableness of the British nation.'

[192] ÖNB: 1022/44–8, Redlich to Molden, 12 May 1929.

[193] HLS, Felix Frankfurter Papers: Box 197, Folder 21, Redlich to Frankfurter, 13 July 1932.   [194] Ibid.

[195] LOC, Felix Frankfurter Papers: Box 92, Redlich to Frankfurter, 18 July 1935.

[196] Redlich, *Austrian War Government*, 131–2.

[197] HLS, Felix Frankfurter Papers: Box 197, Folder 21, Redlich to Frankfurter, 13 July 1932.

[198] Ibid. Redlich to Frankfurter, 1 Aug. 1933.

The seeming failure of even British and American parliamentary democracy to oppose totalitarianism led Redlich, like Karl Popper, to the reluctant conclusion that parliamentary democracy was ill-equipped to face certain challenges. In Popper's words, 'I realised that democracy—even British democracy—was not an institution designed to fight totalitarianism; but it was very sad to find that there was apparently only one man—Winston Churchill—who understood what was happening, and that literally nobody had a good word for him.'[199] 'One of the greatest blessings of the parliamentary institution is that parliamentary government just because it is a party government means a rule by compromise', wrote Redlich.[200] However, there were forces against which compromise was not possible. Redlich could not share liberal optimism over the 'reasonableness' of Hitler and the possibility of negotiation with Nazi Germany. He warned Nicholas Murray Butler about the sterility of the 'Carnegie Approach' (a reference to the Carnegie Institute of Peace, of which Butler was the head), and of underestimating Hitler's Germany.[201] In his own way, Redlich realized what Namier was preaching so stridently—that pre-1914 liberalism had become anachronistic in the tough ideological struggles of the 1930s.

Confronted with the seeming helplessness and lack of will to combat Hitler on the part of the western democracies, Redlich and Namier were led to the belief that '[i]n the end democracy needs a solution of the problem of leadership'.[202] Both Redlich and Namier argued the necessity for strong leadership. Redlich pointed out that there was 'no great business organization that does not require from time to time a strong dictatorial element',[203] and that the victory of the First Reform Bill in 1832 was due to a 'moral dictatorship' in Britain.[204] 'When a nation is shaken to the depth, when the waves of popular passion rise and the masses are in motion, leaders must be robust and single-minded; not lofty or nimble litterateurs, nor acute or versatile thinkers, but athletes in thought and action', wrote Namier. Otherwise, they would founder like 'the Continental Socialists who succumbed to various forms of Fascism because of their own moderation'.[205] Strong leadership in and of itself was not inimical to parliamentary

[199] Karl Popper, *Unended Quest: An Intellectual Autobiography* (Glasgow, 1986), 112.
[200] *The Decline of Parliamentary Government, Discussed by Harold J. Laski and Dr Josef Redlich*, 20.
[201] HLS, Charles C. Burlingham Papers: Box 15, Redlich to Burlingham, 23 Jan. 1927.
[202] *The Decline of Parliamentary Government, Discussed by Harold J. Laski and Dr Josef Redlich*, 21.
[203] Ibid. 20.   [204] Ibid.
[205] L. B. Namier, 'The Russian Revolution: 1917–1942,' *Manchester Guardian* (7 Nov. 1942).

democracy. In Redlich's words, '[w]hat is terrifying in Europe now is less the idea of dictatorship than the consequences of the natural endeavours of dictators to maintain themselves'.[206] Namier agreed, maintaining that parliamentary government would not be endangered as long as the possibility of change and for a free renewal of mandate existed, since '[i]t is change which constitutes the very nature of representative and responsible government'.[207]

Indeed, in the Manichean atmosphere of the 1930s, Redlich was even prepared to regard non-democratic, anti-Hitler regimes as the lesser evil compared to Nazism. Hence, despite alarm at Dollfuss's *Heimwehr*, Redlich could say that 'Austria [under Dollfuss] is quite in order, the "authoritative" government is on the whole for one poor country quite a good form of government'.[208] Namier, far more than Redlich, had always had a love affair with strong leaders—Piłsudski, Churchill, and Zionist leader Chaim Weizmann. In fact, Namier's attachment to the idea of a strong and virile oligarchic ruling elite could have easily taken a Fascist direction, as it had with Pareto, Mosca, and Michels.[209] Nevertheless, both Redlich's and Namier's call for strong leadership with almost dictatorial powers fell strictly within the formal requirements of parliamentary democracy. Their recommendations at this time had much in common with Max Weber's and Joseph Schumpeter's theory of 'competitive leadership', in which the role of elections was reinterpreted as providing legitimation for a party leader, who was then allowed to conduct government more or less independently of popular constraints.[210]

Nazism confronted Redlich with the long-dormant problem of his own Jewish identity as well as with his identification with German culture, especially when close friends, relatives, and eventually his son suffered under the Nazis in Germany.

---

[206] *The Decline of Parliamentary Government, Discussed by Harold J. Laski and Dr Josef Redlich*, 21.

[207] Namier, *Skyscrapers*, 43.

[208] HLS, Roscoe Pound Papers, Box 80, Folder 22: Redlich to Pound, 14 Oct. 1936. This was by no means atypical for Austrian Jews, some of whom were prepared to support Dollfuss and Schuschnigg as the lesser of two evils compared to Nazism, and as a necessary shelter for survival. See Bruce F. Pauley, *From Prejudice to Persecution: A History of Austrian Anti-Semitism* (Chapel Hill, NC, 1992), 260–74.

[209] Nye, *The Anti-Democratic Souces of Elite Theory: Pareto, Mosca, Michels*.

[210] Richard Swedberg, *Joseph A. Schumpeter: His Life and Work* (Cambridge, 1991), 162–3; David Beetham, 'Mosca, Pareto and Weber: A Historical Comparison', in Wolfgang J. Mommsen and Jürgen Osterhammel (ed.), *Max Weber and his Contemporaries* (London, 1987), 156.

His personal identification as German had already been strained to the breaking-point during World War I. This struggle with his German identity can be clearly seen in a letter written in 1920. Redlich first announced that he was probably the first German to be invited to the post-war United States to lecture. Later on, however, commenting on the cosmopolitan background of his newborn daughter by his second marriage, he explained that she had 'an English American godmother . . . as well as a Catholic Viennese godmother . . . and she has a Moravian father and a Moravian German mother and—God willing, she will learn English in America as her first language'.[211] That Redlich characterized himself solely as 'Moravian', a territorial identity, as opposed to 'Moravian German' for his wife, is a sign of his ambivalence towards national identity at the time. But ultimately Redlich could not renounce his own Germanness, although he considered himself a German of a different type from the 'new Germans.'

. . . nobody understands this anger, this spiritual suffering, that I have borne for the last thirty-six years in ever-increasing measure—my hatred and my anger for this appalling new-German people, created by the Hohenzollerns and also unfortunately by the genius Bismarck over the course of the past seventy-seven years . . . I, who was born and brought up German, even if my parents were of the Jewish faith, am still German in a better way than these millions of vicious idiots who are nowadays designated 'Teutons' . . .[212]

Redlich's attitude towards the Jews in the 1920s remained much the same as before—in discussions about Jews he exhibited a kind of cultural anti-Semitism, blaming them for many ills in the German and Austrian characters. However, like many other assimilated Jews, intensified anti-Semitism engendered a defiant pride in his own Jewish heritage. Redlich may have been encouraged in this direction by his friend Felix Frankfurter, himself a committed Zionist activist, who kept Redlich supplied with articles about Jewish affairs.[213] In his memoirs Redlich would dwell nostalgically on Jewish aspects of his childhood, and express pride that he could still read a bit of Hebrew, 'one of the original languages of mankind'.[214]

[211] WSLB, Handschriftensammlung: I.N.198.662, Redlich to Darkow-Singer, 2 Sept. 1920.
[212] Redlich's diary entry for 27 Sept, 1923, quoted in Fellner (ed.), *Dichter und Gelehrter*, 498–9. The reference to thirty-six years presumably refers to the time since Redlich's first stay in Germany as a law student in 1887. The reference to seventy-seven years is more obscure.
[213] HLS, Felix Frankfurter Papers: Box 197, Folder 21, Redlich to Frankfurter, 1 Aug. 1933.
[214] Redlich, 'Aus dem alten Oesterreich', 37.

Whereas in the past he had condemned Jews for corrupting and caricaturing German and Austrian culture, Redlich now praised Stefan Zweig as the supreme talent in German literature, who made even Goethe look like a middling talent.[215] That Redlich accorded such praise to Zweig, someone who came from the same assimilated Jewish liberal elite background as Redlich and shared his liberal humanitarian ideals, can perhaps be seen as a tacit affirmation of what many German-speaking Jews now asserted openly—that they themselves were the true and the best Germans.[216] Similarly, Namier pointed out that the best of what the world considered Viennese high culture had been created by Jews, whereas the 'Austrian "Aryan" lower middle class has produced Hitler'.[217]

Redlich's determined if qualified optimism for Europe (even in 1930 he believed the more limited goal of economic union between the successor states of Austria-Hungary attainable, even if political union was not)[218] gave way to unremitting pessimism in the last years of his life. 'It [Europe] must become far far worse, before it can finally become fundamentally better',[219] he predicted. 'The international tension in Europe is so great, it is difficult to believe that we will be spared a new war of all against all.'[220]

In his old age Redlich would have liked nothing better than to withdraw completely from the world into the past, but his concern for his wife, his young daughters, and his only son by his first marriage continued to draw his attention to the present. In 1920, the 50-year-old Redlich had married his 20-year-old wife—a second marriage that proved a great comfort to him, and which he credited with having saved him from psychological collapse after the break-up of the empire.[221] However, he felt now that his wife and children were hostages to fate and to a dark future. He was deeply pessimistic about the possibility of any viable future for his family. Since his retirement from Harvard Law School, he worried constantly about personal finances and wondered how he could possibly provide for them after his death. 'My daughters have graduated with distinction from the gymnasium, but what is the outlook for the future! I always shudder, when I think of the hard future awaiting this whole generation in poor

---

[215] Redlich to Bahr, 7 Nov. 1928, in Fellner (ed.), *Dichter und Gelehrter*, 568.
[216] Beller, *Vienna and the Jews*, 162–4.
[217] Namier, *In the Margin of History*, 81–3.
[218] Redlich to Schober, 15 Sept. 1930, in 'Johann Schober und Josef Redlich: Aus den Tagebüchern und Briefwechsel', *Zeitgeschichte*, 11–12 (1977), 378.
[219] WSLB, Handschriftensammlung: I.N.198.707, Redlich to Darkow-Singer, 5 Nov. 1931.
[220] Ibid., I.N.198.741, Redlich to Darkow-Singer, 1 July 1936.
[221] Redlich to Hofmannsthal, 28 Apr. 1929, in Fußgänger (ed.), *Briefwechsel*, 122.

Austria!'[222] Redlich did all he could to help find academic posts in the United States for displaced German Jewish scholars, but was always acutely aware of his own impotence to do more.[223] He failed in the case closest to his heart—to help his son, made redundant in Germany by the new racial laws, to escape to the West.[224] This was the last straw for the ailing man. 'I am . . . too old and too tired a man to help my beloved son',[225] he wrote shortly before his death. He died on the anniversary of the end of World War I, on 11 November 1936. 'For *his* sake I must say I cannot wish him back', wrote his friend Helena Hirst. 'He was a very, very sick and a desolately lonely man for some time, longing, I fear, for the end.'[226] 'To a man so sensitive and so hopeless, death came as a deliverance', wrote Charles C. Burlingham, Redlich's closest friend in the United States.[227]

Still, Redlich was spared the Holocaust, which forced all German Jews to confront the utter bankruptcy of their identification with *Deutschtum*. Redlich was too clear-sighted not to have read the writing on the wall, but his identification with Germandom and his commitment to assimilation was too deep-rooted for him to renounce, despite stirrings of Jewish feeling and Jewish pride. By contrast, Namier had no difficulty in pronouncing that '[t]he nineteenth-century connexion with the Germans was a disaster for us'.[228] Namier's quarrel was not merely with the Jewish connection to the Germans, but with the century-long hope that the Jews had invested in German *Bildung*, in the Enlightenment, and in liberalism, the political expression of the Enlightenment.

The emancipation of the Jews and their entry into the mainstream of European society was a result of the victory of liberalism. Jewish assimilation, however, came at a price—renunciation of Jewish particularism, communal autonomy, and the national connotations of their identity. Even then they were not accorded full acceptance, but only conditional tolerance.[229] Namier's Zionism resulted from the failure of Jewish assimilation.

---

[222] WSLB, Handschriftensammlung: I.N.198.741, Redlich to Darkow-Singer, 1 July 1936.

[223] Ibid., I.N.198.713, Redlich to Darkow-Singer, 17 May 1933.

[224] Hans Ferdinand Redlich managed to emigrate to Great Britain in 1938, partly through the influence of Seton-Watson. See Hugh Seton-Watson and Christopher Seton-Watson, *The Making of a New Europe,*' 438, n. 23.

[225] WSLB, Handschriftensammlung: I.N.198.743, Redlich to Darkow-Singer, 25 Sept. 1936.

[226] LOC, Felix Frankfurter Papers: Box 92, Helena Hirst letter, 12 Nov. 1936.

[227] Charles C. Burlingham, 'Josef Redlich—Obituary', *Harvard Law Review*, 50: 3 (Jan. 1937), 394.

[228] Namier, *In the Margin of History*, 65.

[229] Wistrich, *The Jews of Vienna in the Age of Franz Josef*, ch. 5.

One of Namier's reasons for becoming a socialist in Galicia was the perceived lack of anti-Semitism in its ranks. However, both Polish socialists and National Democrats united in their denial of the occurrence of pogroms, reports of which flooded the Foreign Office in 1919 and 1920.[230] He clung to his socialist faith a little longer by making a distinction between the Polish national socialists and socialists proper[231]—the former were the ones who condoned, and many times joined in, the pogroms, whereas the latter sometimes helped the Jews in their time of crisis.[232] Nevertheless, he was sadly forced to the conclusion that 'there is no reason why an ultra-nationalist, anti-Semitic Communism should not arise. Capitalism, in its individualist outlook, was international; Communism, aiming at a nationalized economy, is basically national, and its internationalism will probably disappear like that of the French Revolution. And then woe to him who in a Socialist community will be considered as a stranger!'[233]

Given the failure of individual assimilation, Namier then proposed the halfway house between Zionism and assimilation—Jewish national autonomy within Poland. In the immediate aftermath of World War I Namier tried to secure Jewish cultural rights in the Polish treaty, insisting that the Jews had to be given collective as well as individual rights, since the mainspring of Jewish life was communal, an argument Namier presented to Paderewski himself in Paris.[234] To the demurs of Headlam-Morley (and others less friendly), that Jewish 'national' autonomy would militate against good Polish citizenship,[235] Namier maintained that Jews could be good Polish citizens and still be culturally Jewish, just as 'a man may be a Welshman, a Boer or a French Canadian and claim Welsh, Dutch or Franch [*sic*] schools under autonomous administration and yet be a good Britisher, though he certainly is not an Englishman'.[236] (Headlam-Morley later persuaded Namier to use the term Jewish cultural rather than national autonomy.)[237]

[230] PRO: FO 371/3281/205848, Namier comment on *New York Times* article, 19 Dec. 1918.
[231] PRO: FO 371/4377/110, Namier note to Tilley, 8 Feb. 1919, pp. 252–53.
[232] PRO: FO 371/3903/80643, Namier memo on Jewish pogroms in Poland, 22 May 1919, p. 2.
[233] Namier, *In the Margin of History*, 76.
[234] PRO: FO 371/4379/364, Headlam-Morley note, 22 Apr.1919.
[235] Headlam-Morley to Namier, 24 Mar. 1919, in Headlam-Morley, *A Memoir of the Paris Peace Conference, 1919*, 54–55.
[236] PRO: FO 371/3903/38028, Namier note to Tilley, 14 Mar. 1919.
[237] Such debates, of course, echo discussions about whether the Jews were a national or religious/cultural minority in the Habsburg Monarchy. See Gerald Stourzh, 'Galten die Juden als Nationalität Altösterreichs?', *Studia Judaica Austriaca*, 10 (1984), 73–98.

This distinction between civic and cultural/national identity was similar to that which Redlich had made in the context of multinational Austria,
but as every emigrant and national minority knows, such a distinction is
rarely satisfactory in situations where the purported civic identity of a
minority is the national identity for the majority. Namier's contention that
Jews could remain Jews and still be good Polish citizens was frequently
answered with his own argument in 1916—that such hyphenation of identity 'does not work for good citizenship'.[238] Namier, with his own urgent
need to belong to a community, could not personally be satisfied either with
a purely civic identity. He once pointed out with a touch of bitterness that,
whilst others could identify themselves as 'English' or 'Scottish', he
himself had be content with being 'British'.[239]

To Namier, the failure to secure Jews the rights of a national minority
within Poland marked the bankruptcy of any policy to solve the Jewish
problem within the nation-states of others.[240] Not even in Britain, the
country where 'Jews are given the fairest deal',[241] did 'the Jew enjoy the
same moral freedom to express his views, especially in politics, as the non-
Jew'.[242] Namier's viciousness against liberalism and the Enlightenment
ideals of universal humanity, faith in reason, in education, and in progress,
can be read as the outcome of a sense of betrayal by these ideals. 'In the age
of "enlightenment" the place of the Messianic creed was taken by a belief
in humanity and progress, in democracy and the rights and brotherhood of
man . . . But we cannot wait for the humanization of mankind',[243] wrote
Namier. Jews seeking assimilation and amalgamation had been met with
only a half-open door. 'It was the semi-toleration accepted by the assimilated Jews which turned so many of them into neurotics.'[244]

Unlike many liberal Jews who continued to hope that anti-Semitism was
caused by ignorance and backwardness and would melt away in the light of
reason and education, Namier thought anti-Semitism pathological,
endemic, and rooted in the human delight in cruelty. Namier's profoundly
Hobbesian and pessimistic view of human nature, and his antagonism
towards the irrational masses, are directly related to the Jewish situation in
his lifetime. Namier's bile was hence aimed at the kind of Jew which
Redlich represented. He could very well have had Redlich in mind when
penning the following passage:

[238] Namier, *Skyscrapers*, 12.   [239] Namier, *Conflicts*, 166.
[240] Israel Bartal and Magda Opalaski, *Poles and Jews: A Failed Brotherhood*, (Hanover, NH,
1992).
[241] Namier, *Conflicts*, 122–3.   [242] Ibid. 123.
[243] Namier, *In the Margin of History*, 76   [244] Namier, *Conflicts*, 126.

On my first visit to Vienna after the war, I happened to engage in a discussion about Jewish Nationalism and Zionism with one of those high-minded, broad-minded, open-minded, shallow-minded Jews who prefer to call themselves anything rather than Jews. 'First and foremost', he declared in a pompous manner, 'I am a human being.' I replied . . . 'I, too, once thought so; but I have since discovered that all are agreed that I am a Jew, and not all that I am a human being. I have therefore come to consider myself first a Jew, and only in the second place a human being.'[245]

The only way for Jews to stop being cannon-fodder in the nationality conflict in Europe was to band together. 'Scattered groups without a centre must not be exposed to the impact of nations.'[246] Despite this interpretation of Zionism as self-defence, however, Namier's Zionism did exhibit the kind of xenophobia which he would condemn in other nationalisms. The following anecdote by Isaiah Berlin is illuminating:

I well recollect a meeting to interview candidates for a post in English in the University of Jerusalem, at which Namier would fix some timid lecturer from, say, Nottingham, with his baleful, annihilating glare, and say: 'Mr Levy, can you shoot?' The candidate would mutter something—'Because if you take this post, you will have to shoot. You will have to shoot our Arab cousins. Because if you do not shoot them, they will shoot you.' Stunned silence. 'Mr Levy, will you please answer my question: can you shoot?' Some of the candidates withdrew. No appointment was made.[247]

Nevertheless, in less impassioned moments Namier recognized the fact that 'Jewish prosperity in Palestine ultimately depends on the Jews reaching an understanding with the Arabs. They cannot be truly safe, even if they are a majority in Palestine, with a vast and discontented minority in their midst, which can, moreover, appeal for help from surrounding countries.'[248] The solution that Namier proposed, both for the Arab problem within Palestine and the problem of an isolated Jewish state within a sea of Arab states, was that Palestine should be included within the British empire as its seventh dominion.[249] The British Crown would guarantee political

---

[245] Ibid. 163. Namier's reaction to the Jewish plight of the inter-war years was by no means unique. 'What I was forced to learn during the past year, I have now at last understood and shall never forget it again. Namely, that I am no German, no European, maybe not even a human being—at any rate the Europeans prefer the worst of their own race to me—but that I am a Jew', wrote Arnold Schoenberg. Letter from Arnold Schoenberg to Wassily Kandinsky, 20 Apr. 1923, in *Schoenberg Briefe*, 90, quoted in Wistrich, *The Jews of Vienna in the Age of Franz Josef*, 632.
[246] Namier, *Conflicts*, 136.
[247] Berlin, 'Lewis Namier', 222.
[248] Namier, *In the Margin of History*, 91.
[249] Namier, 'Palestine and the British Empire', in *In the Margin of History*, 84–93.

parity irrespective of numbers within Palestine, and would safeguard the new Jewish state from the hostility of its Arab neighbours. Namier's burning faith in the role of the British Crown and the British empire in protecting the Jews echoes Austrian Jewish devotion to the multinational Habsburg empire as a haven protecting them from the hostility of their neighbours.[250]

Ultimately, however, his Zionism remained an intellectual passion, and he never made any attempts to relocate to Palestine, fending off Chaim Weizmann's threats and blandishments to join the nascent Palestinian academic community.[251] He argued that once the Jews had a state of their own, the rest could 'dissolve with dignity' and melt seamlessly into their community—in Namier's case, the British community, which continued, despite everything, to be his primary love. Namier had a crying need to belong to a stable, rooted community—the English establishment which did not want him. Berlin has written of Namier's naive courting of London clubmen who viewed him with distaste.[252] In 1919 it was a Conservative member of parliament who raised questions about Namier's reliability as an employee of the Foreign Office because of his foreign ancestry, charges against which two Liberal members of parliament defended him.[253] Oxbridge never gave him the professorship that he craved, and he had to content himself with being a professor at the University of Manchester. 'His failure to obtain an Oxford Chair ate into his soul',[254] wrote Isaiah Berlin. With his huge burden of self-hatred, perhaps Namier was unconsciously acting according to Groucho Marx's quip, that he would not want to be a member of any club that wanted him. It is thus typical that Namier, despite his passionate identification with the Jews and his commitment to Zionism, did not basically like what he thought of as the Jewish national character—over-intellectualized, petit bourgeois, foxes in Pareto's sense instead of lions.[255]

---

[250] Cf. Karl Popper, who embraced empires (both Austrian and British) as a cosmopolitan civilising force but opposed nationalism and nation-states. Malachi Hacohen, 'Dilemmas of Cosmopolitanism: Karl Popper, Jewish Identity, and "Central European Culture" ', *JMH* 71: 1 (Mar. 1999), 136–9.

[251] Rose, *Lewis Namier and Zionism*, 114–5.

[252] Berlin, 'Lewis Namier', 221.

[253] Parliamentary Debates Commons, v. 120. c. 1648–9, 6 Nov. 1919. See also PRO: FO 371/4383/642.

[254] Berlin, 'Lewis Namier', 226.

[255] Ved Mehta, *Fly and the Fly Bottle: Encounters with British Intellectuals* (London, 1963), 210.

In the 1920s, it had been easy enough to reconcile British and Jewish interests—after all, the Balfour Declaration had made the Jewish national home a British mandate. Namier's most cherished hope was for Palestine to become the seventh dominion of the British empire. His great hero was Disraeli, the Jew (albeit converted) who later rose to become prime minister. In the 1930s, however, as British foreign policy became anti-Zionist, Namier found it increasingly difficult to reconcile his two loves. He tried to explain this away by insisting that the British supporters of Zionism were mostly patricians like Churchill, whereas the anti-Zionists were the same middle-class and petit-bourgeois pen-pushers who were appeasing Hitler. Indeed, the Zionists, like the Czechs, felt themselves sacrificed on the altar of appeasement, since the British could not offend the Arab and Muslim world stretching from Egypt to India.[256] Hence, Namier managed to construct a grand synthesis in which '[t]he Cecils, Churchill, true aristocracy, pride, respect for human dignity, traditional virtues, resistance, Zionism, personal grandeur, [and] no nonsense realism', were fused together into one amalgam.[257]

Jewish terrorism directed against British administrators in Palestine and the anti-British birth of Israel finally shattered Namier's painstaking attempts to reconcile his two loves. Namier never felt close to the new Israel, regarding himself as too much of a European to identify with the very 'oriental' state that had emerged.[258]

In the last years of his life Namier was showered with honorary degrees from Oxford and Cambridge, a knighthood, and invitations to deliver a string of prestigious lectures.[259] All this, combined with a very happy second marriage, somewhat softened his annihilating bitterness against himself and the world. His wife recorded, however, that Namier still contemplated suicide at various times,[260] and attributed his cancer of the pancreas, of which he eventually died, to his decision not to live beyond 1960.[261]

Namier's despair stemmed from the complete demise of his loved old world. 'The century which has closed was that of German predominance in Europe, the age which has closed that of European predominance in the

[256] Rose, *Lewis Namier and Zionism*, 86
[257] Berlin, 'Lewis Namier', 220.
[258] J. Namier, *Lewis Namier*, 319.
[259] The Raleigh Lecture on '1848: The Revolution of the Intellectuals', the Waynflete Lectures on 'The German Problem in 1848–50', and the Academia dei Lincei lecture in Rome on 'Nationality and Liberty'.
[260] J. Namier, *Lewis Namier*, 308.
[261] Ibid. 328.

world . . . The German century and the German bid for world dominion have ended in the physical destruction of Europe, and its moral and intellectual desolation',[262] he wrote. Namier referred most probably to continental Europe in this sentence, but he was too much of a European, despite his British patriotism, not to feel the loss heavily.

He had witnessed the demise of the Austrian empire and lived to (covertly) regret it; he now witnessed the decline of the British empire, and Great Britain's eclipse on the international stage by two extra-European powers, the United States and the Soviet Union. Throughout the 1930s, he had entertained inflated notions of British international power, and believed that Britain could have prevented war single-handedly had she chosen to oppose Hitler earlier.[263] Redlich, however, realized that the United States had become the supreme power after the Great War, and feared presciently an 'Americanization' of Europe.[264] Now Namier was also forced to face the fact that the age of European supremacy was over. 'The Macedonian age, and the Hellenistic age, which followed after the life of Hellas had been sapped in the Peloponnesian Wars, was wider, more varied, rich in its own way, but it lacked the intensity which there had been in Greek city culture. There opens now an extra-European, Europaistic [*sic*] age',[265] wrote Namier, and indeed he, the most intense of historians, felt himself out of place in the new age.

Both Redlich and Namier had been bitter critics of Europe all their lives. In the last analysis, however, the old Europe, with all its faults and its glaring injustices, was still their world. That world was now triply lost to them—the Great War had destroyed the old Europe without replacing it with anything better, Europe as hegemonic power in the world had yielded to extra-European powers, and continental Europe had severed its centuries-long connection with the Jews. To Central and East European Jews in the inter-war years and during World War II, the Anglo-American lands promised freedom and safety from death and destruction, and yet they could not rejoice at leaving. 'The triumphant feeling of liberation is mixed too strongly with sorrow, since the prison, out of which one would be released, is still despite everything beloved',[266] wrote Freud on leaving

---

[262] BOD: MS Eng Hist.d.341, Namier, 'Waynflete Lecture', 1.

[263] Namier, *Europe in Decay*, 150–70.

[264] Redlich, *Schicksalsjahre Österreichs*, 5 Feb. 1917, II, 189; Josef Redlich, 'Sovereignty, Democracy, and the Rights of Minorities', 379.

[265] BOD: MS Eng Hist.d.341, Namier, 'Waynflete Lecture', 1.

[266] Sigmund Freud to Max Eitingon, 6 June, 1938, *Briefe, 1873–1939* (Frankfurt, 1960), 439. Quoted in Malachi Hacohen, 'Dilemmas of Cosmopolitanism: Karl Popper, Jewish Identity, and "Central European Culture" ', 134.

Vienna in 1938. No hagiographers of the old Europe, Redlich and Namier
had struggled alternately to transform it and to escape its miseries without
ever being able to renounce it. When it disappeared, they went into lifelong
mourning for their lost world, for, despite everything, it had been beloved.

Yet, notwithstanding Redlich's deep mourning for the culture of grace
that had disappeared with the old Austria, he largely overcame the temptations of nostalgia to which his friends Hofmannsthal and Bahr succumbed
so completely.[267] Although the emotional need to commemorate his
beloved old Austria drove his intense scholarship, his historical works were
no exercises in nostalgia but sober analyses dissecting the causes of the
Habsburg empire's decline, the degeneration of liberalism, and the irra-
tionality of nationalism. His biography of Franz Joseph was his 'most
personal book',[268] but Redlich thought that he had been able 'fully to rise
above the subjective in my book'.[269] He was also occupied with the problem
of reinterpreting and re-examining liberal pluralism and multinational
coexistence for modern times. Unlike Hofmannsthal who founded the
Salzburg Festival in an attempt at neo-baroque cultural reconstruction, or
Bahr, author of books such as *Austria For Eternity*,[270] Redlich looked not
towards a glorious, medieval, and universal Catholic empire,[271] but towards
the Austria of the Kremsier Constitution as the prototype of a modern,
democratic, multinational federation. Redlich was never an 'Austrian
anthropologist',[272] and his concerns for political liberty and national coexistence transcended the lost empire. 'Being human, very human, [Redlich]
had his loyalties of time and place, of local and national institutions that

[267] Michael Steinberg argues that the post-war correspondence between Bahr,
Hofmannsthal, and Redlich over Austrian cultural reconstruction and the relation between
Germans and Czechs is a confrontation between 'Catholic conservatism and genuine liberal
pluralism, with the rhetoric of liberal pluralism controlling the language of all three men.
Redlich spoke with a voice of genuine legal and political pluralism and did not emphasize the
cultural questions that remained of paramount importance for Hofmannsthal and Bahr, and
which prevented them from wedding their liberal rhetoric to truly pluralist attitudes.' See
Michael P. Steinberg, *The Meaning of the Salzburg Festival: Austria as Theater and Ideology,
1890–1938* (Ithaca, NY, 1990), 132.
[268] Redlich to Schober, 7 Dec. 1928, in Fellner (ed.), 'Johann Schober und Josef Redlich:
Aus den Tagebüchern und Briefwechsel', *Zeitgeschichte*, 11–12 (1977), 373. Josef Redlich,
Kaiser Franz Joseph von Österreich (Berlin, 1928).
[269] Redlich to Hofmannsthal, 20 June 1928, in *Fußgänger* (ed.), *Briefwechsel*, 103
[270] Hermann Bahr, *Österreich in Ewigkeit. Roman* (Hildesheim: Borgmeyer, 1929).
[271] Malachi Hacohen, 'Dilemmas of Cosmopolitanism: Karl Popper, Jewish Identity, and
"Central European Culture" ', 114.
[272] Steinberg, *The Meaning of the Salzburg Festival: Austria as Theater and Ideology,
1890–1938*, 129; Stanley Suval, ' The Search for a Fatherland', AHY 4–5 (1968–9), 275–99,
and Jacques Le Rider, 'Hugo von Hofmannsthal and the Austrian Idea of Central Europe', in
R. Robertson and E. Timms (eds.), *The Habsburg Legacy* (Edinburgh, 1994), 121–35.

were dear to him', wrote Felix Frankfurter. 'But they were all in subordination to, because they were expressions of, those forces of civilization which transcend parochial bounds of every kind, racial, religious, or national.'[273] Namier eventually did succumb to nostalgia. His critique of nationalism as a centralizing, levelling force, breaking down both class distinctions as well as regional loyalties, is really a critique of modernity.[274] Significantly, Namier identified himself as a 'Tory Radical'—that is, as a spiritual descendent of the movement which had campaigned against the very Poor Law of 1834 that Redlich had defended as a necessary step in the evolution of a great industrial state;[275] a campaign rooted in preference for the historical role of local self-government by the landed society, and the defence of small communities over power exercised by the central organs of the state.[276] Ultimately, Namier had far more in common with great nostalgic writers like Hofmannsthal, Bahr, and Joseph Roth than did Redlich, although his object of desire was not Austria or the Holy Roman Empire, but the lost Arcadia of eighteenth-century English history. Isaiah Berlin once wrote that Namier had a Proustian appreciation of the English aristocracy.[277] Like Proust, Namier, because of his awareness of the irretrievable nature of time,[278] went in search of lost time, and embalmed eighteenth-century England in a golden halo of an arrested past.

---

[273] Felix Frankfurter, 'Josef Redlich—Obituary', *Harvard Law Review*, 50: 3 (Jan. 1937), 389.

[274] Namier, *Vanished Supremacies*, 36–7. See esp. p. 37: 'For men rooted in the soil . . . things are individual and concrete in the village or the small, old-fashioned town. But in the great modern cities men grow anonymous, become ciphers, and are regimented; thinking becomes more abstract and is forced into generalizations; inherited beliefs are shaken and old ties are broken; there is a void, uncertainty, and hidden fear which man tries to master by rational thought.'

[275] Redlich, *Local Government in England*, i. 129–33.

[276] Robert Stewart, *The Foundation of the Conservative Party 1830–1867* (London and New York, 1978), 165–71.

[277] Berlin, 'Lewis Namier', 221.

[278] J. Namier, *Lewis Namier*, 46: '[Namier's] overwhelming sense of time's swift retrocession increased till it acquired the concreteness of physical sensations. More than once, when decisive and sustained action was imperative, he felt paralysed by too clear an awareness of time's implacable course.'

5

Nationality, Liberty, and Rationality

The fundamental question which engrossed Redlich and Namier was the same one preoccupying many European Anglophiles—why, despite the triumph of constitutional government over the forces of absolutism in most of nineteenth-century Europe, did continental Europe fail to evolve the kind of political liberty to be found in Great Britain?[1] Through their studies of British parliamentary history Redlich and Namier sought to discover the preconditions for and characteristics of representative self-government; through their studies of nineteenth- and twentieth-century European history they tried to explain why political liberty failed in Central and Eastern Europe. Both regarded modern nationalism, especially German nationalism, as one of the biggest culprits for the failure of political liberty in Europe. Significantly, both Redlich and Namier revered Great Britain and not France as the paragon of liberty, although France and her revolutions exerted such a magnetic influence on so many Central and East European intellectuals. On the contrary, Redlich and Namier traced the beginnings of modern nationalism to the French Revolution and to French rationalist philosophy, and the spread of nationalist ideas throughout Europe to Napoleon and his armies.[2] Both took issue with the Enlightenment doctrine of natural rights that underlay French revolutionary political theory and praxis, contrasting French rationalism unfavourably with British empiricism and respect for tradition. Like their fellow Habsburg political thinker Baron József Eötvös, they argued that the French interpretation of liberty, equality, nationalism, and sovereignty was inferior to the British interpretation of these concepts. Whereas in Britain liberty was understood as freedom from arbitrary coercion and the absence of any absolute power in the state, French revolutionaries thought that liberty could be achieved through

[1] Ian Buruma, *Voltaire's Coconuts or Anglomania in Europe* (London, 1999).

[2] Paul Bödy, *Joseph Eötvös and the Modernization of Hungary, 1840–1870: A Study of Ideas of Individuality and Social Pluralism in Modern Politics* (Boulder, Col., 1985), 66; József Eötvös, *The Dominant Ideas of the Nineteenth Century and their Impact on the State*, vol. I, trans., ed., and annotated with introductory essay by D. Mervyn Jones (Boulder, Col., 1996), ch. 6.

the principle of absolute popular sovereignty.[3] Whereas equality in Britain referred pre-eminently to equality before the law, in France equality was understood as the right of every citizen to participate in the exercise of popular sovereignty. Most importantly, in Britain nationalism manifested itself as loyalty to a historic territory, whereas in France it was redefined along linguistic lines by the French revolutionaries. As Namier pointed out, the shift from 'King of France' to 'Emperor of the French' implied a shift from a territorial to a linguistic conception of the nation.[4]

Redlich's critique and Namier's rejection of popular sovereignty has already been discussed in the previous chapter. It was to nationalism, however, that they devoted the bulk of their attention. Again like József Eötvös, they agreed that modern nationalism's will to rule and exclusiveness of national claims were fundamentally incompatible with the principles of liberty and equality.[5] Namier explained that a nation which based its unity on language could not easily tolerate an alien minority within the state or renounce groups of co-nationals intermingled with those of the neighbouring nation. Domestically this led to repression of the alien minority, 'which are apt to abase the standards of government; while fellow-countrymen across the border awaiting liberation keep up international tensions, which again are destructive of a free civic life'.[6] Redlich defined the main features of modern European nationalism as 'defensiveness yet simultaneously the will to conquer of every people and every linguistic unit against the neighbour';[7] 'a drive to expansion and political self-determination . . . over the entire territory which it [the nation] claims even if many nations live there, always under the principle of including de-nationalized former co-nationals or subordinating migrant alien elements'.[8]

Moreover, nationalism was not conducive to the development of parliamentary government. As we have seen, Redlich wrote his pre-war work on British parliamentary procedure partly to prove that integral nationalism

---

[3] Cf. F. A. Hayek, *New Studies in Philosophy, Politics, Economics and the History of Ideas* (London, 1978), 120: 'While to the older British tradition the freedom of the individual in the sense of a protection by law against all arbitrary coercion was the chief value, in the Continental tradition the demand of the self-determination of each group concerning its form of government occupied the highest place.'

[4] Namier, *Vanished Supremacies*, 38.

[5] Redlich, *Das österreichische Staats- und Reichsproblem*, I, 554. See also Bödy, *Joseph Eötvös*, 64, where Bödy points out the similarities between Eötvös's and Namier's views on the mutually exclusive natures of nationalism and political liberty. See too József Eötvös, *The Dominant Ideas of the Nineteenth Century*, i. ch. 3.

[6] Namier, *Vanished Supremacies*, 53.

[7] Redlich, *Das österreichische Staats- und Reichsproblem*, I, 137.

[8] Ibid. 171.

undermined parliamentary government because it questioned the constitutional and territorial basis upon which parliament rested.[9] '[N]ationalist
radicalism hinders the necessary precondition for a fruitful development of
our state existence, namely the mutual compromise between the claims of
individual national parties and between them and the State',[10] wrote
Redlich with regard to nationalist obstruction of the Austrian parliament.
Namier pointed out that the fundamental mistake made by the revolutionaries of 1848 was to assume that the right to self-government and the right
to self-determination were 'cognate causes favouring each other',[11] since
both tended to undermine the rule of 'reactionary' dynasties. However,
self-government, 'which means constitutional development within an
existing territorial framework', is antithetical to self-determination, 'for
which there is no occasion unless that framework is called in question and
territorial changes are demanded; and acute disputes concerning the territorial framework naturally retard, or even preclude, constitutional development'.[12] 'A constitutional régime is secure when its ways have become
engrained in the habits and instinctive reactions—*dans les moeurs*—of the
political nation: it safeguards civilized life, but it presupposes agreement
and stability as much as it secures them.'[13]

The ideas of the French Revolution were spread throughout Europe by
Napoleon's armies, not only through propaganda and nationalist reaction
to French conquests, but also because the administrative rationalization
that Napoleon instigated in the conquered areas destroyed local territorial
allegiances, creating a vacuum for modern nationalism to fill.[14] One of
Namier's outstanding scholarly achievements was to demonstrate, through
a painstaking piece of prosopography (never published), that the majority
of leaders for the movement for German unity in 1848 were people whose
native districts had been rationalized by Napoleon or transferred in the
Congress of Vienna in 1815.[15] Namier argued that any territorial unit, no
matter how small, 'was capable of developing a specific patriotism in those
truly rooted in it'.[16] Moreover, those entrenched in a specific territory were

---

[9] Redlich, *The Procedure of the House of Commons*, i. pp. xxiv–xxv, 133–63; III, 196–201.
[10] Redlich to Bahr, 18 Sept. 1911, in Fellner (ed.), *Dichter und Gelehrter*, 76.
[11] Namier, *1848: Revolution of the Intellectuals*, 26.
[12] Namier, *Personalities and Powers* (London, 1955), 106. See also 'Nationality and
Liberty', in Namier, *Vanished Supremacies*, 31–53. Original version: *Nationality and Liberty*
(Rome: Accademia Nazionale Dei Lincei, 1948).
[13] Namier, *1848: Revolution of the Intellectual*, 31.
[14] Namier, *Vanished Supremacies*, 43.
[15] BOD., MS Eng Hist.d.341, Namier, notes for Waynflete Lecture, esp. 119–227.
[16] Namier, *Vanished Supremacies*, 48.

relatively immune to the blandishments of a nationalism based on the abstract principles of language or race. Napoleon, by combining many of the German pygmy states into larger units, and the Congress of Vienna, by confirming many of Napoleon's changes, destroyed these feelings of allegiances to a specific homeland, thus leaving the way wide open for adherence to German nationalism. Correspondingly, there was less interest in German unity amongst Prussians, Bavarians, and Austrians, all subjects of states with a territorial consciousness.[17]

Thus the 1848 revolutions operated within the area of Napoleon's work and influence, 'for he had sapped inherited forms and loyalties, regrouped territories, established modern administrations, and familiarized tens of millions of men with change in political and social conditions—and new ideas are not nearly as potent as broken habits'.[18] The effect was most marked in Germany, where the territorial resettlement of the Napoleonic period was much more extensive and permanent than elsewhere.[19] Redlich noted a similar effect among the Illyrian provinces of Napoleon's conquest and the subsequent galvanizing of South Slav nationalism,[20] as well as the impetus that the Napoleonic administrative apparatus gave to Lorenz von Stein's counter-French reforms, which initiated the movement for self-government and municipal autonomy in Germany.[21]

Namier viewed 1848 as the conflict between two basic principles: 'the one [dynastic property] feudal in origin, historic in its growth and survival, deeply rooted, but difficult to defend in argument; the other [national sovereignty] grounded in reason and ideas, simple and convincing, but as unsuited to living organisms as chemically pure water.'[22] Given his sympathies with territorial nationalism over linguistic nationalism, it comes as no surprise that Namier's evaluation of 1848 was purely negative. He would have agreed with Eötvös's claim that the underlying purpose of the 1848 revolutions was not the struggle to obtain and protect liberty, but to augment the power of the state through the principle of national sovereignty.[23]

Whilst paying tribute to the sincerity and fervour of Mazzini and other like-minded liberal nationalists, Namier agreed with Mazzini's own self-

[17] Ibid. 43–6.
[18] Namier, *1848: Revolution of the Intellectuals*, 23.
[19] Ibid. 43.
[20] Redlich, *Das österreichische Staats- und Reichsproblem*, i. 136; ii. 421.
[21] Ibid., i. 664–5.
[22] Namier, *1848: Revolution of the Intellectuals*, 24.
[23] Bödy, *Joseph Eötvös*, 66.

assessment that 'his heart was stronger than his head'.[24] At best the liberal nationalist idealism produced a lot of hot air—the resultant Manifesto of the Pan-Slav Congress, 'an exceedingly vague, verbose, and ineffective document',[25] being a prime example. At worst, however, such idealism served as a smokescreen for modern imperialist nationalisms. Mazzini's 'words of faith and action rather than of thought' concealed from contemporaries 'how deficient his teachings were in substance correlated to everyday reality, and what dangerous germs they contained'.[26] '[W]hat remains after the idealistic gilt of nationalism has worn off is the claim to superiority, hence to dominion.'[27]

Although willing to acknowledge the genuine (if misguided) idealism motivating many Latin and Slav nationalists, Namier insisted that German nationalism was from the beginning devoid of internationalist idealism. He argued that the German nationalists and would-be revolutionaries of 1848 showed no trace of the 'enlightened pacific humanitarianism which, in spite of grandiloquent phrases, was prominent in the French revolution of 1848'.[28] Hegel ('who mistook the Kingdom of Prussia for the Kingdom of Heaven'[29]) and Fichte had already laid the foundations of the German deification of the State and nation. '[I]t is the Germans, from Hegel and Fichte down to Treitschke and the Nazis, who have deified the State and nation; of this the ultimate expression is Hitler's maxim that whatever benefits the German nation is morally good and just.'[30]

Namier maintained that the 'Freiheit' of the German slogan 'Einheit, Freiheit, and Macht' meant something quite different from the 'liberty' of 'liberty, equality, and fraternity'.[31] It implied neither equality nor self-government—'in 1848 it [self-government] was adventitious and often described as such'.[32] Moreover, even in 1848 'Macht' was already considered the most important of the trinity.[33] Everyone, from the most moderate Liberals to the extreme left, favoured war against Russia as a means of rallying all Germans and thus uniting Germany.[34]

[24] Namier, *Vanished Supremacies*, 39.
[25] Namier, *1848: Revolution of the Intellectuals*, 114.
[26] Namier, *Vanished Supremacies*, 39–40.
[27] Ibid. 43.
[28] BOD, MS Eng Hist.d.341, notes for Waynflete Lecture, 11.
[29] Ibid. 84.
[30] Namier, *Conflicts*, 91.
[31] BOD, MS Eng Hist.d.341, notes for Waynflete Lecture, 8.
[32] Ibid. 9.
[33] Ibid. 7.
[34] Ibid. See also Namier, *Vanished Supremacies*, 44–5.

Namier saw 1848 as the beginning of the German bid for supremacy in Europe, which ended in 'the physical destruction of Europe, and its moral and intellectual desolation'.[35] His main thesis was that the German 'liberals' of 1848 anticipated Hitler in their worship of power and the German nation, and in their imperialism over other nations. Namier contemptuously refuted the argument that 1848 was potentially a chance for the unification of Germany along liberal lines. 'States are not created or destroyed, and frontiers redrawn or obliterated, by argument and majority votes; nations are freed, united, or broken by blood and iron, and not by a generous application of liberty and tomato-sauce; violence is the instrument of national movements.'[36] Moreover, German 'liberalism' was merely a 'German counterfeit of Western liberalism'.[37] He traced the waning German liberal commitment to the equality of all nations, chronicling in detail the diminishing part the German liberals were willing to accord Poland in the case of the proposed partition of Posnania between Germans and Poles. He also charted the German reaction to the Czech national movement: at first moderate and conciliatory, later increasing in wrath after Palacký's famous refusal to attend the National Assembly in Frankfurt, culminating in a proposal to send troops into Bohemia to rescue Germans embroiled in the Prague riots.

In short, 'the debility of German liberalism can be clearly discerned in those early months of the "glorious revolution" of 1848, when the professorial lambs at Frankfort, bitten by the Pan-German dog, caught rabies'.[38] Namier quoted the Austro-German liberal leader Schuselka, that a great nation requires space (*Raum*) to fulfil its world destiny (*Weltberuf*). 'How far was Frankfort from the *Lebensraum*?'[39] he asked rhetorically. About the positive liberal achievements of 1848—such as the emancipation of the Jews—Namier was completely silent.

Namier's unrelenting attack on the German liberals was part of his larger argument that there was no second and better Germany of *Dichter und Denker* to offset the imperialist Germany of Wilhelm II and Hitler. Rather, it was precisely German poets and thinkers and 'liberal' intellectuals who

---

[35] BOD, MS Eng Hist.d.341, notes for Waynflete Lecture, 1.

[36] Namier, *1848: Revolution of the Intellectuals*, 31. (The reader may recall Redlich's more cautious pronouncements on this point, when he expressed doubts if 'struggles involving the existence or destruction of a state or of a union of states can be carried through under the forms of parliamentary government'); Redlich, *The Procedure of the House of Commons*, iii. 200.

[37] Namier, *Facing East*, 43.

[38] Namier, *1848: Revolution of the Intellectuals*, 57.

[39] Ibid. 87. See also Namier, *Vanished Supremacies*, 47.

had provided German imperialism with its ideology, rather than the much-maligned 'Prussian militarism' which merely provided the means. As far back as World War I, Namier had argued that the essence of Prussian militarism was 'brutal egotism, but its brutality [was] sane'.[40] The danger lay with the 'unpractical [*sic*] German "thinker," the inhuman German sentimentalist, the neurasthenic individual who dreams of power [Nietzsche], the complex mind which, tired of its own shallow complexity, yearns for the simplicity of force'.[41] 'Modern German Imperialism is the outcome of the union between Germany and Prussia; it is Prussian in its methods, but German in its ideology and aims.'[42] As noted in the previous chapter, Namier found it significant that none of Hitler's core group of followers were Prussian. He always emphasized the Austrian and South German *völkisch* nationalist roots of Nazism, which was in many ways opposed to the Prussian conception of nationalism. Hitler was 'the posthumous revenge of the Hapsburgs on the Prussia of Frederick the Great, and on the Germany of Bismarck: he piped them to their doom along paths once blazed out by the Hapsburgs.'[43]

Namier even cited Goethe (that the people had a right to be well governed, not to govern themselves) and Kant (on the importance of the state being based on the rule of law rather than self-government), two giants of the German Enlightenment, to support his point that self-government never entered the German conception of freedom.[44] To Namier, it was no accident that the Frankfurt Parliament was a highly academic assembly—the German revolution was the 'revolution of the intellectuals'.[45] The only reason why they did not consummate '*la trahison des clercs*' was because reaction did win, thereby saving the reputation of the German revolution of 1848. 'Had not Hitler and his associates blindly accepted the legend which latter-day liberals, German and foreign, had spun round 1848, they might well have found a great deal to extol in the *deutsche Männer und Freunde* of the Frankfort Assembly.'[46]

---

[40] Namier, *Germany and Eastern Europe*, 62.
[41] Ibid. 63.
[42] Ibid. 64.
[43] BOD, MS Eng. Hist. d. 341. See also Peter Pulzer, *The Rise of Political Anti-Semitism in Germany and Austria*, 320.
[44] Namier, *Facing East*, 42; BOD, MS Eng Hist.d.341, notes for Waynflete Lecture, 9.
[45] Namier, *1848: Revolution of the Intellectuals*, 86–7 (footnote): 'The Frankfort Parliament was a highly academic assembly—it contained 49 University Professors and Lecturers, and 57 schoolmasters, and at least three-fourths of its members had been to a University . . . The presence of a great many historians and jurists set a mark on its debate . . .'
[46] Ibid. 123–4.

Namier believed that 'Hitler's unparalleled rise is due to the fact that he has given expression to some of the deepest instincts of the Germans'.[47] The impulse to be both slave and master according to their place in a rigidly ordained hierarchy was deeply ingrained in German psychology, and arose from the complete lack of moral autonomy on the part of the individual. 'Characteristic of the German social groups is the utter, conscious subordination of the individual, the iron discipline which they enforce, the high degree of organisation and efficiency which they attain, and their resultant inhumanity.'[48]

'It is the lack of moral courage, self-assurance, and independence in the individual German which makes him seek safety, self-assertion, and superlative power in and through his State and nation, and which makes him glorify them beyond all bounds of sense and reason.'[49] Namier's analysis is strikingly similar to that of the psychologist Eric Fromm, who postulated that German national psychology was 'other-directed'—that is, oriented towards obeying orders from above, and of looking to external authorities to determine right and wrong.[50]

Redlich too, without recourse to psychological terminology, deduced the same traits in German philosophy and jurisprudence. We have already seen his sustained scholarly and political attack on the German philosophy of subordinating all other aims to the state. Like Namier, Redlich realized that what made German nationalism so dangerous was its alliance with a political philosophy of state supremacy and of freedom through submission to the state. Indeed, Redlich insisted that Hitler was not merely a nationalist dictator like Piłsudski in Poland or even Mussolini in Italy, since Nazism was the political and philosophical fruit of a long-standing and deep-rooted veneration of the absolutist state.[51] Redlich traced the roots of German nationalism and state veneration not so much to the German Enlightenment (Goethe and Kant) but to German romanticism,[52] to the 'great new streams of political and philosophical thought on law and history in Germany represented by Fichte, Hegel, Savigny and the great school of "Romanticism" '.[53] He agreed that *Dichter und Denker* had a large share of responsibility in Germany's unhealthy political development.[54]

---

[47] Namier, *Conflicts*, 81.   [48] Ibid. 79.
[49] Ibid. 90.   [50] Eric Fromm, *Escape from Freedom* (New York, 1941).
[51] *The Decline of Parliamentary Government, Discussed by Harold J. Laski and Dr Josef Redlich*, 17–18.
[52] Ibid. 23.
[53] Redlich, 'Sovereignty, Democracy, and the Rights of Minorities', 382.
[54] Even now historians are divided over whether Nazism was a temporary aberration or connected to deeper structures and continuities in German history. See John Hiden and John

Redlich also argued that nationalism was a far stronger motive force than liberalism in the Frankfurt Parliament[55]—indeed, Robert Kann, usually so deferential to Redlich's opinions, maintains that he ignored the genuine attempts by certain Austrian-German liberals like Giskra, Mühlfeld, Sommaruga, and Unterrichter at Frankfurt to arrive at the idea of national equality in a federalized Austria.[56] Redlich noted that the divergence between German political development and the mainstream of European thought was already noticeable in 1848, as a comparison between Bakunin and Mazzini with German liberalism demonstrated.[57] German liberals were only too ready to fall back upon the 'political power philosophy' of Hegel and Fichte when confronted by the nationalisms of the other peoples.[58]

The transformation of German jurisprudence by Gerber, Laband, and Redlich's unloved teacher Jellinek into a formal science, to the exclusion of social, political, or moral problems, marked yet another stage in the degeneration of German liberalism.[59] It gave rise to an emphasis on the form rather than the content of law, the doctrine that the state as the source of law could only be limited by self-imposed constraints, as well as to a dangerous moral relativism which stressed obedience to law whatever its content.[60] Redlich censured the German liberals of the 1860s for forsaking the struggle against absolutism and being content with the reality created from 'above' as long as they had a 'truly written and signed' constitution. 'They wanted a constitution . . . but they were indifferent as to in what way such a constitution would come about.'[61] Moreover, they had enshrined the 'feeble miserable efforts of Schmerling-Perthaler in 1861' as the 'untouchable Palladium for liberal politics, and thought the quality of "constitutional loyalty" could compensate for all other mental and moral factors in politics'.[62] 'Nothing could better illustrate the traditional sterility of political life in Austria, or the paralysing hold of merely formal and juristic

---

Farquharson, *Explaining Hitler's Germany: Historians and the Third Reich*, 2nd edn. (London, 1989). See too D. C. Watt, 'British Historians, the War Guilt Issue, and Post-war Germanophobia: A Documentary Note', *Historical Journal* 36: 1 (1993) 179–185.

[55] Redlich, *Das österreichische Staats- und Reichsproblem*, i. 154–162, 186.
[56] Kann, *The Multinational Empire*, i. 83–4.
[57] Redlich to Bahr, 16 Aug. 1919 in Fellner (ed.), *Dichter und Gelehrter*, 374–5.
[58] Redlich, *Das österreichische Staats- und Reichsproblem*, i. 182.
[59] Redlich, *Schicksalsjahre Österreichs*, 14 Jan. 1910, I, 77–8. See also Redlich to Bahr, 16 Nov. 1920, in Fellner (ed.), *Dichter und Gelehrter*, 434.
[60] John H. Hallowell, *The Decline of Liberalism as an Ideology with Particular Reference to German Politico-Legal Thought* (Berkeley and Los Angeles, 1943), 77–87.
[61] Redlich, *Das österreichische Staats- und Reichsproblem*, ii. 442.
[62] Ibid. 643.

notions in its parliamentary legislation, than the steady rejection by the Upper House of the bills of the Judicial Committee designed to mitigate the dictatorship, and their rejection exclusively on technical grounds.'[63] Similarly, Redlich designated Kelsen's 'pure legal theory of the state' as a 'great absurdity',[64] since Kelsen's morally relativistic approach to law could and did force him to regard Nazism as a legitimate form of government.[65] Although Redlich rejected the metaphysics of Natural Law theory, he accepted its basic ethical axioms, such as the state's duty to respect the dignity of the individual and the notion of a universal minimal ethical standard applicable to all humanity regardless of nation or race.[66] To Redlich, law was both objective norm as well as subjective authority, and hence was inextricably interwoven with history and politics.[67]

All the same, Redlich's judgement on the German liberals is more complex and nuanced than Namier's. He assigned a greater role to genuinely liberal impulses in the German and Austrian revolutions of 1848, citing the conduct of the Austro-German liberals at the Kremsier constitutional assembly as proof of their basic good will towards the other nationalities and their commitment to liberal principles.[68] Given the widespread German prejudice towards Slavs as country bumpkins,[69] Redlich argued that it was a great step forward in and of itself that the Germans at both Frankfurt and Kremsier had so readily accepted the *principle* of national equality, even if they fell short in actual implementation.[70] The degeneration of German liberalism was the product mostly of the 1850s and 1860s, when in both Prussia and Austria it became divested almost wholly of its cosmopolitan traits and humanitarian-philosophical rationalism, to be replaced by a *realpolitisch* nationalism instead.[71] In both Germany and Austria, Bismarck's career led quickly to a depreciation of parliamentary government and a strong appreciation of one-man rule,[72]

---

[63] Redlich, *Austrian War Government*, 159.

[64] Redlich to Schober, 7 Dec. 1928, in Fellner (ed.), 'Johann Schober und Josef Redlich: Aus den Tagebüchern und Briefwechsel', *Zeitgeschichte*, 11–12 (1977), 373.

[65] R. A. Métall, *Hans Kelsen: Leben und Werk* (Vienna 1969).

[66] See Georg G. Iggers, *The German Conception of History: The National Tradition of Historical Thought from Herder to the Present* (Middletown, Conn., 1968), 269–86, for an interesting comparison and contrast between German and 'Western' (French and British) political thought.

[67] Frankfurter, 'Josef Redlich—obituary', 390.

[68] Redlich, *Das österreichische Staats- und Reichsproblem*, i. 236.

[69] 107, in which Redlich noted the popular comic figure of the migrant 'Böhm'.

[70] Ibid. 152–3, 236–7.

[71] Ibid. 182.

[72] *The Decline of Parliamentary Government, Discussed by Harold J. Laski and Dr Josef Redlich*, 16.

whilst Redlich's old nemesis Rudolf von Gneist created a theoretical 'liberal' underpinning for monarchical rule.[73]

Since the nationality problem of 1848 emerged almost wholly within the sphere of the Habsburg Monarchy, the dynasty was naturally the target of attack. However, of all the nationalist movements excited to a fever-pitch in 1848, it was only those of the socio-economically dominant nations in Central and Eastern Europe (dubbed by Namier the 'master nations'), such as the Germans, Italians, Poles, and Magyars, which attacked the dynastic principle. The Habsburg dynasty was the greatest obstacle to the programmes of three of the four master nationalities—German and Italian unity, and Hungarian independence. Only the question of Polish independence lay largely outside the Habsburg sphere.[74] The successful realization of the German, Italian, Hungarian, and Polish programmes would have resulted in the disruption of the Habsburg empire. The other nationalities in the empire, realizing that their social and economic oppression by the master nationalities would be even more absolute if reinforced by political domination, came out on the side of the dynasty.[75]

On the whole, Namier endorsed the choice of the non-dominant nationalities. We have seen how negative he had been about the Habsburg Monarchy during World War I. In the post-war years, however, he modified his position.[76] 'Why thus wipe out a chapter of Polish history—in which the Poles learnt and achieved a great deal?' wrote Namier in response to hostile Polish historiography on the Habsburg Monarchy. 'The Cracow Conservatives (the so-called *Stanczyki*) were one of the most cultured political groups which Poland ever produced, her enlightened Tories.'[77] The Habsburgs had learnt that 'dominion to be far-flung has to be at least tolerable'.[78] The 'dominant, non-nationalistic Germanism' of the Habsburgs was infinitely preferable to the imperialism of pan-Germanism.[79]

Namier applauded the fact that the Habsburgs and other monarchical anti-revolutionaries did win in 1848, thereby preserving the peace of Europe.[80] The reprieve that the oppressed nationalities received from the

---

[73] Redlich, *Das österreichische Staats- und Reichsproblem*, i. 668.
[74] Namier, *Personalities and Powers*, 109.
[75] Ibid. 113; Namier, *Vanished Supremacies*, 49.
[76] See Namier, *Vanished Supremacies*, 48–50.
[77] Namier, *Facing East*, 95.
[78] Namier, *Conflicts*, 36.
[79] Ibid. 38.
[80] Namier, *1848: Revolution of the Intellectuals*, 31.

master nationalities did not last long, however. The dynastic principle alone soon proved too weak a basis for the Monarchy, which was forced to adopt the modified programmes of the four master nations between 1859 and 1867. The Habsburgs were expelled from Germany and Italy but retained the German and Italian provinces which were part of their old hereditary dominions, Hungary achieved constitutional independence within the framework of the empire, and the Poles were handed Galicia.[81]

The gradual disintegration of the Ottoman empire meant that yet more oppressed nationalities surfaced politically, all demanding their place in the sun. 'By 1914 the Balkan nations were free, and the problem of the Greek-Orthodox Serbs and Rumans [*sic*] in the Habsburg Monarchy came to the fore: the survival of the Habsburg Monarchy reconstituted in terms of the dominant nations was now at stake.'[82] This ultimately led to the disintegration of Austria-Hungary, and the triumph of the principle of the nation-state in Central and Eastern Europe. 'The process which formed the essence of European history since the French Revolution has now reached its term.'[83]

Although Namier came to prefer the Habsburg Monarchy to the new nation-states, in the last analysis he still believed that the Monarchy was an artificial creation of a dynasty intent only on its own glory.[84] Redlich, however, indignantly refuted the view, 'now so frequently expressed, that the Habsburg multinational empire was a politically unnatural entity. For three hundred years the opposite was true—the empire achieved an enormous cultural task.'[85] Redlich regarded the Habsburg Monarchy as an admittedly very imperfect embodiment of the ideal of multinational coexistence.[86] The great problem he set himself was to understand why the old dynastic multinational empire had failed to evolve common civic ties and a common territorial loyalty strong enough to overcome the centrifugal forces of linguistic nationalism.[87]

Through their studies of British history, both Redlich and Namier concluded that territorial nationalism was the product, in Namier's words, of a long historical development and an active civic life within a historically given territory.[88] Redlich argued that the House of Commons had originally

---

[81] Namier, *Personalities and Power*, 114.
[82] Ibid. 116.
[83] Ibid. 116–7.
[84] Namier, *Germany and Eastern Europe*, 124.
[85] Redlich, *Das österreichische Staats- und Reichsproblem*, i. p.vii
[86] Ibid., p. v.
[87] Ibid., p. vi.
[88] Namier, *Vanished Supremacies*, 31–3.

consisted of representatives of ancient local communities, so that it was initially a 'House of confederated States', with parliament acting as a connecting link between the local communities. A change gradually came about in the fourteenth century, as members began to regard themselves as representatives not merely of the locality but of the nation as a whole, thus laying the foundation of British state patriotism.[89]

The Habsburg Monarchy certainly fulfilled the requirement of a 'long historic development'. What the Monarchy lacked, however, was the welding force of an active civic life. Redlich had hoped that a common constitution and a common parliament could play the same integrating role in Austria as they had in Britain. Namier thought these hopes had been futile all along, because the Habsburgs were a German dynasty. Possessing the qualities of 'German political incapacity and deadness, and of German administrative efficiency', the Habsburgs and the other German dynasties that governed most of Central and Eastern Europe had 'emptied the territorial State of communal contents and converted it into sheer dynastic property', resulting in 'the denationalised State with an unpolitical [*sic*] population'.[90] Even the German nobility never played the part of opposition to the Crown. 'Nowhere outside Germany has the nobility always sided with autocracy and with a centralised bureaucracy against self-government', charged Namier.[91] In fact, he accused the 'German guild of princes' of further widening the gap between the ruler and his subjects by imposing upon Europe 'a German "racial" theory, utterly alien to the traditions of most other nations, about the blood of sovereigns having to be "uncontaminated" by that of non-princely [even though otherwise aristocratic] families'.[92] Thus, although Namier sometimes veered towards Redlich's position that Metternich's repression of active civic life was a lost opportunity for the development of Austrian territorial patriotism,[93] he rejected this as a false might-have-been, since the Germanic nature of the Habsburgs predestined them to hostility towards self-government. Ultimately, Namier could never accept the Habsburg Monarchy completely, because he regarded it as a Germanic power.

[89] Redlich, *Local Government in England*, i. 46; L. B. Namier, *The Structure of Politics at the Accession of George III*, 2nd edn. (London, 1957), 5: 'The Commons were the *communitas communitatum*, originally a quasi-federation of shires and boroughs.'
[90] Namier, *Vanished Supremacies*, 33.
[91] BOD., MS Eng Hist.d.341, Namier, notes for Waynflete Lecture, 98.
[92] Namier, *Conflicts*, 34.
[93] Namier, *1848: Revolution of the Intellectuals*, 26.

Given Redlich's lifelong, though severely strained, identification with German culture and his deep allegiance to the Austrian empire, he quite naturally displayed far more ambivalence about the German contribution to the Monarchy and towards the role of the Habsburgs themselves than Namier.

This spiritually hard fate was thereby laid upon those German Austrians, who had in their persons and in their activities affirmed the Austrian idea with all their strength, but at the same time earnestly struggled against the Austrian reality—to realize that the greatness and creativity of the founding of the Habsburg empire and state had come about through the mental and material energy of the Germans, but simultaneously also to recognize the disastrous and impeding effect of German political thought and action on the further development of the fruitful structure of thought, which the old empire, even if in a very incomplete form, had embodied.[94]

Redlich too described monarchy in the sense of 'one-man rule' as a Germanic invention; 'especially after the revolutions of the seventeenth and eighteenth centuries it always has been reinvigorated by the Teutonic influence'.[95] Originally, however, the Habsburgs, despite being absolutist rulers, had contributed greatly to the welfare of their peoples. Redlich credited the Habsburgs' 'apparently purely dynastic policies' with achieving an enormous cultural task and fulfilling a true European need by keeping the Turks at bay for 300 years, and ensuring peace in the Danubian region for a quarter-of-a-millennium.[96] He saw real potential in Maria Theresa's and Joseph II's reforms, in which they had attempted to create a truly unitary, organic state out of their conglomerate of lands and kingdoms through a bureaucracy which was advanced and enlightened for the time. He recognized that their government, although absolutist, was also enlightened—both monarchs felt a passionate concern for the welfare of their subjects, although of course they reserved the right to determine how their subjects' welfare could best be achieved.[97]

Redlich dated the degeneration of Habsburg policies to the French Revolution, when fear of revolution so dominated Emperor Franz II that he repudiated the Enlightenment heritage of Maria Theresa and Joseph II, and looked with suspicion on any form of Austrian patriotism not directly dynastic, thus preventing the growth of an Austrian territorial patriotism.[98] Ultimately, Redlich traced the fall of the Austrian empire to Habsburg

---

[94] Redlich, *Das österreichische Staats-und Reichsproblem*, p. v.
[95] *The Decline of Parliamentary Government, Discussed by Harold J. Laski and Dr Josef Redlich*, 17.
[96] Redlich, *Das österreichische Staats- und Reichsproblem*, i. p. vii.
[97] Ibid. 26–39.　　　[98] Ibid. 40–7, 66–75.

policy since Franz II,[99] and portrayed Franz Joseph as the single biggest obstacle to any attempt to transform the old dynastic empire into a modern, democratic, multinational federation.[100]

To Redlich, as to Namier, 1848–9 were fateful years for the history of Austria and the history of Europe. Three intersecting events determined the fate of Austria—the entrance of nationalism and democracy onto the political agenda of Europe, the accession of Franz Joseph, and the creation and suppression of the Kremsier Constitution. 'The March revolution of Vienna in 1848 opened the sluices of nationalist passion throughout the Danubian empire',[101] thus raising the question 'whether the national and democratic ideas which flared up in all the peoples of Austria would be capable of creating a new Austria as a community of politically free and nationally equal peoples', in the place of the 'hitherto purely mechanical "State" superimposed from above'.[102] Although nationalism, Pan-Germanism, Pan-Slavism, and the desire for Hungarian independence at first enticed Habsburg subjects away from the historically given empire, the partial triumph of reactionary forces forced a more sober assessment of the nationality problem in Austria and a renewed affirmation of the historically given territory of Austria, at least among the Germans and Slavs. 'No doubt, affirmation out of disappointment and resignation on all sides: but nonetheless, affirmation!'[103] Thus, the way was prepared for the meeting of minds at Kremsier.

Redlich was not blind to the shortcomings of the Kremsier Constitution, especially the exclusion of Hungary from its sphere of concern. The Kremsier constitutional makers, deprived of all practical political experience by the absolutist state, were also prone to overvaluation of the legislative components of constitution-writing without paying enough attention to implementation and administration. Moreover, the state of political philosophy prevalent in Austria at the time suffered from two basic flaws—one, a complete misunderstanding of the English political institutions they sought to imitate; two, a lack of federal models, the examples of Switzerland and the United States being too little known to counter the French liberal dogma of a strong state being a centralized state.[104]

Despite its flaws, however, Redlich judged the Kremsier Constitution

[99] Redlich, *Das österreichische Staats- und Reichsproblem*, i. p. vii.
[100] See Redlich, *Emperor Francis Joseph of Austria*, esp. the epilogue.
[101] Redlich, 'Sovereignty, Democracy, and the Rights of Minorities', 384.
[102] Redlich, *Das österreichische Staats- und Reichsproblem*, i. 99.
[103] Ibid. 187.
[104] Ibid. 99–100.

worthy to rank next to the American Constitution and the French Constitution of 1791.[105] The Kremsier Constitution was the only great reform plan resulting from the free association of the peoples within the Habsburg Monarchy,[106] and contained the potential for a truly liberal multinational state. Although Austrian Germans and Slavs differed in their conceptions of a future constitutional Austria—the Germans wanting a centralized state, the Slavs a federal one[107]—there was enough mutual good will to lead to a viable compromise at Kremsier, resulting in a programme of decentralized power in a unitary state, with autonomy provisions for the crownlands, for the *Kreise* (nationally demarcated administrative areas), and for the commune.[108]

Unlike Namier, Redlich thought it fatal that reaction should have won in 1848–9. The Kremsier Constitution was the moral and political high-point of recent Habsburg history, 'the outcome of a truly rare measure of good will to reach an understanding between all nations, parties, and individualities, as well as a high measure of idealistic devotion to a high principle'. The success of reactionary forces in suppressing the constitution and blackening its reputation negated its vast potential for good.[109] Instead of viewing 1849–67 as a brief reprieve from the programmes of the 'master nations', Redlich regarded this period as fatal to Austrian and European history, and laid the blame squarely at the feet of Franz Joseph.

Franz Joseph began his reign with a lie—his claim to be a constitutional monarch—although he and the entire dynasty had no intention of giving in to constitutionalism. Redlich described 'the bad faith with which Franz Joseph met his people on the threshold of his rule' as the ' "evil deed that forever bears fresh evil" to be realised in this life of eighty-six years'.[110] The period of Franz Joseph's absolutist rule witnessed a great degeneration in the moral and idealistic forces of both German conservatism and German liberalism,[111] and alienated the non-German nationalities not merely from the reality of the Austrian absolutist state, but from the idea of Austria as a multinational state, feeding fresh currents into embittered nationalisms.[112]

---

[105] Ibid. 93.
[106] Ibid. 92.
[107] Ibid. 202.
[108] Ibid. 221–323.
[109] Ibid. 322. Historians have differed in their evaluation of Kremsier. Many have agreed with Redlich's evaluation of Kremsier as a real potential turning-point for Austria—See Kann, *The Multinational Empire*, ii. 21–39; Karl Tschuppik, *Franz Josef I. Der Untergang eines Reiches* (Dresden-Hellerau, 1928), 41; Rudolf Schlesinger, *Federalism in Central and Eastern Europe* (London, 1945), 170–7. For a less starry-eyed view, see Okey, *The Habsburg Monarchy*, 155–6.
[110] Redlich, *Emperor Francis Joseph of Austria*, 33.
[111] Redlich, *Das österreichische Staats- und Reichsproblem*, i. 182.
[112] Ibid. 454.

Redlich should rather have said the degeneration of German neo-conservatism as well as German neo-liberalism. He saw clearly what Namier did not or chose not to see—that the counter-revolution of Franz Joseph was not a return to the status quo, but 'a revolution to the right, conducted from above, carried through in the interest of the imperial person, and constituting a veritable coup d'état'.[113] The young emperor, imbued with eighteenth-century ideas of absolute monarchical sovereignty, imagined that his new bureaucratically centralized state was a return to pre-revolutionary days. Bad historian that Franz Joseph was, however, he completely failed to take into account that never had the entire Habsburg empire been ruled as a unitary state; never had the reach of the state been so extensive or weighed so heavily upon the subjects.[114] Although his grandfather Franz I was reactionary from the standpoint of the new ideas imported by Napoleon, he was conservative with regard to Austrian history. He observed all the historic rights of his peoples—the estates constitutions in the hereditary provinces remained in force, as did the 800-year-old Hungarian constitution. 'But what Francis Joseph did on the advice of his conservative counsellors, was anything but conservative. He abolished all the rights that had existed from time immemorial between the monarch and his kingdoms and territories by the self-same stroke with which he destroyed the entire achievement his people had won through the revolution.'[115]

This new state, 'superimposed on a great number of countries of definite and historic individuality, and comprising eight distinct peoples, was a mechanical construction, and in no sense a living or politically coordinated unity'.[116] Under this Schwarzenberg–Kübeck–Bach regime, 'the alienation of the people from the "State" . . . proceeded far faster and was more extensive than during the Austrian *Ancien Regime*, whose patriarchal character and atrophy of will caused discontent and finally contempt, but no hatred'.[117]

Redlich noted that 'many of them [the Habsburgs] had traits of the genuine artist in their make-up in so far as they had a powerful impulse to mold the inchoate in accordance with their will', as well as 'an almost esthetic conception of politics as a means to the realization of the idea of

[113] Redlich, *Emperor Francis Joseph of Austria*, 92.
[114] Ibid. 92; Redlich, *Das österreichische Staats- und Reichsproblem*, i. 399.
[115] Redlich, *Emperor Francis Joseph of Austria*, 93.
[116] Redlich, *Austrian War Government*, 7.
[117] Redlich, *Das österreichische Staats- und Reichsproblem*, i. 454.

domination for its own sake, with Catholicism as its support'.[118] In Franz Joseph's case,

> [t]he material here was the men and nations, the subjects and territories with all their historic rights and ethnic peculiarities, which Francis Joseph had inherited with his many crowns; the esthetic idea, that of an unlimited dominion conditioned by no obsolescent or new created rights on the parts of others but as free from any influence of the Estates as it was from 'public opinion,' from feudal rights in the aristocracy or any dependence on the popular will.[119]

Austria was never allowed to develop organically according to its own inner historical logic, but was repeatedly altered by the will of Franz Joseph, in his younger days so prone to sudden structural overhauling of his empire. Redlich appreciated what Namier chose not to emphasize, that doctrinarism could just as easily appear amongst conservatives as well as liberals.[120]

Redlich's disapproval of Franz Joseph's radical breaks with the past inclined him sympathetically towards the 'old conservatives' who were appalled at Franz Joseph's suppression of prescriptive rights, and who pressed for the restoration of their historic rights. Moreover, he praised them for their understanding of the essentially multinational, federal nature of the empire. Still, their 'feudal-imperial' outlook was fundamentally contradictory to the idea of a modern multinational state.[121] They were antiquarian romantics out of touch with the modern currents of the age, battling against a quarter-of-a-millennium of reality (the reality of the unified Habsburg state). Their programme would have resulted in an empire without a state.[122]

The real enemy of progress, however, was not this group of politically ineffectual old conservatives, but the so-called liberals. Franz Joseph, in his pursuit of a technically efficient autocracy, relied heavily on the state bureaucracy. This bureaucracy was increasingly supported by the German liberals, who saw their only salvation in a heavily centralized, German-administered empire.

Prior to 1848, proto-federalist liberal sentiments were not lacking even amongst the Germans—Baron Andrian-Werburg's proposals to strengthen the provincial diets, and his friend Karl Möring's recognition of the diets as forums for the national principle to express itself being good

---

[118] Redlich, *Emperor Francis Joseph of Austria*, 222.
[119] Ibid. 223.
[120] Redlich, *Das österreichische Staats- und Reichsproblem*, ii. 438.
[121] Ibid. i. 544.
[122] Ibid. 545.

examples. After the psychological shock of 1848, however, in which the Austrian Germans found themselves caught between *Kleindeutsch* sentiments in the Frankfurt Parliament and Austro-Slavism at home, they quickly and fatefully began to see the bureaucratic-centralist state as a national asset to the Germans.[123] This identification with bureaucratic centralism was made easier by the fact that the bureaucracy, though politically oppressive, was ethnically German, economically liberal, and was becoming increasingly bourgeois in composition.[124] On its part the bureaucracy, alarmed by Franz Joseph's flirtations with the feudal aristocrats and their Slav partners after Bach's fall from grace, also wished for a closer rapprochement with the liberals.[125]

Anton von Schmerling and German bourgeois acceptance of his constitution consummated the marriage between bureaucratic centralism and German liberalism. By accepting the Schmerling Constitution, which was basically a reconstitution of the Schwarzenberg–Bach unitary state with a liberal constitutional gloss,[126] the German liberals made themselves complicit in the 'sin of violence' by which the bureaucracy, army, and dynasty had created the new unified empire of Austria.[127] Redlich attributed the eventual provisions for provincial and communal autonomy as well as the article proclaiming national equality in the 1867 Constitution not so much to German liberalism, but to fear. Having lived through so many sudden and sweeping changes of government in Austria, they were afraid that Franz Joseph, once he found himself in a stronger position, would enforce absolutism—hence the defensive need for provincial and communal autonomy, and the strategic necessity not to alienate the other nationalities too much. The German-Austrian liberals were very aware of how precarious their base of power was, having seen the magic of Schmerling's 'electoral geometry' at work, which could produce either an aristocratic-feudal-Slav majority or a German bourgeois majority in parliament according to the dictates of the emperor.[128]

The Schmerling Constitution, which aimed at a unitary empire incorporating Hungary, foundered on the rock of Magyar opposition. Despite Redlich's pronounced anti-Magyar sentiments in his political life, his post-

[123] Ibid. 173–4. See also Kann, *The Multinational Empire*, ii. 89–93.

[124] Redlich, *Austrian War Government*, 8–10.

[125] Redlich, *Das österreichische Staats- und Reichsproblem*, i. 486; Redlich, *Austrian War Government*, 10.

[126] Redlich, *Das österreichische Staats- und Reichsproblem*, i. 698.

[127] Ibid. ii. 161.

[128] Ibid. 644–5.

war treatment of the Hungarian problem was surprisingly mild—so much
so that Oskar Jaszi could describe him as 'a scholar . . . friendly to the
Magyars' and a 'sincere admirer of the greatness of Francis Deák and
József Eötvös'.[129] Whilst it was certainly an exaggeration to term Redlich a
scholar friendly to the Magyars, since his admiration was confined to what
were arguably non-representative Magyars (Deák, Eötvös, and Jaszi
himself), he did retreat from his pre-war tendency to blame all the empire's
problems on the Magyars, recasting the Germans instead as the chief
culprits.

Redlich recognized that the historical development of Hungary was
completely different from Austria's,[130] that Hungary had always enjoyed a
kind of dualism with Austria, and condemned Joseph II's centralizing
Germanizing policy as rash and 'absurd'.[131] Joseph II's policy awakened a
Magyar nationalism that became increasingly intolerant towards the other
nationalities inhabiting Hungary in the early nineteenth century. Redlich
described the unitary state imposed upon the Hungarians as a great, unhis-
torical wrong, and compared the Hungarian constitutional struggle under
Deák's leadership to Eliot's, Pym's, and Hampden's defence of the people's
right in their struggle against the autocracy of Charles I.[132] For Deák's
personality, Redlich had nothing but praise;[133] he was also generous in his
evaluation of Andrássy as a statesman.[134] However, the same cannot be said
of his judgement of Deák's programme of dualism. Redlich counted it as
one of the greatest tragedies in Habsburg history that Eötvös, whose
programme of historical autonomy commanded his highest respect, went
over to Deák's party.[135] While convinced that both Deák and Eötvös
sincerely intended to respect the rights of the other nationalities in
Hungary, as enshrined in the 1868 nationality law authored by Eötvös,
Redlich criticized them for overlooking the fact that the logic of dualism,
based on Magyar and German hegemony in the two halves of the empire,
would inevitably lead to the oppression of the other nationalities once the
'era of good feelings' in the liberal Hungary of the 1860s had passed
away.[136]

Redlich agreed with Namier that the dualism of 1867, an unholy pact
between the emperor and the Germans, Magyars (and later the Poles), was
very detrimental to the Monarchy. It was not the mere division of the

---

[129] Jaszi, *The Dissolution of the Habsburg Empire*, 336.
[130] Redlich, *Das österreichische Staats- und Reichsproblem*, i. 97, 543–5.
[131] Ibid. ii. 202.   [132] Ibid. 465.
[133] Ibid. 51–64.   [134] Ibid. 505.
[135] Ibid. 174.   [136] Ibid. 259.

empire into two that distressed Redlich so greatly—he actually defended foreign minister Count Beust from the charges made by Great Austrians that only a foreigner could cut apart the 'living' body of the Monarchy, pointing out that 'the monarchy as a unitary state with a unitary centralised domestic government, as Bach had created it, was never a living and growing, but always an artificial body created by a short-sighted power based purely on military power'.[137] Moreover, Beust was appointed by Franz Joseph for the express purpose of building up the Monarchy's strength for the next bout with Prussia. A seasoned statesman, Beust was quick to realize that the German liberals in Cisleithania and the Hungarian Deákists were the most powerful groups in the Monarchy—hence it made sense to seek their co-operation rather than to court Bohemian conservative feudal aristocrats out of touch with the modern world.[138] From Beust's and Franz Joseph's short-term view, dualism made a lot of sense. Moreover, Franz Joseph at the time probably viewed dualism as yet one more in a series of constitutional experiments that might not prove more lasting than the others. Dualism did last, however, proving itself incapable of reform. It fatally froze the momentary power relations between the different nationalities in 1867 into a permanent structure. Although the Slavs in Cisleithania managed to carve out political space for themselves through the autonomy provisions of the 1867 Constitution, the Magyar stranglehold on the whole of Hungary grew stronger and stronger. Redlich accounted it Franz Joseph's greatest political sin that he ignored the nationality problem in Hungary[139]—a mortal error, for Magyar oppression aggravated the South Slav problem to such a degree that it would finally bring down the Monarchy.

Ever since its fall, one of the main historiographical debates in late imperial Habsburg history has revolved around the inevitability of its collapse. Redlich laid the ultimate blame for the fall of the empire on Franz Joseph's repressive policies against constitutionalism in his country—albeit with much help from German nationalism, and the mostly German bureaucracy which embraced the German philosophy of state supremacy, which 'from 1870 on imposed a rigid theory of state and empire on Austria that impeded an understanding of the special existence of the historically given Habsburg empire and state, at a time when an organic solution, with the

---

[137] Redlich, *Das österreichische Staats- und Reichsproblem*, i. 581.
[138] Ibid. 532.
[139] Redlich, *Emperor Francis Joseph of Austria*, 463.

help of the great creative idea of a federation of equal peoples could still have, if earnestly undertaken, been achieved'.)[140]

Although Redlich treated the person of Franz Joseph with respect, even affection, in his biography (to such an extent that Oscar Jaszi would charge him with overindulgence towards his subject),[141] he would have agreed with Karl Tschuppik's assessment of Franz Joseph's fatal impact on Austria: 'Nothing could be more false than the view that Kremsier was a mere episode, an unfulfilled youthful dream of a new Austria. Kremsier was Austria's reality, and what followed it was the dream of an autocrat that the will of the dynastic house must prevail and the will of the people bend before it.'[142] Whilst Redlich respected Franz Joseph's personal character and integrity, he condemned the doctrine of the divine right of kings which drove the emperor as a dangerous and anachronistic doctrine in the nineteenth century.[143]

Franz Joseph did learn in time to 'impose compromises upon himself and upon his peoples that could only be regarded as temporising expedients, means of coping with an immediate difficulty'.[144] However, 'a creative application of modern ideas to the old Habsburg conception of the realm of the peoples of the West and East, lay beyond his mental scope'.[145] Even after the suppression of the Kremsier Constitution, the empire could still have been rescued had constitutional government really taken root after 1867, had the Bohemian *Ausgleich* succeeded, and had there been a government committed to true national equality and reconciliation. Instead, with Franz Joseph's support, Count Taaffe had instigated the demoralizing 'divide-and-rule' policy amongst the nationalities, let loose the 'battle of languages',[146] and substituted bureaucratic for parliamentary government, thereby increasing and accelerating 'the common alienation of the peoples from an authority which all felt to be the purely external, family rule of an hereditary State', an alienation 'not in the least diminished by the fact that, merely because the aged monarch needed peace and quiet, the bureaucratic State . . . doled out crumbs to all the parliamentary parties in turn, in the shape of progressive or social reforms, designed to keep the constituencies in good temper'.[147] The Bohemian *Ausgleich* failed, in the last analysis,

[140] Redlich, *Das österreichische Staats- und Reichsproblem*, i. pp. xiii–xiv.
[141] Jaszi, *The Dissolution of the Habsburg Empire*, 324.
[142] Tschuppik, *Franz Josef I. Der Untergang eines Reiches*, 41.
[143] Redlich, *Emperor Francis Joseph of Austria*, 539–40.
[144] Ibid. p.xii.
[145] Ibid.
[146] Redlich, *Austrian War Government*, 26.
[147] Ibid. 51.

because Franz Joseph feared such a compromise, afraid that he would lose a decisive measure of power in the Bohemian lands as he had in Hungary.[148] It could have been otherwise. Franz Joseph's potential to exert his powerful will for constructive measures had been seen in his pushing through universal suffrage, in the teeth of great opposition, in 1907. Until the end of the empire, 'the strongest motive force for good or evil in Austrian State life lay in the Crown'.[149]

Namier, on the other hand, blamed the fall of the Habsburg Monarchy not so much on the dynasty but on the nationality problem. Whilst Redlich portrayed the Compromise of 1867 as resulting from a combination of Franz Joseph's need for revenge against Prussia, Beust's cynical calculation of power realities within the empire, Deák's moral leadership, and Magyar tactical brilliance, Namier argued that in 1867, 'at half-time between Vienna and Versailles',[150] the dynasty was forced by the logic of the situation to make a deal with the Germans, Magyars, and later the Poles. 'The political developments of Austria-Hungary obeyed the necessities of its internal structure; *illusions there were of dynastic power to shape them*—in reality these developments were pre-determined as the movements of the stars, and subject to iron laws'[151] (my italics). Moreover, '[o]n the two rocks of the Dualist system and of German Bohemia every attempt at reforming Austria-Hungary from within was bound to founder, however sincerely undertaken. But, in fact, no such attempt was honestly made.'[152]

The divide between Redlich and Namier on Habsburg history in many ways echoes the century-long *Historikerstreit* over whether the Austrian empire was the germ of a League of Nations, or whether it was really a 'prison of peoples'. Closely related to this question is the 'inevitability' of Austria's fall.[153] Nevertheless, neither Redlich nor Namier can be classified clearly in one camp or the other. Although Redlich thought the dissolution of the empire a historic error, he did not regard Franz Joseph's Austria as a prototype for a future, equal, and democratic United States of Europe but as a crime against the Austrian state *idea*. Moreover, despite dwelling upon all the missed opportunities for empire reform, Redlich never arrived at a final judgement regarding the 'inevitability' of the empire's fall. Writing

---

[148] Redlich, *Emperor Francis Joseph of Austria*, 452.
[149] Redlich, *Austrian War Government*, 159.
[150] Namier, *Personalities and Powers*, 116.
[151] Namier, *Vanished Supremacies*, 115.
[152] Ibid. 133.
[153] For summaries of this historiographical debate, see Kann, *The Multinational Empire*, ii. 286–8; Steven Beller, *Francis Joseph* (London and New York, 1996), 3–9; Le Rider, 'Hugo von Hofmannsthal and the Austrian Idea of Central Europe', 124–8.

about the 'might-have-been' of 1848 in Austria, Redlich pointed out that a government sincerely committed to constitutional reform could have taken advantage of the rapprochement between the Slavs and the regime and the strengthening of the moderate elements amongst the Austrian German leaders in the autumn of 1848, and could have easily achieved a careful dismantling of the revolution whilst consolidating the revolution's positive achievements. Had this government put through a constitution guaranteeing national equality, it would have had the backing of all the nationalities and European opinion behind it to win Hungary back to the empire idea. 'Whoever does not deny free will' could easily argue that 'it would have been possible to have proceeded in quite a different manner from Franz Joseph I and Schwarzenberg at this juncture. On the other hand, the historian could also demonstrate that the chief characteristics exhibited by Franz Joseph's advisers at this point—carelessness, short-sightedness, and a lack of principles—were the unavoidable result of the way the Austrian population had been governed for more than two centuries, and thus conclude that the whole recent development of Austria was inevitable.[154]

Namier had always regarded the Habsburg Monarchy not as a prison but as a 'boarding-house' of nations.[155] As we have seen, he thought Habsburg imperial rule preferable to German nationalist hegemony, and that imperial times had been far better than the era of the successor states. He recognized too that almost every nationality within the Habsburg Monarchy (with the exceptions of the Italians and the Serbs) had, at one time or another, a direct interest in the preservation of Austria, and hence had developed different varieties of pro-Austrian feelings.[156] Nevertheless, he thought that the development of an inclusive Austrian territorial nationality was doomed to failure because of the ingrained sense of superiority of the 'master' nations.

No civic territorial nationality could unite the different nationalities of Austria-Hungary, for such community is possible only between linguistic groups acknowledging each other as equals, whereas the Germans, Magyars, and Poles claimed cultural, social, and political superiority over those on whom they looked down as 'a-historic' subject races, not entitled to an independent national existence.[157]

These national inequities had become enshrined in the Dual Monarchy. 'I recommend a reading of the essay to those who regret the destruction of

---

[154] Redlich, *Das österreichische Staats- und Reichsproblem*, i. 221–3.
[155] Namier, *Germany and Eastern Europe*, 124.
[156] Namier, *Vanished Supremacies*, 48–50.
[157] Ibid. 50.

the Habsburg Monarchy, and imagine that a federation of free and equal nations could have been established within a framework of which national supremacies were the sense and the justification',[158] wrote Namier in 1958 on the republication of his 1920 analysis of the downfall of the Habsburg Monarchy.[159]

Hence, Redlich's and Namier's disagreement centred not so much on the 'inevitability' of the downfall of the empire, the *desirability* of supranational empires, or even the faults and merits of the actual Dual Monarchy, but on the *viability* of the Austrian state *idea* and, by extension, the viability of multinational states. One of Redlich's avowed intentions in writing his Austrian histories was to hammer home the point that 'it was not the old Austrian idea, but its practical form through Franz Joseph's hopeless art of government that constitutes the reason for the collapse of the empire'.[160] The Kremsier Constitution was proof that a modern multinational state could emerge if enough people of good will sought a solution to the problems of multinational existence. Namier, on the other hand, stressed that the nationality problem was intractable. Like his fellow Galician Jewish compatriot Ludwig Gumplowicz,[161] Namier viewed the Habsburg Monarchy in social-Darwinist terms, and regarded the history of Europe and even of humankind as a *Rassenkampf*.

In theory there was nothing in Namier's definition of territorial nationalism to preclude a multinational state—in both Great Britain and in Switzerland 'it is the State which has created the nationality, and not *vice versa*'.[162] However, Namier, so quick to discern historical 'laws' that doomed continental Europe to eternal strife, was far less certain as to how happy outcomes had come about. Certainly, the geographical characters of Great Britain and Switzerland were important determinants for the evolution of territorial nationalism, '[b]ut the argument must not be pressed too far: for in the adjoining island a similar mixture of Celt, Anglo-Saxon, and Norman has failed to evolve an Irish territorial nationality . . . the frontiers of Switzerland are by no means preordained, nor amenable to a strict rational explanation.'[163] Great Britain and Switzerland were unique products of a serendipitous combination of factors. As a general rule, however, Namier

[158] Namier, *Vanished Supremacies*, p. v.

[159] Namier, 'The Downfall of the Habsburg Monarchy', in Temperley (ed.), *A History of the Peace Conference of Paris*, vol. iv, part 3, pp. 58–119; repr. in Namier, *Vanished Supremacies*, 112–64.

[160] Redlich to Hofmannsthal, 3 Dec. 1926, in Fußgänger (ed.), *Briefwechsel*, 81.

[161] Johnston, *The Austrian Mind*, 323–6.

[162] Namier, *Vanished Supremacies*, 32.

[163] Ibid. 32–3.

thought that '[f]reedom is safest in the self-contained community with a territorial nationality; and where this has not by some miracle or the grace of God grown up spontaneously, it might perhaps best be secured by a transfer of populations'.[164]

In fact, Namier not only blamed nationality conflict on modern nationalism and its absolutist claims, but also implied that nations were primordial entities doomed to eternal struggle. In his Creighton Lecture of 1952 Namier traced the roots of the European nationality problem all the way to the great era of migrations in European history—the universal European *Drang nach Osten* from the eighth century onwards, and the continual Asiatic incursions of the Avars, Magyars, and Turks into South-Eastern Europe. From West to East, the French pressed against Flemings and Germans, the Germans against Lithuanians and Slavs, the Lithuanians and Poles against the Russians, the Russians against the Finnish tribes and ultimately also against the Mongols, whilst the Swedes spread across the Baltic and the Italians across the Adriatic. To this movement Namier attributed the origins of the Flemish–Walloon problem in Belgium and the Franco-German problem in Alsace, the problems of Germany's ragged eastern border, Poland's problems on both her western and eastern flanks, and the conflict between the Yugoslavs and the Italians.[165] To the Asiatic invasions Namier ascribed the birth of the Habsburg Monarchy, since German resistance at the gate of the Danube against Asian invasions was the origin of Austria, whose core was the Ostmark round Vienna. The Germans and Magyars in their head-on collision split off the Northern from the Southern Slavs and established their dominion over that middle zone; the subjection of the Southern Slavs and the Romanians was completed by the Turkish conquest of the Balkans.[166]

Each conquest was integral within certain districts and partial over much wider areas. 'In the case of partial conquests the upper classes and the urban population were as a rule the first to be replaced or assimilated by the conquerors, while the peasantries retained their original nationality.'[167] The result: a dozen Irelands and Ulsters all over Europe. Even before the nineteenth-century age of nationalisms, venomous proto-nationalist conflicts did occur, although at the time communities were defined more by religion and class (peasants against landlords, town against country) than nationality.

---

[164] Ibid. 53.   [165] Namier, *Personalities and Powers*, 108.
[166] Ibid. 108.   [167] Namier, *Conflicts*, 4–5.

This astonishing historical scenario, in which Namier traced the roots of modern nationality conflicts to migration patterns of over a millennium ago, rather than to the more recent determination of state borders through warfare and diplomacy, shows that he assumed nations and nationalities to have a historical ethnic kernel, rather than being merely categories constructed by modernity.[168] Namier's criterion for determining the boundaries of the new nation-states after World War I is an even clearer example of his positivist, not to say mechanistic, approach to nations and nationalities. He assumed that nations were 'objective' entities. Hence, the question of state boundaries had one true solution that could be deduced from demographic data alone. Like Wilson, Namier opposed plebiscites because they introduced a subjective element into a problem that was solvable by objective data. Commenting on the plebiscite in Upper Silesia in which the majority of the Polish-speaking population chose to belong to Germany rather than Poland, Namier wrote:

The Polish national revival in Upper Silesia was progressing steadily, but was still far from having reached its natural term in 1919. There is such a thing as a nationality *in posse* besides a nationality *in esse*, and a plebiscite is not justified in districts which are in a state of change and transition. Whatever injustice may have been committed against Germany in the execution or interpretation of the Silesia plebiscite, the plebiscite itself was an injustice against Poland.[169]

He did acknowledge that nationality and religion had no 'independent existence and permanent, immutable contents; they reflect certain things in the lives of communities, and often the same things under changed names'.[170] These shifting names, however, denoted 'a living reality, which merely centres and finds its symbol in some acknowledged principle or combination of principles—consanguinity, real or presumed; the profession of a creed; the use of a language; the manner of securing one's livelihood'.[171]

To Namier, the nationality conflict was permanent because it was one face of 'the eternal, insoluble problem how mass organisms can co-exist within the same or contiguous territory'.[172] 'The relations of groups of men to plots of land, of organised communities to units of territory, form

---

[168] See R. J. W. Evans, 'Frontiers and National Identities in Central Europe', *International History Review*, 14: 3 (1992), 480–502, for a completely different view of the conflict between territorial border demarcation and national identity in Central Europe.

[169] Namier, *In the Margin of History*, 46–7.   [170] Namier, *Skyscrapers*, 55.

[171] Ibid. 55.   [172] Ibid.

the basic content of political history', [173] wrote Namier. He cited an anonymous Irish pamphleteer in 1779: 'The political body has no heart . . . and nations have affections for themselves, though they have none for each other. . . . There is no such thing as political humanity.' [174] The 'strongly knitted mass formations of the neo-horde are based on positive feelings which keep the nation together; but the negative feelings, which have to be suppressed within the group, turn with increased virulence against "the stranger in our midst", or against the neighbour'. [175] Ireland, 'geographically isolated and not subjected to any further encroachments', still caused havoc in British political life in the nineteenth century—how much more so, then, Europe with two-dozen Irelands! [176]

Redlich never succumbed to such a Hobbesian view of the nationality conflict. He insisted that the nationality problem in Austria was in actuality a problem of the empire and state. [177] In other words, the problem was not the multinational character of the Monarchy in and of itself, but the failure to evolve political institutions that would ensure national equality and civic liberty to all its citizens. The problem also lay in the doctrine of modern nationalism, especially the passionate attachment to national sovereignty. In Austria this had manifested itself in the crownlands and in Hungary, where the nations claiming the territory as their own had exhibited great intolerance towards the other nationalities on the land. The break-up of Austria-Hungary had merely exacerbated the problems—the newly created nation-states were even more fiercely protective of their national sovereignty, thus making the plight of the national minorities within these new states direr than ever before.

Redlich believed that the only way to rid the world of the curse of nations and states in fierce conflict with each other was to weaken or even abolish the hold of the doctrine of sovereignty. Hence he preferred the notion of federation over confederation, both within the Habsburg Monarchy as well as in the future hoped-for United States of Europe. To Redlich, a confederation implied too weak a bond between essentially sovereign states for effective action externally or internally—the impotence of the League of Nations to restrain its own members or to conduct a common policy being a good example.

---

[173] Namier, *England in the Age of the American Revolution*, 2nd edn. (London, 1961), 18.

[174] Namier, *Conflicts*, 136.

[175] Namier, *Vanished Supremacies*, 53.

[176] Namier, *Personalities and Powers*, 107.

[177] Redlich, *Das österreichische Staats- und Reichsproblem*, i. 134.

Redlich viewed nationalism, nationality, and the doctrine of national sovereignty as distinctly modern phenomena. Although he never explicitly arrived at Karl Popper's conclusion that nationalism was something invented by the historians for the purposes of the state, or the contemporary understanding of nationalism as the result of invented tradition and an imagined community, he was markedly ironic about the doctrine of nations and nationalism as self-evident, 'unproblematic', and a 'political force of nature'.[178] His own conscious exit from the Jewish community sensitized him too to the role of agency and subjectivity in determining nationality. He implicitly recognized the constructed quality of nationalism by pointing out anomalies within the various national movements. He noted the incongruity of the Bohemian feudal aristocracy championing Bohemian state rights, when their own ancestors had been the greatest beneficiaries of the destruction of the native Czech aristocrats after the Battle of White Mountain. He viewed the dwelling upon historical injustices like the tragedy of White Mountain as a kind of unhealthy romanticism which diminished the record of the centuries-long peaceful national coexistence within the Habsburg empire since.

Ultimately, Redlich's and Namier's diametrically opposed views on nationality conflict can be traced to different conceptions of rationality in human nature. Although Redlich rejected French-style rationalism, he did not regard human rationality as an illusion. He would have agreed with his one-time ministerial colleague Ignaz Seipel, who wrote: 'One must not shut rational human beings, in spite of their conflicts of interest in the past, into cages to prevent their tearing each other to pieces at the first meeting.'[179] Namier, on the other hand, believed human beings to be irrational, and hence better off segregated.

Nowhere is this differing evaluation of human rationality more apparent than in their conceptions of English history. Whilst both agreed that the organically evolved English Constitution was not 'an ingenious device, the product of creative thought'[180] or 'called into existence by the mere authority of a doctrinaire',[181] they differed in their approaches towards exploring constitutional growth. Redlich explicitly located his constitutional history in the nexus between political ideas and power politics—on the one hand, he was dedicated to tracing the hitherto ignored influence of

[178] Redlich, *Das österreichische Staats- und Reichsproblem*, i. 134.

[179] Ignaz Seipel, *Nation und Staat* (Vienna, 1916), 137.

[180] L. B. Namier, *Crossroads of Power: Essays on Eighteenth-Century England* (London, 1962), 234.

[181] Redlich, *Local Government in England*, i. 3.

liberal, radical, and socialist ideas on the development of the English Constitution and administration;[182] on the other hand, he sought to consider the Constitution as a product of political conflict:

A constitution must be understood as an attempt to fix by a system of rules and legal institutions, the different social, economic, political and spiritual forces that permeate the body of a nation at the given moment of constitutional legislation . . . The actual history of a nation, moreover, is a continual adaptation of this compromise to the more or less continuous change of the conditions under which the life of that nation is developing.[183]

An outstanding example of Redlich's dual interest in power politics and political ideas is his narrative of events leading up to the First Reform Act of 1832. After tracing how the growth of radicalism (with its impetus from the American and French revolutions) and the rise of the middle classes led to increasing pressure to democratize the parliamentary franchise, '[t]he final fate of the Reform bill was decided by the Whigs; for wealth and organisation easily gave them the leadership, when once they were convinced that they could only return to power as reformers. The campaign of 1830–32 was the result of party egoism—that desire of a political party for self-preservation and power which has so often proved the salvation of the country.'[184] Similarly, the 1867 Reform Act was introduced by Disraeli and the Tories, who had learnt 'to be the instrument where it could not be the successful opponent of democracy'.[185] Like Namier, Redlich acknowledged the key role that new wealth played in the changing composition of parliament between the eighteenth and nineteenth centuries,[186] and indeed, did devote a token chapter to the 'The Social Structure of the House of Commons'.[187] Nevertheless, Redlich concentrated almost exclusively on the political and constitutional aspects of history, largely ignoring the economic aspects—he failed to mention municipal trading at all, for instance, in his history of English local government, although it was the most controversial question in local government at the time of writing.[188]

---

[182] Ibid. i. p. xxii.
[183] Redlich, 'Sovereignty, Democracy, and the Rights of Minorities', 377–8.
[184] Redlich, *Local Government in England*, i. 79.
[185] Ibid. 175.
[186] Ibid. 59–60.
[187] Redlich, *The Procedure of the House of Commons*, ii. 115–130.
[188] Bryan Keith-Lucas, 'Introduction', in *The History of Local Government in England: Being a reissue of Book I of Local Government in England by Josef Redlich and Francis W. Hirst*, ed. with introduction and epilogue by Bryan Keith-Lucas (London, 1958), p. xiii.

Namier, on the other hand, decrying the hitherto exclusive concentration on 'kings and statesmen and wars', 'institutions, inventions and "reforms" ', called for a new kind of social history of the British 'political nation', and most particularly the House of Commons.[189] In this kind of history, obscure members of parliament 'in the margin of history' (to use a favourite phrase of Namier's) would feature for the first time, because he was convinced that only the sum total of all the transactions, feelings, and thoughts of individual members of parliament over time could explain the transition from royal to parliamentary government in England. He had read and greatly admired the work of Charles Beard, who famously argued that the American founding fathers were motivated by economic and class interests rather than political philosophical convictions.[190] Like Beard, Namier depreciated political ideas and all reform movements, claiming that 'on a careful inquiry it will be found that the coming in of American wheat has wrought a greater change in the composition of the British House of Commons than the first two Reform Acts'.[191]

Fiercely denying the primacy of ideas to shape events, Namier wanted to rewrite history on a strictly empirical basis, in terms of the acts, thoughts, and feelings of individual human beings transacting with other individual human beings. The sum total of all these realities would be history as it actually happened, in the Rankean sense. Appointed in April 1929 to the Committee on Records of Past Members of the House of Commons, Namier soon clashed with Josiah Wedgwood, the instigator of the whole project. Whereas Namier wanted to examine the House of Commons as a corporate entity, with special attention to the grass-roots and financial interests of individual members, Wedgwood wanted the history to be a pageant of English political striving for democracy and freedom.[192] Scorning the myths of progress and human rationality which, in his view, underlay the Whig interpretation of history, Namier stressed the degree to which tradition and prescription had shaped English political institutions, and how, conversely, 'in the earlier stages the growth of constitutional monarchy was impeded rather than aided by conscious political thought'.[193] Namier consistently ignored sources such as legislature, political memoranda, and political literature (sources favoured by Redlich) on principle in favour of more personal sources such as diaries and letters.

[189] Namier, *Crossroads of Power*, 4.
[190] Colley, *Lewis Namier*, 25.
[191] Namier, *Crossroads of Power*, 3.
[192] J. Namier, *Lewis Namier*, 199–200; MGA: B/N8A/301, Namier to Crozier, 5 Nov. 1942.
[193] Namier, *Crossroads of Power*, 213.

Moreover, Namier was interested not so much in the conscious but the unconscious contents of his sources—for instance, he dismissed the conscious political theory in Horace Walpole's letters and memoirs as 'the current cant of the period about prerogative, oligarchy etc.', but then went on to praise Walpole's 'intuitive, subconsciously formed [political] theory' about the nature of the English parliament in the eighteenth century, such as the true difference between Whigs and Tories.[194] As for Redlich's admired Burke and Bentham, Namier thought both were 'rightly distrusted by sensible, practical politicians', since they 'peddled mere ideas rooted in nothing'.[195]

Although Redlich, like Namier, admired the English respect for tradition and prescription, his interpretation of English history was essentially Whiggish. The English were admirable because they managed to adapt to the spirit of each new age within the framework of the ancient Constitution. Redlich regarded the nineteenth century as the crown of English political history, where rational and highly moral men such as Jeremy Bentham, Edwin Chadwick, and John Stuart Mill managed to radically reshape English institutions to accommodate the needs of a democratic and industrial age. As we have seen in Chapter 1, Redlich's English history was written as a polemic against Rudolf von Gneist, who decried nineteenth-century reforms as alien innovations which threatened traditional English forms of government and liberty. By extension, Redlich was also attacking English romantic constitutionalists such as Joshua Toulmin-Smith, who were fighting against the centralizing policy of Chadwick, and who glorified the Common Law methods of parochial government.[196] In his polemical and democratic zeal, Redlich represented the eighteenth century as corrupt and autocratic, where aristocrats monopolized all local administration to perpetrate a patriarchal tyranny, neither subject to any central control, since the parliament was elected from the same narrow franchise as the local administrators, nor accountable to the mass of inhabitants living under their rule. This corrupt, inefficient, and wasteful one-class oligarchic rule was unable to fulfil the most elementary tasks of local government such as effective policing, provision of streetlights, or hygiene, but resisted any reform in the name of the sanctity of the Constitution and of local autonomy.[197]

---

[194] Farmington Library, Yale University: Lewis Namier to Wilmarth S. Lewis, 30 Dec. 1954.
[195] Isaiah Berlin, 'Lewis Namier: A Personal Impression', 219.
[196] Redlich, *Local Government in England*, i. 145.
[197] Ibid. *passim.*

Namier, on the other hand, was much closer in spirit to romantic constitutionalists like Toulmin-Smith. Although he shared the common view that nineteenth-century parliaments were much 'superior in moral tone'[198] to their eighteenth-century counterparts—indeed, he described the eighteenth century as a 'naively corrupt but very amusing age'[199]—and recognized that eighteenth-century modes of government were woefully inadequate for ruling an empire, he took up arms in defence of 'one of the most gifted, active, inventive generations in British history'. He sought to dismantle that 'unduly derogatory legend' which had grown up around the eighteenth century,[200] put forth by zealous nineteenth-century parliamentary reformers who had 'set out to expose the absurdities of the system and its corruption' whilst neglecting to show 'how practice softened and modified them'.[201]

Namier denounced the tendency to judge eighteenth-century political practices by contemporary moral standards. He defended eighteenth-century corruption by pointing out that corruption was not, in fact, as prevalent as it was made out to be—the notorious secret service accounts under the Duke of Newcastle were not used to buy votes in parliament but for charitable pensions to support aristocratic paupers.[202] Moreover, Namier claimed that corruption in the eighteenth century could be seen as a mark of English freedom and independence, 'for no one bribes where he can bully'.[203] Like Burke, Namier believed that the rotten boroughs served an essential and beneficial structural purpose which had not been successfully replaced by modern party organizations: 'The rotten boroughs of Government opened the gates of the House to budding statesmen and to hard-working civil servants, admirals and pro-consuls, law officers of the Crown—in short, to the men who had the widest and most varied experience of administrative work.'[204] Through the rotten boroughs the *nouveau riche* of each generation entered parliament, thereby preventing the English aristocracy from becoming an exclusive caste. 'The principle established in France by the Great Revolution—"a fair field to ability"—was realized, *without reasoning*, in the eighteenth-century British Parliament.'[205] (my italics).

---

[198] Namier, *The Structure of Politics*, 7.
[199] Ibid. 7.
[200] Namier, *Crossroads of Power*, 24.
[201] Namier, *The Structure of Politics*, 75.
[202] Ibid., ch. 4.
[203] Namier, *England in the Age of the American Revolution*, 4.
[204] Ibid. 4–5.
[205] Namier, *The Structure of Politics*, 11.

Still, Namier was prevented from idealizing the English eighteenth century by the magnitude of its political failure to retain the American colonies. He thought the loss of America the greatest tragedy for the English-speaking communities on both sides of the Atlantic. In America, the admixture of 'French ideas, adaptable in their rootless superficiality', was by no means conducive to the development of American democracy.[206] (Redlich too believed that American, and indeed continental European, reliance on Montesquieu's misinterpretation of the English Constitution and the subsequent enshrinement of the separation of powers was a grave mistake.)[207]

As we have seen, Namier was first drawn to the study of English history by the mystery of the 'phoenix empire' (the failure of the first British empire in the eighteenth, and the resurrection of the second in the nineteenth century), and had set out to study the different plans for imperial federation on the eve of the American Revolution.

However, he discovered that 'the constitutional and political formulas of the problem were exceedingly simple, and the contemporary discussions of it very trite—which usually happens where masses act but are supposed to reason'.[208] 'In 1774, after ten years of discussions of the colonial problem, on the eve of events unsurpassed in greatness by anything since the break-up of the Roman dominions into a Western and an Eastern Empire, not a single election in Great Britain was turned, or even influenced to any marked extent, by the American issue.'[209] Even in parliament, arguments about the American problem had been very pedestrian. This led Namier to conclude that '[t]he basic elements of the Imperial Problem during the American Revolution must be sought not so much in conscious opinions and professed views bearing directly on it, as in the very structure and life of the Empire'.[210] The basic problem underlying the conflict between England and the colonies was, in Namier's Freudian-influenced view, the question of freedom from paternal authority, for 'all authority is to human beings paternal in character'.[211]

The development of every man, in his individual life, obviously proceeds from subjection to freedom, and it proves arrested growth if full freedom is never reached, and if inwardly he carries on the revolutionary (or counter-revolutionary) struggle long after he himself should have attained uncontending authority. For in

[206] Namier, *England in the Age of the American Revolution*, 39.
[207] Redlich, *Local Government in England*, i. 40, 72
[208] Namier, *The Structure of Politics*, p. ix.
[209] Namier, *Skyscrapers*, 36.
[210] Namier, *England in the Age of the American Revolution*, 40.
[211] Ibid. 27.

the life of every man comes a night when at the ford of the stream he has to strive 'with God and with men'; if he prevails and receives the blessing of the father-spirit, he is henceforth free and at peace. . . . Above individual men rises the community, the State. There the struggle is repeated, on an infinitely wider stage, in terms similar to those of man's individual life, and yet in dimensions which are beyond the understanding of the average man . . .[212]

By the mid-eighteenth-century the Americans wished for a more equal relationship to England, whereas British politicians persisted in regarding the American colonies as dependent 'offspring' which should be used to advance trade and profit the Mother Country. Hence, the Americans began increasingly to resent British parliamentary sovereignty over the colonies. Namier was at pains to emphasize that what was at issue was not royal claims, but the claims of 'subjects in one part of the King's dominions to be sovereigns over their fellow-subjects in another part of his dominions'. 'The sovereignty of the Crown I understand', wrote Benjamin Franklin; 'the sovereignty of Britain I do not understand . . . We have the same King, but not the same legislature.'[213] In other words, Franklin had already anticipated the eventual solution of Dominion status for former white colonies in the second British empire. In this arrangement, although the different constituent parts of the British empire enjoyed 'direct governmental power which in a free country is wielded by the sons of the soil', they still acknowledged the 'distant, sublimated authority of the Crown, symbolically "paternal" '.[214] 'The fact that the "paternal" authority of the State centres in the Crown, whose bearer does not, and must not, in any way personally exercise it, establishes a psychological equality between the actual rulers of the State and those governed by them . . . it secures both the idea of authority and the unity of the nation.'[215]

The tragedy of America was that it never received the 'blessing of the father-spirit' on the threshold to freedom, but seized freedom in a revolutionary struggle which resulted in the Americans being 'disinherited' from the English past, their common Anglo-Saxon heritage. 'In the unconscious depths, the bitterness which is still alive in Americans of pure Anglo-Saxon lineage over the Revolution does not refer to the incidents of 1774, nor even to the calamities of war, but to the lasting exclusion of Americans from the common English inheritance.'[216]

---

[212] Namier, *England in the Age of the American Revolution*, 28.
[213] Benjamin Franklin to the Revd Samuel Cooper of Boston, 8 June 1770, quoted by Namier, *Crossroads of Power*, 128.
[214] Namier, *England in the Age of the American Revolution*, 25–26.
[215] Ibid. 28.   [216] Namier, *Skyscrapers*, 32.

The loss of the American colonies was a real tragedy, the more so because no blame can be attached to either side. During the eighteenth century Dominion status was not possible because of the very structure of English politics at the time. A remodelling of the empire as a federation of self-governing states under a Crown detached from the actual government of any part only became possible when the king ceased to be a real factor in power politics.

In the absence of parties in the modern sense, however, the king inevitably had to broker the transfer of power between successive sets of ministers. Namier took great pains to establish that, contrary to received wisdom, George III was not a tyrant according to the standards of the time.[217] The right of the Crown to choose ministers was acknowledged by both Whigs and Tories, although ministers needed the support of a parliamentary majority. By trying to influence the outcome of parliamentary elections to ensure support for his own chosen ministers, George III 'merely acted the . . . first among the borough-mongering, electioneering gentlemen of England. While the Stuarts tried to browbeat the House and circumscribe the range of its action, George III fully accepted its constitution and recognised its powers, and merely tried to work it in accordance with the customs of the time.'[218]

In a throwback to his youthful reverence for the English puritans, Namier claimed that the only significant group who held the 'modern British view of the Empire' in the eighteenth century were the English Dissenters; 'to them alone, who knew no hierarchy either in religion or politics, the Colonists were so many "congregations of brethren beyond the seas".'[219] 'In the spirit of the Dissenters alone could a solution of the Imperial problem have been found in 1770.'[220] Ultimately, however, Namier thought it beneficial that the English Dissenters had not managed to gain the upper hand in the eighteenth century:

After the spiritual and political upheavals of the preceding age, this was the time of England's inner consolidation, when common sense and ready toleration—in other words, insistence on a conformity of a singularly unexacting type—effected a reconciliation in this country such as France was never to reach after her great Revolution. To some, non-jurors or 'tender consciences' on the Dissenting side may be more attractive, and they probably were intellectually more consistent, than

---

[217] Linda Colley has accused Namier of consistently using evidence selectively to portray George III in the most favourable light possible. See Colley, *Lewis Namier*, 62–3.
[218] Namier, *England in the Age of the American Revolution*, 4.
[219] Ibid. 39.
[220] Ibid.

the ecclesiastic statesmen of the Hanoverian period; but they might easily have plunged England into further civil wars, while the Church, such as it was, helped to heal the divisions and to reunify the nation.[221]

Living in an age torn by ideological strife, Namier found comfort in studying a century where ideology scarcely featured at all. Eighteenth-century England, coming in time between the sectarian passions of the English Civil War and the rise of liberalism in the nineteenth century, suited Namier's anti-ideological cast of mind. 'Men went there [to parliament] to "make a figure", and no more dreamt of a seat in the House in order to benefit humanity than a child dreams of a birthday cake that others may eat it; which is perfectly normal and in no way reprehensible.'[222] In fact, common sense and enlightened self-interest, which were such prominent traits amongst the English landed patrician elite, were the best motive forces of history.

Yet there is a paradox at the heart of Namier's work on eighteenth-century English history. He showed compellingly how this same landed patrician elite lost the first British empire by being too absorbed in their own interests. Moreover, his own portraits of key figures of the period—the Duke of Newcastle, Charles Townshend, George III—belie his picture of the pragmatic English politician acting out of enlightened self-interest. The Duke of Newcastle, whose 'nature and mind were warped, twisted, and stunted',[223] suffered from 'unconscious self-mortification'.[224] George III, of course, went insane in the end. Namier's last attempt at answering the question of why Britain lost America took the form of a psychoanalytical biography of Charles Townshend, the author of the Townshend Acts which brought tension between Britain and the American colonies to a boiling point. In this unfinished biography, Namier traced Townshend's behaviour to his childhood—having suffered from the oppression of an overbearing father, Charles in turn acted the overbearing father to American colonists.[225] Linda Colley, deploring the lack of any discussion concerning the legislative or financial background to the Townshend Acts or their impact on the colonies, remarked: 'Indeed we are left with the impression that perhaps the American Revolution broke out because Britain in the 1760s was governed by an oligarchy of neurotics. There may of course be some truth in this, but surely not the whole truth?'[226]

[221] Namier, *Crossroads of Power*, 184.   [222] Namier, *The Structure of Politics*, 2.
[223] Namier, *England in the Age of the American Revolution*, 68.
[224] Ibid. 83.
[225] L. B. Namier and John Brooke, *Charles Townshend* (London, 1964).
[226] Colley, *Lewis Namier*, 33.

In privileging non-rational unconscious factors in historical agency, Namier was heeding Pareto's advice that the new history and social science should concentrate on the 'residues'—that which was unchanging, or which changed very slowly, in human conduct, rather than the 'derivations'—the constantly varying explanations and rationalizations of irrational behaviour, which had previously been the object of historical study.[227] Namier became associated with the devaluation of ideas to such an extent that A. J. P. Taylor famously charged him with 'taking the mind out of history'.[228]

Namier's student John Brooke argued that he was in fact 'among the first to take into history the post-Freudian conception of the mind'.[229] There is much truth in this statement. Namier came to believe that psychology bore the same relation to the humanities as did mathematics to the sciences.[230] Like Dilthey, who had hoped that psychology could be established as the foundation of all the human sciences, Namier thought that *Ideengeschichte* (the history of ideas) should be replaced by *Geistesgeschichte* (the history of the mind).[231] Namier would send samples of his subjects' handwriting to a graphologist, one Dr Mannheim for psychological analysis, frequently incorporating the graphologist's analysis into his history.[232]

Namier's interest in psychology was not confined to the psychology of the individual, but to mass psychology as well. In fact, he declared that mass psychology was the 'most basic factor in history'.[233] An understanding of 'the differences between the forms of communal life which nations have developed, and the variations in the degree of freedom or of moral sense which these forms present, preserve, or attain' was of the utmost importance in the study of history. The characteristic patterns of England are 'Parliament and the team', of Germany 'the State and the army'.[234] Just as childhood patterns in the Freudian view determine the way an individual reacts throughout life, so national patterns, once crystallized, are almost impossible to change. 'There are situations inherent in the structure of Europe, and enduring tendencies in the character of nations',[235] wrote Namier.

[227] H. Stuart Hughes, *Consciousness and Society*, 257.
[228] Namier, *Personalities and Powers*, 5.
[229] Brooke, 'Namier and Namierism', 339.
[230] Ibid., 338; Namier, *Avenues of History*, 9.
[231] Hajo Holborn, 'Wilhelm Dilthey and the Critique of Historical Reason', in W. Warren Wagar (ed.), *European Intellectual History Since Darwin and Marx* (New York, 1967), 85.
[232] Namier, *Personalities and Power*, p.vii.   [233] Ibid. 4.
[234] Namier, *Conflicts*, 78–9.
[235] Ibid. 53.

Namier's psychological determinism was the culmination of a lifelong predisposition towards determinism in history. His tendency towards economic determinism has been amply illustrated in my account of his political activities during World War I. From a geopolitical determinist point of view, Namier thought that the destiny of nations was written on the globe. 'The English Channel and vast Eurasian spaces have placed Britain and Russia beyond the reach of Europe and enabled them to check and destroy its would-be world conquerors.' Spain, France, and Italy all had geographical frameworks that were distinct and permanent, whereas the centrifugal configuration of Germany favoured expansion but impeded unity.[236]

This led Namier to the conclusion that 'whatever theories of "free will" theologians and philosophers may develop with regard to the individual there is no free will in the thinking and actions of masses, any more than in the revolutions of planets, in the migrations of birds, and in the plunging of hordes of lemmings into the sea'.[237] Of course, in the actual writing of history, and in his personal life, Namier found it harder to be a doctrinaire determinist.[238] Thus, for instance, he maintained that World War II was 'the unnecessary war',[239] since it would never have happened had the Poles accepted the Curzon line proposed by Hamish Paton and himself as Poland's eastern border,[240] had the West tried to engage with the Soviet Union,[241] and had the western powers intervened earlier against Hitler.[242]

In this respect, Redlich was the polar opposite of Namier. Redlich held free will to be real although limited by social and economic forces, by geography, and by mass psychological passions. Defending the view that 'history is made by men', Redlich maintained that '[e]ven in a period preoccupied as is our own with research into the development and function of ideas and of institutions, economic, social and political, history cannot omit personality, since it is the instrument through which the will of a nation or

[236] Namier, *Facing East*, 83.
[237] Namier, *England in the Age of the American Revolution*, 40–1.
[238] John C. Cairns, 'Sir Lewis Namier and the History of Europe', *Historical Reflections*, 1: 1 (June 1974), 7; Berlin, 'Lewis Namier', 230.
[239] Namier, *Europe in Decay*, 150–70.
[240] MGA, B/N8A/305, Namier to Crozier, 18 Jan. 1944: 'I am deeply convinced that but for the Riga Line we could have avoided this war, because Russia could have been got into a system of nations united against German aggression. It was Poland's uneasy conscience over these Eastern provinces and Beck's super-clever finessing, joined to Chamberlain's and Halifax's fundamental dislike of Russia, which enabled Hitler and Ribbentrop to pull off their coup with Russia in August 1939.'
[241] Namier, 'The Russian Revolution: 1917–1942'.
[242] Namier, *Europe in Decay*, 150–70.

a state has to be exercised'.[243] The presence of might-have-beens in Redlich's history and their corresponding absence in Namier's is the greatest difference between their works.

Thus, Namier insisted that one could not sensibly speak of another route that Germany might have taken. During World War I, he traced the roots of the German–Slav conflict and German–Magyar co-operation to the medieval past. Redlich, on the other hand, rejected such arguments about the Germans being 'an enigma of evil'.[244] He attributed the difference in continental versus British political development to the revival of Roman Law during the Renaissance, which led to the repression of democratic elements on the European continent, [245] 'whereas in England . . . the fundamentally Germanic ideas of law and polity, of local self-government and of individual liberty, emphasized by specific spiritual forces flowing from Calvinism, prevailed'.[246] Redlich would also have rejected as nonsense Namier's argument that the 1848 liberals foreshadowed Wilhelm II and Hitler. He wrote: 'I have known the old generation that revered the liberal era of Germany in the nineteenth century, and I have seen my own contemporaries in universities growing fully into the neo-German spirit of high-handed, self-righteous monarchical rule by bureaucratic cabinets. *It was not necessary that this neo-German spirit ended in its Wilhelmian form and essence, but that it ended so is a fact'* (my italics).[247]

To Redlich, 'national character' was a reality but one formed by concrete historical events, not an immutable inheritance encoded in cultural genes. He attributed the political character of the Austrian people—a double distrust of the 'State' as the epitome of organized power, as well as of any ability to affect things in a politically creative manner—to the disastrous decade of the Bach system.[248] It was this political character which Redlich had sought in vain to change during his time as an active politician.

---

[243] Redlich, *Emperor Francis Joseph of Austria*, p. viii.

[244] Namier, *Facing East*, 26.

[245] Redlich, 'Sovereignty, Democracy, and the Rights of Minorities', 378.

[246] Ibid. 379. See too Redlich, *The Common Law and the Case Method*, 35–42, for a discussion of the differences between the Common Law and continental law as influenced by Roman Law. See esp. p. 36: 'To the German and the Frenchman of our time, therefore, the law appears always in popular thought as the abstract rule, as the general principles, to which all individual relationships of the citizens are *a priori* and for its own sake subordinated. To the Englishman and the American, on the other hand, the law appears rather as the single case of law, as the single subjective suit, conducted by the regular judge, and depending only upon his "finding of the law".'

[247] *The Decline of Parliamentary Government, Discussed by Harold J. Laski and Dr Josef Redlich*, 18.

[248] Redlich, *Das österreichische Staats- und Reichsproblem*, i. 455.

By the time Redlich and Namier wrote the bulk of their European history, their lives as active politicians were over. Still, as *engagé* intellectuals they found it impossible to examine the past without drawing conclusions for the present and the future. Moreover, the very attempt to use the past to illuminate the present inevitably confronted them with the question of the uses of history. They were both agreed on the superiority of historical thinking over the methodology of logical deduction or of natural science in the understanding of human affairs and institutions. '[T]he past is on top of us and with us all the time; and there is only one way of mastering it even remotely in any one sector: by knowing how these things have come to be, which helps to understand their nature, character, and their correlation, or lack of correlation, to the present realities of life',[249] wrote Namier; while Redlich stated simply: 'We have learned to think of the State and its institutions as a growth.'[250]

They were also very aware of the dangers of bad history—the misunderstanding of the past and the drawing of spurious historical analogies to the present or the future, so that 'by a double process of repetition, they imagine the past and remember the future'.[251] Redlich's denunciation of the effect of Gneist's misreading of English political history on an entire generation of jurists and politicians in Germany and Austria is a case in point.

Both were aware of the tension between history as something unique and unrepeatable and the need to generalize from history. 'The subject matter of history is . . . concrete events fixed in time and space, and their grounding in the thoughts and feelings of men—not things universal and generalized.'[252] However, 'in all intelligent historical quest there is, underneath, a discreet, tentative search for the typical and recurrent in the psyche and actions of man (even in his unreason), and a search for a morphology of human affairs'.[253]

Was this 'search for a morphology of human affairs' through a study of history justified? '[A]ll attempts to derive a universal principle from a description of the development of one State are attempts beyond the range and the power of scientific inquiry', wrote Redlich. However, 'a historical analysis and comparison of individual States' could yield 'a better and more actual conception of what a State is and of the laws and institutions which

---

[249] Namier, *Avenues of History*, 2.
[250] Redlich, *Local Government in England*, i. 1.
[251] Namier, *Conflicts*, 69–70.
[252] Namier, *Avenues of History*, 1.
[253] Ibid. 1.

compose it'.[254] Hence, Redlich's purpose in writing history had always been one of direct application—so it was with his English parliamentary and local administrative history, from which he drew conclusions immediately applicable to the Austrian parliament and administration; so it was with his *Staats- und Reichsproblem*. Redlich started on his magnum opus during World War I, hoping that the insights gained into the Austrian state problem could help in the federal reconstruction of the empire.

Namier, less optimistic, believed that the best that could result from the study of history, in fact, 'the crowning attainment of historical study'—was 'an intuitive understanding of how things do not happen'.[255] The value to be derived from the study of history is not factual content, but a historical sense and a historical way of thinking. 'One of the aims of sound historical education must be to wean men from expecting automatic repetition and from juggling with uncorrelated precedents and analogies; they must be trained to fit things into long-range historical processes, and not to think in isolated word-concepts working in a void'.[256] His approach to the study of history was a valiant attempt to rewrite history on the sound empirical basis of individual human beings interacting with each other. Arguably he was defeated by the sheer scope of his task. Toynbee memorably described Namier's prosopographical parliamentary project as a quixotic attempt to assault infinity with his bare fists.[257] Namier never lived to see the study of parliamentary members finished, and hence never managed to synthesize answers out of his mass of data as to why England lost America, and how parliamentary evolved out of royal government. 'I have chosen for my subject [constitutional monarchy] a story with a happy ending, with a striking denouement, unforeseen and unpredictable while it was shaping',[258] announced Namier at the beginning of a lecture entitled 'Monarchy and the Party System', only to admit at the end that he could not really explain why royal had given way to parliamentary government, since the necessary prosopographical work had not yet been done. 'Its [parliamentary government's] bases are deep down in the political structure of the nation, which was being gradually transformed during the period of so-called mixed government. An electorate thinking in terms of nation-wide parties is its indispensable basis; and it is therefore at least as much in the constituencies as in parliament that the growth of these parties will have to be traced.'[259]

---

[254] Redlich, *Local Government in England*, ii. 378.
[256] Ibid. 7.
[258] Namier, *Personalities and Powers*, 13.
[259] Ibid. 37.

[255] Namier, *Avenues of History*, 4.
[257] Toynbee, *Acquaintances*, 85

Lastly, Namier saw in history a psychoanalytical function. 'A neurotic, according to Freud, is a man dominated by unconscious memories, fixated on the past, and incapable of overcoming it: the regular condition of human communities.' However, history, like psychoanalysis, is 'better able to diagnose than to cure: the beneficial therapeutic effects of history have so far been small; and it is in the nature of things that it should be so.'[260] In the last analysis, then, Namier depreciated the value of history, and depreciated the value of his own work. With great insight and perspicacity he had analysed the causes and nature of the nationality conflict and had concluded—that nothing could be done about it. Human beings and human communities were destined to a Hobbesian struggle, despite their best efforts to escape the human condition:

At times, when the burden of the past becomes unbearable, men stand forth determined to brush 'the clouds away of precedent and custom', and to live by 'the great beacon light God set in all'; the Puritans called it conscience, the French of 1789 called it reason. But even conscience and reason move in the grooves of inherited, historically conditioned ideas and words; and when man has wiped the slate clean and tries to write his own message, the past which lives in him and has moulded him will bring back the very things he has tried to obliterate.[261]

In Namier's eyes, the only successful attempts to mitigate the destructive effects of conflict between individuals, classes, and nations had been the British parliament and the British empire. To Namier, the British parliament was 'a brilliant expression of mankind's urge to suspend aggression by debate, and a source for sketches illustrative of efforts to find acceptable solutions to tangled affairs—private and public—by means of words, not the fist'.[262] Such a sustained effort to find alternatives to violence, however, depended upon self-discipline, 'which, in the last resort, is the one power adequate to hold in check the cruelty inherent in every member of the human race'.[263] In the 1950s, Namier thought he could detect signs everywhere that self-discipline was breaking down among the young, and that officialdom condoned its collapse. He had originally conceived of his massive History of Parliament project as 'a living translucent skyscraper in which to cherish the roots of contemporary parliamentary history'. Later he thought he was building an era's mausoleum.[264]

Similarly, the British empire had been the one great civilizing and peaceful force in the world, and the British Commonwealth a symbol of

[260] Namier, *Avenues of History*, 5.　　[261] Ibid. 3.
[262] J. Namier, *Lewis Namier*, 187.　　[263] Ibid. 300–1.
[264] Ibid. 321.

worldwide freedom and worldwide co-operation.[265] Its disintegration was to Namier the ultimate confirmation of the futility of multinational empires, no matter how benevolent and beneficial to their constituent nations. Namier had always praised British territorial nationalism for being based not upon language or race, but upon territory—hence, the Celtic Scots and Welsh were considered British, and the Americans descended from English stock were not. In his heart, however, he was an English nationalist, who believed that English liberties were the unique fruit of English blood and soil[266]—he blamed the Scottish officers in the American colonies for lacking an English 'spirit of sympathetic toleration and restraint' towards the colonists. 'At home the rights and interests of the Colonies were hardly ever championed by a Scotsman or Irish-Scot . . . In office they were authoritarians, and showed little understanding for the constitutional refinements and the "sound doctrine of Mr. Locke", which were of English, and not of Scottish origin.'[267] If even the non-English Britons could not truly appreciate English liberty, how then could British parliamentary institutions ever be exported to Europe?[268] Hence, Namier argued that '[a]ll the past and all the present assign to this country a place in the community of *English-speaking* nations' (my italics).[269] The success of the British empire lay in part to its common '*racial* and ideological'[270] origin (my italics). In multinational Europe, however, such a free union would be impossible: 'Neither for good nor for evil has Europe ever been able to form a free union: not even against the conquering Turk, when religion and the common tradition seemed almost to demand it. European co-operation can sometimes be achieved through a concert of the Great Powers exercising a temperate measure of control. But integral European union would require coercion.'[271]

[265] Namier, *In the Margin of History*, 56.

[266] Gerald Newman, *The Rise of English Nationalism* (London, 1987).

[267] Namier, *England in the Age of the American Revolution*, 265. Contrast with the following statement by Redlich: 'I never forget Scotland. With a good many Scotchmen sitting in Westminster I don't believe much nonsense will be made . . . Prime Minister Ramsay MacDonald fortunately is a Scotchman and there are several leading Scotchmen in the Labor party. You certainly understand why I am an optimist for the future of British parliamentary government and its traditions!' *The Decline of Parliamentary Government, Discussed by Harold J. Laski and Dr. Josef Redlich*, 16.

[268] See Buruma, *Voltaire's Coconuts or Anglomania in Europe*, 36–7, 49, 160, 205, for the difference between Enlightenment Anglophilia like Voltaire's, which assumed that British-style political liberty could take root elsewhere given the right institutional arrangements, and a more Herderian appreciation of English liberty as a result of 'national character', organic and unique.

[269] NP: Creighton Lectures, 1/1b/1, p. 17.

[270] Namier, *England in the Age of the American Revolution*, 29.

[271] Namier, *Facing East*, 100.

As we have seen throughout, Redlich too was no optimist with regard to the possibility of a complete renewal of humanity in the way that socialists and idealistic liberals demanded.[272] Indeed, he thought there was an unchanging core of evil in human beings.[273] Nevertheless, having perceived far more clearly than Namier the implications of modern warfare technology, Redlich believed that such a federation must be *made* possible, since the alternative was 'the physical and moral suicide of nations'.[274] 'Unless human beings find another way to live with each other in the future, humankind will become extinct',[275] he wrote. One was not absolved from the responsibility of trying, no matter how small the probability of success. As Felix Frankfurter wrote:

He [Redlich] was a child of the Enlightenment . . . his abiding allegiance was to Reason . . . He was content neither to find nor to leave the world a chaos, nor even a crazy-quilt. The refusal of society to conform to the doctrinaire simplifications of dreamers or fanatics, did not lead him to abandon the search for the meaning of experience nor exchange the wisdom of the wisest for the humourless absolutism of the moment, however triumphant.[276]

There is a great emotional and intellectual unity between the politician and the historian in both Redlich and Namier. Redlich's approach to politics and to history was incremental and constructive because he was fighting for something he wished to preserve and to improve. Namier's approach was destructive. 'Easeful pleasure is suited for men who safely possess; destruction is the instinct, the living art and the wild joy of the dispossessed—the dark, cynical, defiant face of Michael Angelo's statue of Brutus menaces the exquisite and aristocratic beauty of Leonardo da Vinci.'[277] Both felt themselves many times to be Cassandras in a mad world. Redlich, however, always proceeded as if *this time* Cassandra might be heeded, whereas Namier tended increasingly towards the role of Jonah, perversely looking forward to the destruction of a degenerate world. As a determinist, Namier insisted several times that one could not judge history. 'Those who are out to apportion guilt in history have to keep to views and

---

[272] Redlich, *Schicksalsjahre Österreichs*, 18 Mar. 1919, II, 337.

[273] Ibid., 5 Feb. 1917, II, 189.

[274] Redlich, 'Heinrich Lammasch', in *World Unity: Non-Partisan Discussion of International Movements*, 273.

[275] Redlich, *Schicksalsjahre Österreichs*, 5 Feb. 1917, II, 189. See Rudolf Schlesinger, *Federalism in Central and Eastern Europe*, 244–5, who argued that the western powers could not have created a federation against the will of the small states.

[276] Frankfurter, 'Josef Redlich—Obituary', 389.

[277] 'N', 'Trotski', 10.

opinions, judge the collisions of planets by the rules of the street traffic, make history into something like a column of motoring accidents, and discuss it in the atmosphere of a police court.'[278] Yet few historians have judged history more harshly than Namier.

[278] Namier, *England in the Age of the American Revolution*, 40.

Conclusion

Redlich was born in 1869, Namier in 1888. Yet in a very important sense their stories began in 1848, since their lives were so intertwined with the demands for individual freedom and national liberation from dynastic absolutism which first took centre-stage politically in the Habsburg lands in that year. These demands reached an apogee during World War I, and resulted in the dismantling of the multinational Habsburg Monarchy and the establishment of democratic nation-states, which gave way in turn to nationalist dictatorships and totalitarian governments. Contrary to the dominant intellectual trends of their times, Redlich and Namier argued that nationalism was inimical to political liberty, and that the sovereignty of the people could lead to even worse tyrannies than that of absolute monarchy. They were anti-nationalist historians in an age of nationalism, and staunch defenders of parliamentary democracy in an era when parliamentary democracy came under attack from both the political right and left.

Redlich and Namier regarded Great Britain as the paragon of political liberty and her parliament as the Mother of Parliaments. Philosophically, they identified with the British empiricist as opposed to the French rationalist or the German metaphysical traditions. They greatly preferred the civic, territorial definition of nationality in Great Britain to the linguistic, racial, and cultural nationalisms on the European continent. Their historical research encompassed British parliamentary as well as European history. But while British thinkers themselves, with the notable exception of Lord Acton (himself with strong Central European ties), did not tackle the problem of integral nationalism, Redlich and Namier grappled with the questions of how far British parliamentary government could be adopted in a multinational framework and whether civic allegiance to a multinational state could grow out of active participation by all nationalities in the political life of the state.

Redlich's and Namier's advocacy of British civic nationalism over continental linguistic nationalism as a model for state patriotism in a multinational state was not unique. From Eötvös in the mid-nineteenth century to Popper, Jaszi, and Hayek closer to our times, an important minority of Habsburg intellectuals regarded the Anglo-American political tradition as a positive alternative to the authoritarian politics and raging nationalisms of continental European history. Moreover, they also belong to a larger

European Anglophile tradition which had sought an answer to the very same question which preoccupied Redlich and Namier—why, despite the introduction of the forms of parliamentary government in most of nineteenth-century Europe, did the kind of political liberty enjoyed by the British fail to take firm root in continental Europe?

Both Redlich and Namier singled out German nationalism as the force most inimical to political liberty in Central and Eastern Europe, since it was inextricably intertwined with a philosophy which deified the state and nation above all other moral claims. Redlich launched a systematic attack on German jurisprudence, constitutional theory, and theory of the state as well as on their metaphysical underpinnings, whereas Namier's attack centred on the collective psychology of the Germans—their extreme submissiveness to authority, exaltation of power, the utter subordination of the individual to the needs of the collective, and the high degree of organization and efficiency which they attained in the resultant Leviathan state. Redlich and Namier were both pioneers of the German *Sonderweg* theory—the theory that Nazism was the product of political, cultural, and societal trends in German history and not a historical aberration.

In comparing Redlich's and Namier's ideas, I have taken to heart one of Namier's favourite aphorisms, that ideas are not like Pallas Athene, springing full—born from the head of Zeus, but have their roots in the perplexities and desires of individuals rooted in specific milieus. Redlich and Namier were not only historians but participants in and, in some respects, victims of the collisions and collusions between nationalism and supranationalism, nation-states and multinational empires, liberalism and autocracy, democracy and demagogy. As Jews, they were members of the group which felt the loss of the protective aegis of the multinational Habsburg empire most keenly, and which suffered the most from integral nationalism, especially German nationalism.

It has become almost a truism of Habsburg historiography to say that Jews were the most loyal and committed of Habsburg subjects[1] and later became the most ardent internationalists.[2] Some historians have advanced the essentialist argument that Judaism has a fundamental affinity with

---

[1] Magris, *Der Habsburgische Mythos in der österreichischen Literatur*, 244, 267.

[2] David Rechter, 'Kaisertreu: The Dynastic Loyalty of Austrian Jewry', in Klaus Hödl (ed.), *Jüdische Identitäten: Einblicke in die Bewusstseinslandschaft des österreichischen Judentums* (Innsbruck, 2000), 189–208; Wistrich, *The Jews of Vienna in the Age of Franz Joseph*, 272–3, 665; Rozenblit, 'The Jews of the Dual Monarchy', *AHY* 23 (1992), 160–80; Werner J. Cahnmann, 'Adolf Fischhof and his Jewish Followers', *Leo Baeck Institute Year Book*, 4 (1959), 111–39; Jászi, *The Dissolution of the Habsburg Monarchy*, 170.

liberal humanitarian and Enlightenment traditions, and that this heritage survived even amongst the most assimilated Jews.[3] Others have argued along structural lines, pointing out that the Jews, being a dispersed minority, naturally hoped for the preservation or resurrection of the multinational empire out of enlightened self-interest.

The cases of Redlich and Namier show the dangers of both approaches. While Redlich was a cosmopolitan liberal, Namier was temperamentally intolerant, tended towards extremism, and held the liberal humanist tradition in contempt—a living rebuttal of the essentialist argument. Moreover, by presenting Redlich's and Namier's ideas as a growth, we can see the presentist assumptions of the structural argument. Although it is obvious now, with the benefit of hindsight, that Jews were far better off in a multinational empire than in a nation-state, it was not as obvious at the time to Redlich and Namier. The difference in Redlich's and Namier's initial responses to the nationality problem point to a wider diversity of responses amongst Habsburg Jews than the later, favourable Jewish historiography on the Monarchy may indicate.[4] The later convergence of views on the part of two such temperamentally different individuals is testimony to the terrible pressures on Central and Eastern European Jews in the inter-war years— the anti-Semitic threat both to their physical and moral existence, the destruction of the dream of partaking in the mainstream of European (and especially German) society which had been the hope of so many assimilated Jews.

In their reactions to these threats and dilemmas, however, Redlich and Namier were separated by the generational chasm known in intellectual history as the 'revolt against positivism'. Despite his rejection of the abstract rationalism and more doctrinaire theories of the Enlightenment and his disillusion with the idea of progress, Redlich identified with such core Enlightenment beliefs as human rationality, the educability of human beings, and a common humanity and common ethical code transcending cultures and nations. He had chosen the path of assimilation and amalgamation into German society, and had initially underestimated anti-Semitism as a mere demagogical tool to rouse the uneducated masses.

---

[3] See Beller, *Vienna and the Jews*, ch. 9, for Beller's own arguments bolstered by citations of contemporary Jewish apologists who explicitly asserted this link between Jewishness and the Enlightenment.

[4] For the alternative view that Jewish dynastic loyalty was a post-imperial rather than imperial phenomenon, see Steven Beller, 'The World of Yesterday Revisited: Nostalgia, Memory and the Jews of *Fin-de-Siècle* Vienna', *Jewish Social Studies*, 2 (1996), 37–53, and id., 'Patriotism and the National Identity of Habsburg Jewry, 1860–1914', *Leo Baeck Institute Year Book*, 41 (1996), 215–38.

Namier, on the other hand, denigrated human rationality and rejected liberal humanism and universalist idealism. To him, the destructive impulse was one of the basic drives in the human psyche, and communities were forever doomed to conflict. His Zionism was an unstable compound of populist romanticism, blood-and-soil nationalism, and *realpolitisch* considerations of collective defence against the violence of other nationalisms. Both approaches to the Jewish question ultimately proved inadequate. The rise of Nazism forced Redlich to reassess his (already problematic) identification with Germandom as well as the viability of assimilation, whilst the anti-British genesis and the 'Asiatic' complexion of the new Jewish state alienated Namier from the resurrected Israel.

Their diverging views on the Enlightenment heritage and liberalism had important implications as well for their political views. Redlich believed that the dangers of democracy and populist passions could be mitigated by the political education of the masses; Namier believed freedom to be possible only within an oligarchic (and preferably aristocratic) society. Redlich thought that the British political system and British constitutional development held important lessons for continental liberals; Namier believed that British political liberty was a unique fruit of an organic historical development. Redlich believed in the possibility of peaceful coexistence between nations, either in a federation or in a multinational state, given enough good will, an appropriate constitutional and administrative framework, political education, and socio-economic development. Namier, on the other hand, entertained a Hobbesian view of international relations, and advocated population transfers as the only way to cut the Gordian knot of conflict in nationally intermingled territories.

Seen from our present perspective, we can say that they were both right. Parliamentary democracy has taken root firmly in Western Europe, and is making inroads into Eastern Europe as well. Redlich's hopes for a federation in Europe have succeeded to a certain extent in Western Europe, where debates about the extent of administrative centralization versus autonomy for member states, federation versus confederation, a common constitution, and the efficacy of the European parliament would have all struck him as very familiar. He would have noted the backlash against 'Europe' through recourse to the doctrine of national sovereignty with alarm. He would also have had misgivings about how administrative rule has taken precedence both chronologically and in terms of political power over parliamentary rule in the present European Union, and would probably have suggested much the same measures for administrative reform as he did in late imperial Austria. British isolationism towards Europe would have pained and alarmed him, whereas it would probably have delighted Namier, convinced that Britain's future lay with the United States and the Commonwealth.

Redlich's hopes for federation failed completely, of course, in the area closest to his heart—in the successor states of the Habsburg empire. Despite pious hopes about resurrecting some sort of *Mitteleuropa* in the 1980s and early 1990s (now replaced by the issue of European Union membership), nationalist tensions continue to plague the region. Namier's presentiments have come true, especially his hopelessness about national coexistence in multinational states and his intimations about population transfers. Linda Colley has argued that Namier's 'extreme and emotional' beliefs about Germany's unchanging evil enabled him to discuss pre-war European developments far more accurately and presciently than more liberal observers. 'At a time when unreason and intolerance abounded, prejudice like Namier's could be a historiographical asset while cool rationality was left stranded by events.'⁵ Now that 'unreason and intolerance' are rife again in Eastern Europe, Namier's presentiments may yet prove to be right.

National self-determination and the formation of nation-states was the preferred liberal solution to the nationality problem in Central and Eastern Europe at the end of World War I. Despite the history of nationalistic violence and nationalist dictators in the inter-war years, many of the same liberal nationalist solutions are being proposed after the collapse of Soviet hegemony in the region. Anti-nationalist arguments like Redlich's and Namier's are still relatively ignored. I believe that the study of Redlich and Namier is not only of historical interest, but also of contemporary relevance to the debate regarding nationalism, national self-determination, and nationality conflict in Central and Eastern Europe. After all, the problem of whether parliamentary democratic governments can take root in nationally mixed areas is one with immediate implications for the former Habsburg lands and beyond.

⁵ Colley, *Lewis Namier*, 43.

CHRONOLOGY OF JOSEF REDLICH[1]

1869	Born in Göding, Moravia.
1878	Moves to Vienna.
1881	Enrolled in *Akademisches Gymnasium*, Vienna.
1886–90	Attends the Universities of Vienna, Tübingen, and Leipzig.
1897	Marries Alix Simon.
1891	Dr. Jur., University of Vienna. First visit to England.
1891–3	Legal Officer of Government in Brünn, Moravia (*Konzeptspraktikant der Statthalterei in Brünn*).
1901–5	Lecturer (*Privatdozent*) at the University of Vienna.
1903	Baptism; birth of son, Hans Ferdinand Redlich.
1906	*Titular Extraordinarius* Professor for State Law and Administration, University of Vienna.
1906–18	Member, Diet of Moravia.
1907–18	Member, Lower House of Austrian Parliament.
1908	Divorced from Alix Redlich, retains sole custody of son; Member of Delegations.
1909–18	*Ordinarius* Professor of Constitutional and Administrative law at the *Technisches Hochschule* in Vienna.
1910	Awarded title of *ordentlichen Universitätsprofessor*; delivers Godkin Lectures at Harvard, lectures at State University of Illinois.
1911–17	Leading member of the Imperial Administrative Reform Commission.
1912	Invited by the Carnegie Foundation for the Advancement of Teaching to write a report on American legal studies.
1913	Delivers Schouler Lectures, Johns Hopkins University; Member, Balkan Committee, Carnegie Endowment for International Peace.
1918	Minister of Finance in last imperial Austrian cabinet.
1919	Marries Gertrud Flaschar.
1920	Birth of daughter, Eleonore Helene.
1921	Envoy of Austrian Republic to Washington DC for five months.
1922	Delivers Lowell Lectures in Boston; birth of second daughter, Rosemarie.
1926–34	Fairchild Professor of Comparative Public Law in Harvard Law School.
1928–36	Member, European Center (Paris), Carnegie Endowment for International Peace.

---

[1] I have excluded publication dates of scholarly works since these are listed chronologically in the Bibliography.

1930–6   Elected by Assembly of League of Nations and Council, Deputy
            Judge of Permanent Court of International Justice at the Hague.
1931   May to October, Minister of Finance in Republic of Austria.
1936   Dies 11 November in Vienna.

CHRONOLOGY OF LEWIS NAMIER[1]

1888	Born in Wola Okrzejska (Russian Poland).
1890	Moves to Kobylowloki in Galicia.
1906–7	Attends Lausanne University.
1907–8	Attends London School of Economics; joins Fabian Society.
1908	Enters Balliol College, Oxford.
1910	Changes name to Lewis Bernstein Naymier.
1911	Achieves First Class degree in Modern History.
1913	Becomes British subject; changes spelling of his name to Namier; spends year in the United States working for Louis N. Hammerling.
1914–15	Private in the 20th Royal Fusiliers.
1915–17	Member of the Propaganda Department at Wellington House.
1917–18	Member of Department of Information.
1917	Marries Clara Sophia Edeleff-Poniatowska.
1918–20	Member of the Political Intelligence Department of the Foreign Office.
1920–1	Tutor in Modern History at Balliol College, Oxford; separated from wife.
1921–3	Representative in Prague of cotton business; appointed special correspondent in Vienna of the *Manchester Guardian Commercial*; raises money on Viennese stock exchange; psycho-analysed by Theodor Reik.
1922	Disinherited by father's will.
1924–9	Works on eighteenth-century English history with the financial aid of Rhodes Trust grants and journalism.
1929–31	Political Secretary of the Jewish Agency for Palestine.
1931–53	Professor of Modern History at Manchester University.
1933	Works at Jewish Agency to rescue and re-establish German-Jewish scholars and students.
1934	Ford Lectures, 'The Cabinet in the Eighteenth Century' (never published in full).
1939	Participant in St. James's Palace tripartite Conference between Government, Arabs, and Jews; seconded for liaison work between Foreign Office/Colonial Office and Zionist Organization.
1944	Raleigh Lecture, '1848: The Revolution of the Intellectuals'.
1947	Waynflete Lectures, 'The German Problem in 1848–50' (never

---

[1] I have excluded publication dates of scholarly works since these are listed chronologically in the Bibliography.

published); married Julia de Beausobre; baptized into Anglican
Church.

1948   Delivered the Academia dei Lincei lecture 'Nationality and
            Liberty' in Rome; elected honorary fellow of Balliol College.

1951   Appointed member of the Editorial Board of the *History of
            Parliament*, and editor of three volumes—section 1750–90.

1952   Knighted; Romanes Lecture, 'Monarchy and the Party System';
            Creighton Lecture (London University), 'Some Basic Factors of
            Nineteenth-Century European History'; awarded honorary
            D. Litt. by University of Durham.

1953   Royal Academy of Arts Lecture 'King George III: A Study of
            Personality'.

1955   Awarded D. Litt. by Oxford University.

1956   Receives in Balliol College Festschrift by sixteen leading English
            historians; awarded honorary degree by Rome University.

1957   Awarded Honorary D.Litt. by Cambridge University; works on
            History of Parliament; assigned £4,000 a year for four years by
            Rockefeller Foundation to direct research.

1958   Visits Israel as member of Board of Editors for the Weizmann
            Papers.

1959   Cambridge University, Leslie Stephen Lecture, 'Charles
            Townshend: His Character and Career'.

1960   Awarded D. C. L. by Chancellor of the University of Oxford; dies
            19 August in London.

BIBLIOGRAPHY

MANUSCRIPT AND ARCHIVAL SOURCES:

REDLICH SOURCES

Butler Library, Rare Books and Manuscripts Division, Columbia University, New York:

Carnegie Endowment Committee, Box 89.
James T. Shotwell Papers, Box 50.
Nicholas Murray Butler Papers, Box 'Rea-Red', Folder 'Josef Redlich'.
Division of Economics and History, I.L.—1921; I.O.—1923.
Munroe Smith Papers.
Oskar Jaszi Papers.

Fritz Fellner, Neustiftgasse 47, Vienna:

Redlich Papers.

Harvard Law School Library, Harvard University:

Charles C. Burlingham Papers, Box 15, Folders 11 and 12.
Sheldon Glueck Papers, Box 59, Folder 6.
Oliver Wendell Holmes Jr. Papers, Box 49.
Roscoe Pound Papers, Box 80, Folder 22.
Felix Frankfurter Papers, Box 197, Folder 21.

Houghton Library, Harvard University:

FMS Ger 145.1, 'Report to Chancellor Mayr,' 1921.
FMS Ger 145.2 'The Food situation in Austria,' 1921.
Autograph File, 'Castle, William Richards', Castle to Redlich, 14 Apr. 1921.

Library of Congress, Washington D. C.:

Felix Frankfurter Papers, Boxes 91 and 92.

London University School of Slavonic and East European Studies, London:

R. W. Seton-Watson Papers, SEW/17/10/1, SEW/17/18/7, SEW/17/22/7, SEW/17/26/6.

Österreichische National Bibliothek—Handschriften, Autographen und Nachlass Sammlung, Vienna:

File 1022/44–46. J. Redlich correspondence with Berthold Molden.

Österreichisches Staatsarchiv, Haus, Hof- und Staatsarchiv, Vienna:

Ernest von Plener Papers, Box 19.

Joseph Maria Baernreither Papers, Box 47, 49.

Josef Redlich Papers, 1 box.

Österreichisches Staatsarchiv, Allgemeine Verwaltungs Archiv, Vienna:

Verwaltungsreform-Kommission 1911–1917, Boxes 1–13.

Wiener Stadt-und Landesbibliothek, Handschriftensammlung, Rathaus, Vienna:

I.H. 137.696, Redlich to Franz Servaes, 16 Mar. 1902.

I.H. 159.988 Redlich to Johann von Ankwicz, 17 Oct. 1913.

I.H. 162.884 Redlich to Heinrich Friedjung, 5 Sept. 1915.

I.H. 162.899 Redlich to Heinrich Friedjung, 21 July 1901.

I.H. 163.047 Redlich to Friedjung, 31 Oct. 1918.

I.N. 185.202, Redlich to Michael Holzmann, 19 Sept. 1918.

I.N. 185.205, Redlich to Holzmann, 3 Sept. 1927.

I.N. 185.206, Redlich to Holzmann, 25. July, 1929.

I.N. 198.547–I.N. 198.743, Redlich to Flora Singer-Darkow, correspondence 1887–1936.

NAMIER SOURCES

Beinecke Library, Yale University, New Haven, Connecticut:

Rebecca West Collection, GEN 105, Series No. 1, Box No. 13, Folder No. 60; Box no. 27, Folder no. 117.

Farmington Library, Yale University, Connecticut:

Wilmarth S. Lewis and Lewis Namier correspondence.

John Rylands Library, Manchester University, Manchester:

Manchester Guardian Archives, A/N2, Namier correspondence with C. P. Scott; B/N8a/1–381, Namier correspondence with W. P. Crozier and A.Wadsworth.

John Rylands Library (Deansgate), Manchester University, Manchester:

Lewis Namier Papers

Bodleian Library, Oxford University, Oxford:

MS Eng Hist.d.341–2, f. 22–23

Public Record Office, London:

FO 371/2450; FO 371/2862; FO 371/3001; FO 371/3016; FO 371/3054/

237630; FO 371/3135; FO 371/3278; FO 371/3281; FO 371/3897; FO 371/3907; FO 371/4359; F.O. 371/4363; FO 371/4377; FO 371/4384; FO 371/4385; FO 371/4379; FO 371/23153/C19384; FO 371/24482/C8027; FO 371/24474/C7639; FO 371/23153/C19384. FO 395-10; FO 395/26; FO 395/26/216971; FO 395/108 CAB 24/13–46.

Sterling Memorial Library, Manuscripts and Archives, Yale University, New Haven, Connecticut:

Charles Nagel Papers (MSS 364), Box. No. 11, Folders 105, 166, 168; Box. 12, Folder 169, 170; Box 40, Folder 466.
James Marshall Osborn Correspondence (OSB MSS 7), Box 56, Folder 1145.
Wallace Notestein Papers, (MSS 544), Box 6, Folder 534.

PRINTED PRIMARY SOURCES

BOOKS BY LEWIS BERNSTEIN NAMIER

Germany and Eastern Europe (London, 1915).
The Case of Bohemia (London, 1917).
The Czecho-Slovaks: An Oppressed Nationality (London, 1917).
'The Downfall of the Habsburg Monarchy', in H. W. V. Temperley (ed.), *A History of the Peace Conference of Paris*, 6 vols. (London, 1920–4), vol. iv, Part 3, pp. 58–119.
The Structure of Politics at the Accession of George III, 2nd edn. (London, 1957).
England in the Age of the American Revolution, 2nd edn. (London, 1961).
Skyscrapers and Other Essays (London, 1931).
In the Margin of History (London, 1939).
Conflicts: Studies in Contemporary History (London, 1942).
1848: Revolution of the Intellectuals (London, 1944).
Diplomatic Prelude (London, 1948).
Europe in Decay: A Study in Disintegration 1936–1940 (London, 1950).
Avenues of History (London, 1952).
Personalities and Powers (London, 1955).
Vanished Supremacies, Essays on European History, 1812–1918 (London, 1958).
Facing East (New York, 1966).

ARTICLES BY NAMIER (OTHER THAN THOSE COLLECTED IN HIS BOOKS)

'C'est a L'amour du Vieux Monde . . .', *Blue Book* (Oxford, May 1912), 3–11.
'The Old House and the German Future', *Nineteenth Century* (July 1916), 169–90.
'Danzig, Poland's Outlet to the Sea', *Nineteenth Century* (Feb. 1917), 300–5.

'Revolutionary Forces in Austria', *The New Europe*, 7: 27 (1918), 14–18.

'Trotski', *The New Europe*, 6: 66 (1918), 9–16.

'Poland and Brest-Litovsk', *The New Europe*, 6: 71 (1918), 179–83.

'Germany and Her Vassals', *The New Europe*, 6: 74 (1918), 272–7.

'Inner Meaning of Central Europe's Depreciated Currencies. Trade "Booms" that Bring Bankruptcy: Austria's Dwindling Capital', *Manchester Guardian Commercial* (12 Jan.1922).

'An Interview with Beneš, Little Entente's Policy Towards Russia and Germans', *Manchester Guardian* (14 Feb.1923).

'Agrarian Revolution', *Reconstruction in Europe*, *Manchester Guardian Commercial* (Aug. 1922).

'Economic Decay and the Flight of Capital: Present Plight and Ultimate Fate of Austria', *Manchester Guardian Commercial* (24 Aug. 1922).

'Inflation at Close Quarters', *Manchester Guardian Commercial: Annual Review of Banking and Investment* (31 Jan. 1924).

'How Austria Passed Through Her Financial Crisis: Present-Day Openings for Foreign Capital', *Manchester Guardian Commercial* (20 Nov. 1924).

'The Problem of East-Central Europe', *Round Table* (June 1923), 569–90.

'Obituary: Ignaz Seipel', *Manchester Guardian* (3 Aug. 1932).

'Marshal Piłsudski. Liberator of Poland: Socialist Turned Dictator', *Manchester Guardian* (13 May 1935).

'Obituary: Dr. Roman Dmowski', *Manchester Guardian* (3 Jan.1939).

'The Russian Revolution: 1917–1942', *Manchester Guardian* (7 Nov. 1942).

'The Russian–Polish Frontier: How the "Curzon Line" Was Drawn. Statistics of Population', *The Times* (12 Jan. 1944), 5.

BOOKS BY JOSEF REDLICH

Englische Lokalverwaltung. Darstellung der inneren Verwaltung Englands in ihrer geschichtlichen Entwicklung und in ihrer gegenwärtigen Gestalt (Leipzig, 1901).

Local Government in England, ed. with additions by F. W. Hirst, 2 vols., (London, 1903).

Recht und Technik des englischen Parlamentarismus. Die Geschäftsordnung des House of Commons in ihrer geschichtlichen Entwicklung und gegenwärtigen Gestalt (Leipzig, 1905).

The Procedure of the House of Commons: A Study of its History and Present Form, trans. A. E. Steinthal, 3 vols., (London, 1908).

Das Wesen der oesterreichischen Kommunal-Verfassung (Leipzig, 1910).

Zustand und Reform der österreichischen Verwaltung. Rede des Josef Redlich, gehalten in der Budgetdebatte des Abgeordnetenhauses des österreichischen Reichsrates vom 26. oktober 1911 (Vienna, 1911).

Bericht . . . über die Entwicklung und den gegenwärtigen Stand der Österreichischen Finanzverwaltung sowie Vorschläge der Kommission zur Reform dieser Verwaltung (Vienna, 1913).

The Common Law and the Case Method in American University Law Schools, Carnegie Foundation for the Advancement of Teaching, Bulletin 8, 1914.

Oesterreichische Politische Gesellschaft. Auszug aus den im Juli 1917 gehaltenen Reden der Herren Reichsratsabgeordneten . . . J. Redlich, E.V. Zenker, R. von Lodgmann und R. Renne an den Diskussionsabenden über das Thema: Das nationale Problem in Oesterreich (Vienna, 1917).

Heinrich Lammasch. Seine Aufzeichnungen, sein Wirken und seine Politik (Vienna, 1922).

Östereichische Regierung und Verwaltung im Weltkriege (Vienna, 1925).

Austrian War Government (New Haven, Conn., 1925).

Das österreichische Staats- und Reichsproblem, 2 vols., (Leipzig, 1922, 1926).

Kaiser Franz Joseph von Österreich (Berlin, 1928).

Emperor Francis Joseph of Austria (London, 1929).

ARTICLES AND PAMPHLETS BY REDLICH

'Austria-Hungary and Servia', *Economist* (25 July, 1914), 179–181; (1 Aug. 1914), 232–4.

Österreich und der Friede: Verständigung unter den Völkern Österreichs. Versammlung vom 17. Juli 1917 in der, ÖPG' (Vienna, 1917).

Das Nationale Problem in Österreich (Vienna and Leipzig, 1917).

Rede in der Konstituierenden Versammlung 'Liga für den Volkerbund' am 21. Feb 1919 [brochure] (Vienna, 1919), 7–9.

'The Problem of the Republic of Austria', *Quarterly Review*, 464 (July 1920), 203–20.

'Reconstruction in the Danube Countries', *Foreign Affairs*, 1: 1 (1922), 73–85.

'Austria and Central Europe', *Yale Review*, 12 (1923), 335–44.

'The Destiny of Austria', *Reconstruction in Europe, Manchester Guardian Commercial* (4 Jan. 1923), 730–2.

'Amerikanischer Brief', *Neue Freie Presse* (25 Dec. 1928).

'The Republic of Austria; Its Recent History and its Present Problems', in *The World Today: Encyclopaedia Britannica*, 1: 4 (New York, 1934), 1–4.

'The World-Wide Influence of the United States Constitution', in *Boston University Law Review*, 10: 2 (Apr. 1930), 195–201.

The Decline of Parliamentary Government, Discussed by Harold J. Laski and Dr Josef Redlich, March 28, 1931 . . . New York Luncheon Discussion (New York: Foreign Policy Association, 1931).

'Sovereignty, Democracy, and the Rights of Minorities', in Joseph H. Beale (ed.), *Harvard Legal Essays* (Cambridge, Mass. 1934), 377–97.

OTHER PRINTED PRIMARY SOURCES

Stenographische Protokolle über die Sitzungen des Hauses der Abgeordneten Wien, 1867–1918.

BAERNREITHER, JOSEPH MARIA, *Fragments of a Political Diary*, ed. Josef Redlich (London, 1930).

BENEDIKT, H., *Die Friedensaktion der Meinlgruppe, 1917/18: die Bemühungen um einen Verständigungsfrieden nach Dokumenten, Aktenstücken und Briefen* (Graz, 1962).

DUGDALE, BLANCHE, *'Baffy'. The Diaries of Blanche Dugdale, 1936–47*, ed. Norman Rose (London, 1973).

FELLNER, FRITZ (ed.), 'Johann Schober und Josef Redlich: Aus den Tagebüchern und Briefwechsel', *Zeitgeschichte*, 9–10 (1977), 305–19; 11–12 (1977), 367–84.

—— *Dichter und Gelehrter: Hermann Bahr und Josef Redlich in ihren Briefen 1896–1934* (Salzburg, 1980).

Fußaenger, H. (ed.), *Hugo von Hofmannsthal–Josef Redlich Briefwechsel*, ed. H. Fußgaenger (Frankfurt am Main, 1971).

HEADLAM-MORLEY, JAMES WYCLIFFE, *A Memoir of the Paris Peace Conference, 1919* (London, 1972).

MAITLAND, FREDERIC WILLIAM, *The Letters of Frederic William Maitland*, vol. II, ed. P. N. R. Zutshi (London, 1995).

REDLICH, JOSEF, *Schicksalsjahre Oesterreich. 1908–1919: Das politische Tagebuch Josef Redlich*, ed. Fritz Fellner (Graz and Cologne, 1953).

SECONDARY SOURCES

SECONDARY SOURCES SPECIFICALLY ON LEWIS NAMIER:

BABINGTON-SMITH, CONSTANCE, *Julia de Beausobre: A Russian Christian in the West* (London, 1983).

BAKER, MARK, 'Lewis Namier and the Problem of Eastern Galicia', *Journal of Ukrainian Studies*, 23: 2 (1998), 59–104.

BERLIN, ISAIAH, 'Lewis Namier: A Personal Impression', in *A Century of Conflict, 1850–1950: Essays for A. J. P. Taylor* (London, 1966), 213–230.

BOYER, JOHN W., 'A. J. P. Taylor and the Art of Modern History', *JMH* 49: 1 (1977), 40–72.

BROOKE, JOHN, 'Namier and Namierism', *History and Theory: Studies in the Philosophy of History*, 3 (1964), 331–47.

—— 'Namier and His Critics', *Encounter*, 24 (1965), 47–49.

BUTTERFIELD, H., *George III and the Historians* (New York, 1957).

—— 'Sir Lewis Namier as Historian,' *The Listener*, 65 (May 18, 1961), 873–76.

BUXTON, E., 'A Dig Long Ago in Eastern Galicia', *The Times* (21 Oct. 1963).

CARR, E. H., 'English History's Towering Outsider', *Times Literary Supplement* (21 May 1971).

CHESTERTON, G. K., 'Potash and Perlmutter', *New Witness* (26 Apr. 1918).

COLLEY, LINDA, *Lewis Namier* (London, 1989).

GILMOUR, IAN, 'Sir Lewis Namier' [obituary], *The Spectator* (26 Aug. 1960).

HUNCZAK, TARAS, 'Sir Lewis Namier and the Struggle for Eastern Galicia, 1918–20', *Harvard Ukrainian Studies*, 1 (1977), 198–210.

MANSFIELD, HARVEY C., Jr., 'Sir Lewis Namier Considered,' *Journal of British Studies*, 2: 1 (1962), 28–55.

MEHTA, VED, *The Fly and the Fly-Bottle: Encounters with British Intellectuals* (London, 1963), 182–204.

NAMIER, JULIA, *Lewis Namier: A Biography* (London, 1971).

PARES, RICHARD and A. J. P. TAYLOR (eds.) *Essays Presented to Sir Lewis Namier* (London, 1956).

PLUMB, J. H. 'The Atomic Historian', *New Statesman* (1 Aug. 1969), 141–3.

RAMHARDTER, GÜNTHER, *Geschichtswissenschaft und Patriotismus* (Munich, 1973).

REIFOWITZ, IAN, 'Inventing a Nation: Joseph Samuel Bloch and the Cultivation of a Supraethnic Austrian Identity, 1882–1918', paper given at the Fifth Annual Convention of the Association for the Study of Nationalities (ASN), Columbia University, New York, 14 Apr. 2000.

ROSE, NORMAN, *Lewis Namier and Zionism* (Oxford, 1980).

ROUSSEAU, G. S., 'Namier on Namier', *Studies in Burke and his Time*, 13: 42 (1971), 2016–41.

SHARP, ALAN, 'Some Relevant Historians—the Political Intelligence Department of the Foreign Office, 1918–1920', *Australian Journal of Politics and History*, 34: 3 (1988), 359–68.

SIMS, CATHERINE S., 'Lewis Namier', in Herman Ausubel (ed.), *Some Modern Historians of Britain: Essays in Honour of R. L. Schuyler* (New York, 1951), 341–57.

SUTHERLAND, LUCY S., 'Sir Lewis Namier', in *Proceedings of the British Academy*, *1962* (London, 1963), 371–85.

TAYLOR, A. J. P., 'Namier the Historian', *Observer* (28 Aug. 1960).

TOYNBEE, A. J. 'Sir Lewis Namier', in *Acquaintances* (Oxford, 1967), 62–86.

WALCOTT, ROBERT ' "Sir Lewis Namier Considered" Considered', *Journal of British Studies*, 3: 2 (1964), 85–108. [comment on Mansfield, 1962].

WATT, D. C., 'British Historians, the War Guilt Issue, and Post-War Germanophobia: A Documentary Note', *Historical Journal*, 36: 1 (1993), 179–85.

WINKLER, HENRY R., 'Sir Lewis Namier', *JMH* 35 (Mar. 1963), 1–19.

SECONDARY SOURCES SPECIFICALLY ON JOSEF REDLICH

BOYER, J. W., 'The End of the Old Regime: Visions of Political Reform in Late Imperial Austria', *JMH* 58: 1 (1986), 159–93.

BURLINGHAM, CHARLES C., 'Josef Redlich—Obituary', *Harvard Law Review*, 50: 3 (Jan. 1937), 392–94.

DUMBA, CONSTANTIN, 'Persönliches über Josef Redlich', *Neue Freie Presse* (22 Nov. 1936).

FELLNER, FRITZ, 'The Plan for a Redlich–Apponyi Lecture-Mission in the United States: Origins and Proposals for the Building of an Austro-Hungarian Propaganda Action in Neutral Foreign Countries during WW I', in *Festschrift für Adam Wandruszka zum 60, Geburtstag* (Vienna, Cologne, and Graz, 1974).

FRANKFURTER, FELIX, 'Josef Redlich—Obituary', *Harvard Law Review*, 50: 3 (Jan. 1937), 389–91.

WANK, SOLOMON, 'Josef Redlich', in *Biographical Dictionary of Internationalists* (London, 1983), 602–4,.

OTHER SECONDARY WORKS

ABRAMSON, HENRY, *A Prayer for the Government: Ukrainians and Jews in Revolutionary Times, 1917–1920* (Cambridge, Mass., 1999).

ACTON, JOHN EMERICH EDWARD DALBERG (Lord), *Essays on Freedom and Power* (London 1956).

BAREA ILSA, *Vienna: Legend and Reality* (London, 1966).

BARTAL, ISRAEL and MAGDA OPALASKI, *Poles and Jews: A Failed Brotherhood* (Hanover, NH, 1992).

BAUMGART, MAREK, *Wielka Brytania a Odrodzona Polska 1918–1933* (Szczecin, 1985).

BEETHAM, DAVID, 'Mosca, Pareto and Weber: A Historical Comparison', in Wolfgang J. Mommsen and Jürgen Osterhammel (eds.), *Max Weber and his Contemporaries* (London, 1987).

BELLER, STEVEN, *Vienna and the Jews 1867–1938: A Cultural History* (Cambridge, 1989).

—— 'The World of Yesterday Revisited: Nostalgia, Memory and the Jews of *Fin-de-Siècle* Vienna', *Jewish Social Studies*, 2 (1996), 37–53.

—— 'Patriotism and the National Identity of Habsburg Jewry, 1860–1914', *Leo Baeck Institute Year Book*, 41 (1996), 215–38.

—— 'The Tragic Carnival: Austrian Culture in the First World War', in Aviel Roshwald and Richard Stites (eds.), *European Culture in the Great War: The Arts, Entertainment, and Propaganda, 1914–1918* (Cambridge, 1999).

BERGER, PETER, 'Die Idee einer österreichischen Staatsnation bis 1938', *Donauraum*, 12: 1 and 2 (1967), 57–73.

BERLIN, ISAIAH, 'John Stuart Mill and the Ends of Life', in *Four Essays on Liberty* (Oxford, 1969), 173–206.

—— 'Two Concepts of Liberty', in *Four Essays on Liberty* (Oxford, 1969), 118–72.

BÖDY, PAUL, *Joseph Eötvös and the Modernization of Hungary, 1840–1870: A Study of Ideas of Individuality and Social Pluralism in Modern Politics* (Boulder, Col., 1985).

BOYER, JOHN W., *Political Radicalism in Late Imperial Vienna: Origins of the Christian Social Movement 1848–1897* (Chicago, 1981).

—— *Culture and Political Crisis in Vienna: Christian Socialism in Power, 1897–1918* (Chicago, 1995).

BROCK, PETER, *Nationalism and Populism in Partitioned Poland: Selected Essays* (London, 1973).

BURUMA, IAN, *Voltaire's Coconuts or Anglomania in Europe* (London, 1999).

CAHNMANN, WERNER J., 'Adolf Fischhof and his Jewish Followers', *Leo Baeck Institute Year Book*, 4 (1959), 111–39.

CALDER, K. J., *Britain and the Origins of the New Europe 1914–1918* (Cambridge, 1976).

COPPENS, PETER ROCHE DE, *Ideal Man in Classical Sociology: The Views of Comte, Durkheim, Pareto, and Weber* (University Park and London, 1976).

CORNWALL, MARK, 'News, Rumour and the Control of Information in Austria-Hungary, 1914–1918', *History*, 77 (1992), 50–64.

DAVIS, H. W. C., *A History of Balliol College*, 2nd edn. (Oxford, 1963).

DAVIES, NORMAN, *God's Playground: A History of Poland*, 2 vols. (Oxford, 1981).

EÖTVÖS, JÓZSEF, *The Dominant Ideas of the Nineteenth Century and their Impact on the State*, trans., ed., and annotated with introductory essay by D. Mervyn Jones, 2 vols. (Boulder, Col., 1996).

EVERETT, L. P., 'The Rise of Jewish National Politics in Galicia, 1905–1907', in A. S. Markovits and F. E. Sysyn (eds.), *Nationbuilding and the Politics of Nationalism: Essays on Austrian Galicia* (Cambridge, Mass., 1982), 149–177.

EVANS, R. J. W., The Habsburg Monarchy and the Coming of War', in R. J. W. Evans and Harmut Pogge von Strandman (eds.), *The Coming of the First World War* (Oxford, 1988).

—— 'Frontiers and National Identities in Central Europe', *International History Review*, 14: 3 (1992), 480–502.

—— 'Historians and the State in the Habsburg Lands', in Wim Blockmans and Jean-Philippe Genet (eds.), *Visions sur le développement des états européens: Théories et historiographies de l'état moderne* (Rome, 1993), 203–18.

FELLNER, FRITZ, 'Die Historiographie zur österreichisch-deutschen Problematik als Spiegel der nationalpolitischen Diskussion', in Heinrich Lutz and Helmut Rumpler (eds.), *Österreich und die deutsche Frage im 19. und 20. Jahrhundert* (Vienna, 1982), 33–59.

FRANKEL, JONATHAN, 'The Dilemmas of Jewish National Autonomism: The Case of Ukraine 1917–1920', in Peter J. Potichnyj and Howard Aster (eds.), *Ukrainian–Jewish Relations in Historical Perspective* (Edmonton, 1988).

FRANZ, GEORG, *Liberalismus: Die deutschliberale Bewegung in der habsburgischen Monarchie* (Munich, 1955).

FROMM, ERIC, *Escape from Freedom* (New York, 1941).

GĄSOWSKI, TOMASZ, 'From *Austeria* to the Manor: Jewish Landowners in Autonomous Galicia', *Polin*, 12 (1999), 120–36.

GOOD, DAVID F., *The Economic Rise of the Habsburg Monarchy, 1750–1914* (Berkeley, 1975).

HACOHEN, MALACHI, 'Dilemmas of Cosmopolitanism: Karl Popper, Jewish Identity, and "Central European Culture" ', *JMH* 71: 1 (1999).

HALLOWELL, JOHN H., *The Decline of Liberalism as an Ideology with Particular Reference to German Politico-legal Thought* (Berkeley and Los Angeles, 1943).

HANAK, HARRY, *Great Britain and Austria-Hungary during the First World War: A Study in the Formation of Public Opinion* (London, 1962).

HARRINGTON-MUELLER, D., *Der Fortschrittsklub im Abg. Haus des oesterr. Reichsrat 1873–1910* (Vienna, 1972).

HAYEK, F. A., *New Studies in Philosophy, Politics, Economics and the History of Ideas* (London, 1978).

HEFFTER, HEINRICH, *Die Deutsche Selbstverwaltung im 19. Jahrhundert: Geschichte der Ideen und Institutionen* (Stuttgart, 1950).

HIDEN, JOHN and JOHN FARQUHARSON, *Explaining Hitler's Germany: Historians and the Third Reich* (London, 1983).

HIMKA, JOHN PAUL, *Socialism in Galicia: the Emergence of Polish Social Democracy and Ukrainian Radicalism, 1860–1890* (Cambridge, Mass., 1983).

HOLBORN, HAJO, 'Wilhelm Dilthey and the Critique of Historical Reason', in W. Warren Wagar (ed.), *European Intellectual History Since Darwin and Marx* (New York, 1967).

HOLLEIS, EVA, *Die Sozialpolitische Partei: Sozialliberale Bestrebungen in Wien um 1900* (Munich, 1978).

HOLMES, COLIN, 'The Tredegar Riots of 1911: Anti-Jewish Disturbances in South Wales', *Welsh History Review*, 11: 2 (1982), 214–25.

HRYNIUK, STELLA, 'Polish Lords and Ukrainian Peasants: Conflict, Deference, and Accommodation in Eastern Galicia in the Late Nineteenth Century', *AHY* 24 (1993), 119–32.

HUGHES, H. STUART, *Consciousness and Society: the Reorientation of European Social Thought* (London, 1959).

IGGERS, GEORG G., *The German Conception of History: The National Tradition of Historical Thought from Herder to the Present* (Middletown, Conn. 1968).

JANIK, ALLAN, 'Viennese Culture and the Jewish Self-Hatred Hypothesis: A Critique', in Ivar Oxaal, Michael Pollack, and Gerhard Botz (eds.), *Jews, Anti-Semitism and Culture in Vienna* (London, 1987), 75–88.

—— Vienna 1900 Revisited: Paradigms and Problems', *AHY* 28 (1997), 1–28.

—— and STEPHEN TOULMIN, *Wittgenstein's Vienna* (London, 1973).

JASZI, OSKAR, *The Dissolution of the Habsburg Empire* (Chicago, 1929).

JENKS, WILLIAM A., 'The Jews in the Habsburg Empire, 1879–1918', *Leo Baeck Institute Yearbook* (1971), 155–62.

JENNINGS, J. R., 'Conceptions of England and its Constitution in Nineteenth-Century French Political Thought', *Historical Journal*, 29: 1 (1986), 65–85.

JOHNSTON, W. M., *The Austrian Mind: An Intellectual and Social History* (Berkeley and Los Angeles, 1972).

JUDSON, PIETER, ' "Not Another Square Foot!": German Liberalism and the Rhetoric of National Ownership in Nineteenth-Century Austria', *AHY* 26 (1995), 83–98.

—— *Exclusive Revolutionaries: Liberal Politics, Social Experience, and National Identity in the Austrian Empire, 1848–1914* (Ann Arbor, 1996).

KANN, R. A., *The Multinational Empire: Nationalism and National Reform in the Habsburg Monarchy, 1848–1918*, 2 vols. (New York, 1950).

—— *A Study in Austrian Intellectual History, from Late Baroque to Romanticism*, (New York, 1960).

KOCKA, JÜRGEN. 'German History Before Hitler: The Debate about the German *Sonderweg*', *Journal of Contemporary History*, 23 (1988), 3–16.

KOHN, HANS, *Pan-Slavism: Its History and Ideology*, rev. edn., (New York, 1960).

KONRAD, HELMUT, 'Between "Little International" and Great Power Politics: Austro-Marxism and Stalinism on the National Question', in Richard L. Rudolph and David F. Good (eds.), *Nationalism and Empire: The Habsburg Monarchy and the Soviet Union* (New York, 1992), 269–94.

LE RIDER, JACQUES, 'Hugo von Hofmannsthal and the Austrian Idea of Central Europe', in R. Robertson and E. Timms (eds.), *The Habsburg Legacy* (Edinburgh, 1994), 121–35.

LEVENE, MARK, *War, Jews, and the New Europe: The Diplomacy of Lucien Wolf 1914–1919* (Oxford, 1992).

LUFT, DAVID S., 'Austria as a Region of German Culture: 1900–1938', *AHY* 23 (1992), 135–48.

MAGOCSI, PAUL ROBERT, 'A Subordinate or Submerged People: The Ukrainians of Galicia under Habsburg and Soviet Rule', in Richard L. Rudolph and David F. Good (eds.,) *Nationalism and Empire: The Habsburg Monarchy and the Soviet Union* (New York, 1992).

MAGRIS, CLAUDIO, *Der Habsburgische Mythos in der österreichischen Literatur* (Salzburg, 1966).

MOMMSEN, HANS, *Die Sozialdemokratie und die Nationalitätenfrage im habsburgischen Vielvölkerstaat* (Vienna, 1963).

MOMMSEN, WOLFGANG J., *The Political and Social Theory of Max Weber, Collected Essays* (Cambridge, 1989).

MORGENBROD, BIRGITT, *Wiener Grossbuergertum im Ersten Weltkrieg. Die Geschichte der 'Oesterreichischen Politischen Gesellschaft' 1916–1918* (Vienna, 1994).

MORITSCH, ANDREAS (ed.), *Der Austroslavismus* (Vienna, 1996).

MORRISON, KEN, *Marx Durkheim Weber: Formations of Modern Thought* (London, 1995).

MUNROE SMITH, E., *A General View of European Legal History and Other Papers* (New York, 1927).

MUSGRAVE, T. D., *Self-Determination and National Minorities* (Oxford, 1997).

NOWAK-KIEŁBIKOWA, MARIA, *Polska—Wielka Brytania w latach 1918–1923* (Warsaw, 1975).

NYE, ROBERT A., *The Anti-Democratic Souces of Elite Theory: Pareto, Mosca, Michels* (London, 1977).

OKEY, ROBIN, *The Habsburg Monarchy c.1765–1918: From Enlightenment to Eclipse* (London, 2001).

ORVIS, JULIA SWIFT, 'Partitioned Poland, 1795–1914', in Bernadotte E. Schmitt (ed.) *Poland* (Berkeley and Los Angeles, 1945).

PAUPIE, KURT, *Handbuch der österreichischen Pressgeschichte 1848–1959*, Bd. II (Vienna, 1966).

PAULEY, BRUCE, 'The Social and Economic Background of Austria's Lebensunfähigkeit', in Anson Rabinbach (ed.), *The Austrian Social Experiment* (Boulder, Col., 1985), 21–37.

—— *From Prejudice to Persecution: A History of Austrian Anti-Semitism* (Chapel Hill, NC, 1992).

PISZCZKOWSKI, TADEUSZ, *Anglia a Polska 1914–1939 w świetle dokumentów Brytyjskich* (London, 1975).

POPPER, KARL, *Unended Quest: An Intellectual Autobiography* (Glasgow, 1986).

PULZER, PETER, 'The Austrian Liberals and the Jewish Question, 1867–1914', *Journal of Central European Affairs*, 23: 2 (July 1963), 131–42.

—— *Political Representation and Elections in Britain*, rev. edn. (London, 1972).

—— *The Rise of Political Anti-Semitism in Germany and Austria*, rev. edn. (London, 1988).

RAMHARDTER, GÜNTHER, *Geschichtswissenschaft und Patriotismus* (Munich, 1973).

RAUCHENSTEINER, MANFRIED, *Der Tod des Doppeladlers. Österreich-Ungarn und der Erste Weltkrieg* (Graz, 1993).

RECHTER, DAVID, 'Kaisertreu: The Dynastic Loyalty of Austrian Jewry', in Klaus Hödl (ed.), *Jüdische Identitäten: Einblicke in die Bewusstseinslandschaft des österreichischen Judentums* (Innsbruck, 2000).

ROZENBLIT, MARSHA, *The Jews of Vienna, 1867–1914: Assimilation and Identity* (Albany, NY, 1983).

—— 'The Jews of the Dual Monarchy', *AHY* 23 (1992), 160–180.

SCHLESINGER, RUDOLF, *Federalism in Central and Eastern Europe* (London, 1945).

SCHORSKE, C. E., *Fin-de-siècle Vienna: Politics and Culture* (Cambridge, 1981).

—— 'Grace and the Word: Austria's Two Cultures and Their Modern Fate', *AHY* 22 (1991), 21–34.

—— *Thinking With History* (Princeton, 1998).

SEIPEL, IGNAZ, *Nation und Staat* (Vienna, 1916).

STIRK, PETER M. R. (ed.), *Mitteleuropa: History and Prospects* (Edinburgh, 1994).

STOURZH, GERALD, 'Die Politischen Ideen Josef von Eötvös und das österreichische Staatsproblem', *Donauraum*, 11: 4 (1966), 204–20.

—— 'Galten die Juden als Nationalität Altösterreichs?' *Studia Judaica Austriaca*, 10 (1984), 73–98.

—— 'The Multinational Empire Revisited: Reflections on Late Imperial Austria' *AHY*, 23 (1992), 1–22.

SETON-WATSON, HUGH and CHRISTOPHER, *The Making of a New Europe: R. W. Seton-Watson and the Last Years of Austria-Hungary* (London, 1981).

SKINNER, QUENTIN, 'The Idea of Negative Liberty: Philosophical and Historical Perspectives', in Richard Rorty, J. B. Schneewind and Quentin Skinner (eds.), *Philosophy in History: Essays on the Historiography of Philosophy* (Cambridge, 1984).

STADLER, KARL R., *The Birth of the Austrian Republic 1918–1921* (Leiden, 1966).

STEED, H. WICKHAM, *The Hapsburg Monarchy*, 2nd edn. (London, 1914).

STEINBERG, MICHAEL P., *The Meaning of the Salzburg Festival: Austria as Theater and Ideology, 1890–1938* (Ithaca, NY, 1990).

STRAKOSCH-GRASSMANN, GUSTAV, *Geschichte des Unterrichtswesens in Österreich* (Vienna, 1905).

SUVAL, STANLEY, 'The Search for a Fatherland', *AHY* 4–5 (1968–9), 275–99.

SWEDBERG, RICHARD, *Joseph A. Schumpeter: His Life and Work* (Cambridge, 1991).

TIMMS, EDWARD, *Karl Kraus: Apocalyptic Satirist: Culture and Catastrophe in Habsburg Vienna* (New Haven and London, 1986).

—— 'Citizenship and "Heimatrecht" after the Treaty of St. Germain', in R. Robertson and E. Timms (eds.), *The Habsburg Legacy: National Identity in Historical Perspective* (Edinburgh, 1994).

TSCHUPPIK, KARL, *Franz Josef I. Der Untergang eines Reiches* (Dresden-Hellerau, 1928).

VEROSTA, STEPHAN, 'The German Concept of *Mitteleuropa*, 1917–1918 and its Contemporary Critics', in Robert A. Kann, Béla K. Király, and Paula S. Fichtner (eds.), *The Habsburg Empire in World War I: Essays on the Intellectual, Military, Political and Economic Aspects of the Habsburg War Effort* (New York, 1977), 203–20.

WALTER, EDITH, *Oesterreichische Tageszeitungen der Jahrhundertwende* (Vienna, 1994).

WANDRUSZKA, ADAM and PETER URBANITSCH (eds.), *Die Habsburgermonarchie 1848–1918, Verwaltung und Rechtswesen*, Bd. II, (Vienna, 1975).

—— —— and ALOIS BRUSATTI (eds.), *Die Habsburgermonarchie 1848–1918: Die Wirtschaftliche Entwicklung*, Bd. I, (Vienna, 1973).

WIENER, MARTIN J., *Between Two Worlds: The Political Thought of Graham Wallas* (Oxford, 1971).

WIERER, RUDOLF, *Der Föderalismus im Donauraum* (Graz, 1960).

WISTRICH, ROBERT S., *Socialism and the Jews: The Dilemmas of Assimilation in Germany and Austria-Hungary* (London and Toronto, 1982).

—— *The Jews of Vienna in the Age of Franz Joseph* (New York, 1989).

WROBEL, PIOTR, 'The Jews of Galicia under Austrian-Polish Rule, 1869–1918', *AHY* 25 (1994), 97–138.

ZEMAN, Z. A. B., *The Break-Up of the Habsburg Empire 1914–1918* (London, 1961).

ZOCHOWSKI, STANISLAW, *Brytyjska polityka wobec Polski 1916–1948* (London, 1979).

ZWEIG, STEFAN, *Die Welt von Gestern: Erinnerungen eines Europäers* (Frankfurt am Main, 1970)

UNPUBLISHED THESES

BAKER, MARK ROBERT, 'A Tale of Two Historians: The Involvement of R. W. Seton-Watson and Lewis Namier in the Creation of New Nation-States in Eastern Europe at the end of the First World War', MA thesis, University of Alberta (1993).

HAHN, E. J., 'Rudolf von Gneist (1816–1895): The Political Ideas and Political Activity of a Prussian Liberal in the Bismarck Period', Ph.D. dissertation, Yale University (1971).

LINDSTRÖM, ERIK, 'Empire and Identity. Biographies of Austrian Identity in an Age of Imperial Dissolution', Ph.D. dissertation, Lund University (2002).

McCORMICK, ROBERT BRADLEY, 'Contending with the National Idea: British Intellectuals and Eastern Europe, 1914–1918', Ph.D. dissertation, University of South Carolina (1996).

POPE, GILES, 'The Political Ideas of Lorenz Stein and Their Influence on Rudolf Gneist and Gustav Schmoller', D.Phil. thesis, Oxford University (1985).

INDEX

Printed in the United Kingdom
by Lightning Source UK Ltd.
133980UK00001B/38/A